Gender Stereotypes in Corporate India

Gender Stereotypes in Corporate India

A GLIMPSE

SUJOYA BASU

Response
Business books from SAGE
Los Angeles ■ London ■ New Delhi ■ Singapore
www.sagepublications.com

First published in 2008 by

Response Books
Business books from SAGE
B1/I-1, Mohan Cooperative Industrial Area
Mathura Road, New Delhi 110 044, India

SAGE Publications Inc
2455 Teller Road
Thousand Oaks, California 91320, USA

SAGE Publications Ltd
1 Oliver's Yard, 55 City Road
London EC1Y 1SP, United Kingdom

SAGE Publications Asia-Pacific Pte Ltd
33 Pekin Street
#02-01 Far East Square
Singapore 048763

Published by Vivek Mehra for SAGE Publications, typeset in Aldine401 BT 10/12pt by Star Compugraphics Pvt Ltd and printed at Chaman Enterprises, New Delhi.

Library of Congress Cataloging-in-Publication Data

Basu, Sujoya.
 Gender stereotypes in corporate India: a glimpse/by Sujoya Basu.
  p. cm
 Includes bibliographical references.
1. Women—India.   2. Sex role—India.   3. Sex differences (Psychology)—India.   4. Stereotypes (Social psychology)—India.
I. Title.

HQ1742.B39   331.40954—dc22   2008   2008023508

ISBN: 978-81-7829-851-1 (PB)

The SAGE Team: Sugata Ghosh, Anushree Tiwari and Trinankur
                 Banerjee

To *Baba, Maa* and *Aveek*

Contents

GENDER STEREOTYPES IN CORPORATE INDIA

List of Tables

List of Figures

Preface

As a child, I kept wondering whether being born a girl was something that made a difference and explained why my relatives treated me differently. My parents insisted that it did not really matter being born a girl or a boy, because when it comes to intelligence and achievement, gender differences do not matter.

When I first started working, I still wondered why women were kept out of the information network at work. Some people tried telling me that it did not matter at the workplace as long as intelligence and dedication were combined. Others did not seem to think so. I still wondered.

Even as a management student I wondered why there were so few women on campus in the first place and why most of our colleagues held views of us which were widely divergent from what the reality was. These were future managers—and would this same pattern continue into the organizational management scene?

India was moving ahead in leaps and bounds. It still is. Students from established western business schools were overlooking lucrative internship placements in the west and opting to come to India to understand the booming growth scene. However, to me, except for some pockets and some industry-sectors where women had started making inroads, most Indian organizations largely remained closed to women managers. Women secretaries, women staff…yes, but women managers, mostly no.

I finally decided that I needed to get to the bottom of things and figure out why women were treated differently in Indian organizations. I thought things were different in the west, but needed to compare the two scenarios. The number of women managers in countries other than India seemed to point to a different story, but was it really different as far as men managers and their perceptions were concerned?

It was this curiosity that started it all. There wasn't much in Indian management literature that could help me form an informed opinion. A review of literature on western management seemed to suggest that most negative outcomes for women managers in organizations, right from inception to progression, could largely be a consequence of the inaccurate perceptions regarding women managers. Was it the same in Indian organizations?

I thought a comparison with the Indian scenario was a good way to start and explore what perceptions about women managers existed in Indian organizations. After that, a further exploration of what gave rise to inaccurate perceptions or stereotypes would clear the air even further. Lastly, if we could say with some surety whether such perceptions could be altered to bring about a positive change in organizations, maybe a concrete set of suggestions could be provided for the chain which produces and nurtures managers in organizations.

This book followed the above-mentioned thread. Three studies addressed each of the three issues. The first gave us a set of managerial gender stereotypes held by men and women managers in India. The second study helped us look at the antecedents of inaccurate managerial gender stereotypes. The third study helped verify whether having women managers in organizational task situations help change inaccurate stereotypes in organizations.

The findings have implications for corporates who want to manage gender diversity well. They also have implications for educators and trainers. Finally, the findings also have implications for society in general, especially the legislature.

This book is a token effort in trying to explore the complex world of Indian management. It is offered with humility and hope. It is also a representation of my effort in bridging the gap that exists in the Indian gender-management scenario. Lastly, it is an effort to reach out to the women managers in India...there is hope and they can take heart from the fact that Indian women managers are a different lot, especially when compared to most developed countries.

Many may not agree with what I have to say or suggest. Many may identify with what this book portrays. Many may learn something new from the findings. I live with the hope that this book will serve its titular purpose...whip up an appetite, leave a pleasant aftertaste and fuel a hunger to explore this phenomenon further.

Acknowledgements

This book would have never been possible had it not been for my father's words ringing in my ears. 'Take up the pen...you'll do yourself justice,' he would say. I am glad I listened to him. Baba, I could not take up the pen, but I did befriend the keyboard.

At a point of time, I felt my Mom nagged me constantly with her 'Publish!' theme. I thank her for that. She's been my gateway to the world of print in the first place.

Aveek...what can I say...his never-ending support, his constant encouragement and his ever-tolerant smile...even when I worked on vacation!...I don't know how much longer this would have taken without him.

And of course, the constant gentle reminders of Dr Sugata Ghosh...they spurred me to write even on vacation.

Prof. Indira Parikh, whose unconditional support saw this piece of research through, till the final stages.

Prof. Parvinder Gupta and Prof. Jerome Joseph, who helped with their salient guidance. Lastly, the roots of these studies would not have been made possible without the encouragement of my friends at IIM Ahmedabad...Debyani, Pallavi, Manmohan, Bharat and of course my dear friend from IIT Bombay, Rajiv.

1

Stereotyping is Everyone's Business: An Introduction and Overview

C alvin and Hobbes has been the world's favourite cartoon strip not only for the sheer entertainment factor, but also because it depicts real issues in a humorous fashion. Though Calvin might not be the relevant corporate manager for management research, his behaviour bears extreme relevance to the topic being explored in this book, that is, gender stereotypes. When six-year-old Calvin denounces Susie's art-class drawing of a neat, tidy house in a yard by invoking gender stereotypes of small-thinking, it is indeed humorous. But when this six-year-old grows up to be a young corporate manager and yet clings on to a similar set of gender stereotypes, it has far-reaching consequences. In everyday life in organizations, inaccurate gender stereotypes affect our judgement and evaluations to the extent of us meting out different treatment to men and women managers. Let us explore further.

Even today, a majority of the managerial workforce in Indian organizations consists of men. Despite the emphasis on the inclusion of more women in the workforce in recent times, we still have very few women in the management cadre in organizations. Consider this (Neft and Levine 1997):

> The United States and Canada have two of the highest ratios of women to men in administrative and managerial positions (67 or 68 women for every 100 men, respectively), but these numbers include low-level as well as high-level managers. In New Zealand there are 48 women for every 100 men in managerial positions. In many other countries, the numbers are far lower. For example, in Japan there are 9 women managers for every 100 men; in Poland there are 18; in Cuba there are 23; and in India there are 2 women managers for every 100 men managers.

What is noteworthy is that the aforementioned numbers actually translate to women managers comprising 40 per cent and 1.96 per cent of the total managerial workforce in Canada and India, respectively, the highest and lowest percentages studied. This percentage, however, included women at all levels of management in India. Although it has been a decade since the study was conducted, not much seems to have changed. What is even more noteworthy is that only an insignificant percentage of women managers ever reach the higher echelons of management in most organizations.

The 'glass ceiling' (the subtle and invisible barrier that prevents women and minorities from moving beyond a certain level in the corporate hierarchy) which restricts women from entering the upper echelons in organizations, the differential treatment that women receive in organizations as compared to men, the discrimination in performance evaluation of women in organizations and other such issues exist across the world to a lesser or greater extent and have been researched well in western gender literature.

Even the women who do make it past the glass ceiling to top executive positions apparently do not reach a place where gender equity is the norm. For example, a recent study of executives in a multinational corporation showed that the women who had reached this level faced a second glass ceiling (Lyness and Thompson 1997). These women drew the same salary and received the same bonuses as their male counterparts. However, they managed fewer people, were given fewer stock options and obtained fewer overseas assignments than the men did. They had reached the same level as the men; however, being in the same position did not necessarily imply having the same status and clout in the organization. When surveyed, the women reported more obstacles and less satisfaction than the men did regarding their future career opportunities. Clearly, they had gotten the message that they had moved up as far as they could in their company whereas the men were more likely to see new opportunities ahead. The differences in the way the two groups were rewarded were subtle, but they apparently signalled to men that they were valued for the long term and to women that they were not. Gender researchers (Agars 2004) state that gender stereotypes have been under examined, although they in fact play a powerful role in maintaining the glass ceiling.

Though India provides scant data in this regard, some instances need mention. As recently as May 2006, *The Times of India* reported alleged discrimination in the topmost circles of the administrative services in the financial capital of India. Some excerpts are provided here:

In IAS, gender may be a glass ceiling

Chitkala Zhutshi, Sharwaree Gokhale and Chandra Iyengar may have shattered the glass ceiling by rising to top posts in the male dominated world of babudom. However, far from basking in the glory of being role models for women in governance, these IAS officials complain of gender bias and denial of equal opportunity...

'All that we are asking for is to do away with this gender-role stereotype. The bias is apparent as women IAS officials in Mantralaya are being rotated around in some select posts. How come key posts like municipal commissioner of Mumbai or Thane are never assigned to a woman IAS officer'?

...Unwilling to go on record, the bureaucrat [a senior male IAS official] said that complaints of discrimination were unfounded. 'Most ministers are reluctant to have a woman as secretary of his department, for their own reasons. We cannot impose a lady officer against the will of the minister'...

The Times of India News Network, Mumbai, Tuesday, 2 May 2006

Given that Indian culture has traditionally been known to be strong on the masculinity factor, it has been only recently that women have graced management positions in corporates. Nonetheless, the numbers convey little news for cheer. For that matter, if one looks at the percentage of female students in top management institutes in India, which hardly exceeds 15 per cent, it explains to a certain extent the dismal picture of Indian women managers till date.

However, the overall picture may not be as bleak as it was, say, a decade ago. Given the position that the Indian economy has carved for itself in the world scenario, it is time to have a look at the status of women at management levels in Indian corporates. Moreover, with education in India reaching enviable standards, as is evident from the rising global demand for our technical and management graduates, corporates are being pushed into trying to understand how to manage the gender diversity that is becoming an eminently inevitable part of our educational and consequently our corporate life.

Research studies across the world have documented the many negative outcomes that women managers face in the workplace like career immobility, recruitment and evaluation differences, differences in terms of power, compensation, training and developmental opportunities, feedback and job segregation, to name a few.

Women managers have constantly had to outperform their male peers to even 'make a mark' in the corporate world. Studies have shown that even women students have had to perform at much higher standards to be evaluated at par with their male counterparts by their professors! There are innumerable studies which show, time and again, that women managers usually get paid less than their male peers at the same hierarchical level, even if they do the same work and have to manage the same roles and responsibilities. It is also seen that when it comes to assigning responsibilities in organizations, usually the key roles and responsibilities, which, in turn, have the maximum learning and growth potential, are usually out of bounds for women managers.

The list is endless. The different behaviours towards women managers and the consequent organizational outcomes for women managers are evident in all spheres of corporate life. In the west, over and above being observed, it is well documented. Unfortunately, in the Indian context, such behaviour and outcomes, though evident, are scantily documented. The evidence lies in the numbers quoted in the first data block earlier (2 women managers for every 100 men managers in India), as compared to the west.

Having witnessed and read and spoken to Indian women managers, both practicing and in-the-making, about such differential outcomes and treatment in organizations, the question that arose in my mind was 'WHY'? Why is it that organizational outcomes are different for women managers? Why is it that they are treated differently? Why is it that they behave differently? Why do they face such discrimination?

Gender literature is rife with theories and perspectives which have tried answering these questions. However, despite a plethora of perspectives trying to explain the glass ceiling and such related discriminatory phenomena, ambiguities exist in the interpretation of results based on most of the prevalent perspectives.

Prevalent research for a long time predicted that women exhibited different managerial characteristics in organizations when compared to men, by the simple virtue of their being women, that is, because of their gender and the consequent gender-based socialization. However, when certain variables like age, education and level in organization were controlled, the predicted differences in the managerial characteristics of men and women vanished (Mainiero 1986; Tsui and Gutek 1984). In other words, managers, irrespective of gender, exhibited the same managerial characteristics.

Among the other perspectives that have tried to explain why this occurs, what comes through as making sense is the *Gender Context* perspective, which portrays inaccurate gender stereotyping as the process responsible for such perceptions (Gregory 1990). The problem, therefore, lies not in the gender-based differences of managers, but in the perception that still exists about women managers not possessing the managerial characteristics required to succeed as managers. It is these perceptions that lead to inaccurate gender stereotypes.

So, the next question is: what are stereotypes? And, once we know what they are, how does one measure their inaccuracy? Stereotypes, in simple words, can be related to the concept of 'we' and 'they' that even children very easily identify with.

> All the people like us are *we*,
>   And everyone else is *they*
>   Kipling

Walter Lippmann (Lippmann 1922) first introduced the term 'stereotype' to represent the typical picture that comes to mind when thinking about a particular social group. This social group could be any group, from caste-based to colour, race or gender-based groups. We tend to categorize people according to their membership of a certain group and then consequently attribute that group's perceived characteristics to the individuals under consideration.

However, what we need to remember here is that stereotyping is a pervasive phenomenon. We stereotype all the time to reduce information processing demands on ourselves. Therefore, on the face of it, stereotyping is not only a universal but a neutral phenomenon as well. The negative face of stereotypes exists because of the negative connotations associated with widely held inaccurate stereotypes and their known negative consequences. The problem arises when we start generalizing widely and in the process miss out on respecting and assessing the individuality of the person under consideration.

Inaccurate stereotypes are especially likely to come into play when evaluators are attempting to judge future performance (as opposed to evaluating past performance). Thus, despite excellent track records, executive women may be subject to the expectation that they will not do as well in the future as male executives will.

Unfortunately, most studies exploring managerial gender stereotypes have been conducted in the western context till date. There have been scant efforts to understand the situation prevailing in Indian organizations. So, my first job was to explore, compare and contrast the managerial gender stereotypes existing in Indian organizations with those in the west and other countries. What are the gender stereotypes that Indian male managers hold of their women colleagues? Also, very importantly, what are the gender stereotypes that women managers hold of their fellow women managers?

That was the first step. Once I was better educated about the kind of gender stereotypes that existed in Indian organizations,

I tried to look back and determine what could be the significant contributors to such inaccurate stereotypes. In the traditional, conservative male-dominated Indian society, gender segregation has always been promoted to maintain respectful and cordial relations between the genders. Social psychology, however, promotes just the opposite. The Contact Hypothesis (Allport 1979) in social psychology states that the more the contact between different social groups, the greater the probability of reduction of negative stereotypes held by each of the other. This contact, however, is not merely in terms of numbers, but also of a certain quality. Five such qualities of contact conditions have been outlined in social psychology, which have been found to help in reducing negative stereotypes. Drawing parallels from social psychology, I predicted low quality interaction with women managers as a significant contributor to inaccurate managerial gender stereotypes in India.

Assuming the above prediction to be true, the question that emerged was: can something be done to reduce such inaccurate stereotypes? Is it possible to design teams and tasks in a way in which inaccuracies of managerial gender stereotypes (and their consequent negative outcomes) can be reduced?

An Indian study was therefore conducted to test the veracity of the above prediction and its implications. The broad questions to which answers were sought were:

1. What are the gender stereotypes that exist in Indian organizations as compared to those held in the western context and other countries?
2. Can we say that lack of quality contact between genders in Indian organizations is a significant contributor towards inaccurate managerial gender stereotypes?

3. If yes, is it possible to reduce inaccuracies of these managerial gender stereotypes and their organizational consequences?

This book follows the plan of the questions and is divided into three broad studies. First, I identified the gender stereotypes existing in the Indian context and that refers to stereotypes held by both men and women managers. The next job was to decide on a quantitative measure of the inaccuracy of these identified gender stereotypes. In the second part, I explored the extent to which prior contact or interaction is related to the inaccuracies of managerial gender stereotypes, the hypothesis being that prior contact would significantly explain inaccurate gender stereotypes. In the third and last part of the study, I conducted a short experiment to determine whether the presence or absence of women in work situations helps reduce the inaccuracies of managerial gender stereotypes, the hypothesis being that the presence of women in work situations would help reduce inaccuracies in managerial gender stereotypes.

In Study 1 it was found that for Indian men managers, not much had changed with respect to time or cultural context. They held managerial gender stereotypes very similar to those found in the west and other countries studied in the past. They associated managerial success with men managers much more than they did with women managers. From the responses of the male managerial sample, 20 managerial gender stereotypes (both masculine and feminine) were identified in the Indian context. The first study also identified the gender stereotypes that women managers held about themselves. It seems women managers in India were a progressive lot and they no longer stereotyped the managerial job. While Indian men managers carried on the 'think manager–think male' phenomenon from other countries, Indian women managers did not sex-stereotype the managerial job. They held positive stereotypes of themselves and were found to be balanced in their outlook towards both men and women managers.

Study 2 confirmed the presence of significant inaccuracies in the managerial gender stereotypes held by Indian men managers. This study also showed that the composite independent variable of 'contact' did explain a substantial variance in the dependent variable of 'inaccuracies of gender stereotypes'. Thus, it was not only the quantity of contact with women managers that was strongly correlated with stereotypic inaccuracies, but also quality of contact conditions (as drawn from social psychology literature). In other words, lack of quality professional contact with women managers is a substantial contributor to inaccuracies in managerial gender stereotypes.

Study 3, which was a short experiment, was far more conclusive. It demonstrated that in the short term and in the presence of women, it was possible to bring about a significant reduction in the inaccuracies of managerial gender stereotypes held by men about women managers. Though this phenomenon could be studied in much greater depth to understand the inner workings of the complex stereotype-changing phenomenon, we can at least say conclusively that such a reduction is possible.

Thus, overall, we could say that prior 'contact' with women managers is an important contributor to the existing inaccuracies of managerial gender stereotypes. However, the presence of women in situations where men and women carry out tasks together contributes to a significant reduction in such inaccuracies in gender stereotypes.

The implications of this three-part study are manifold. First, we come to know that managerial gender stereotypes held by Indian men managers do not significantly differ from those held by men managers in the US and other countries (like UK, Germany, China and Japan). Men managers in the west have over time held on to similar negative stereotypes of women managers. Indian men managers seem to be following the same path today. Over time, however, western corporates have increased the numbers of women managers in their ranks. Compared to that, we are yet to overcome gender hurdles in our organizations, and it will take not only time but also a very strong collective will to move the clock forward to even reach the gender proportions that the west can boast of. Our services sector has already taken a major step forward in this direction, as is evident from the very different gender proportions in that sector, but other industries need to catch up.

As for our societal considerations favouring gender segregation (a Bengaluru university has mooted the idea of seating male and female students separately in class…outlined as follows), this study could act as an eye-opener.

B'lore varsity partitions boys, girls

A line of control has been drawn in the Bangalore University between the sexes. A brutal attack on a group of women students of the English department on May 2, has prompted its syndicate, the highest decision making body, to pass a resolution disallowing boys and girls from sitting together during classes. It has also decided to impose a strict dress code for both boys and girls.

The Times of India News Network, Thursday, 18 May 2006

The implications are not only for our corporates where promotion of gender diversity is yet to be questioned. There are strong implications for educational institutions which nurture our future managers and also for our nation's legislature and executive. In the absence of favourable regulations promoting better gender diversity and quality contact, our gender proportions and interactions will leave much to be wanted and in consequence, will lead to perpetuation of inaccurate managerial gender stereotypes, of which the negative consequences are only too evident. The positive outcome of the third study has strong lessons for educational institutes, training institutes and for corporates in general.

Given the strong social and corporate message promoted by this book, we can only hope that the lessons to be learnt are inculcated by the relevant policy and decision makers at all levels in educational and corporate India. We have long miles to go before we sleep.

REFERENCES

Agars, M.D. (2004). 'Reconsidering the Impact of Gender Stereotypes on the Advancement of Women in Organizations', *Psychology of Women Quarterly*, 28(2): 103–11.

Allport, G.W. (1979 [1954]). *The Nature of Prejudice*. Reading, MA: Addison-Wesley.

Gregory, A. (1990). 'Are Women Different and Why Women are Thought To Be Different: Theoretical and Methodological Perspectives', *Journal of Business Ethics*, 9(4&5): 257–66.

Lippmann, W. (1922). *Public Opinion*. New York: Harcourt, Brace.

Lyness, K. and D. Thompson. (1997). 'Above the glass ceiling? A comparison of matched samples of female and male executives', *Journal of Applied Psychology*, 82(3): 359–75.

Mainiero, L. (1986). 'Coping with powerlessness: The relationship of gender and job dependency to empowerment strategy usage', *Administrative Science Quarterly*, 31(4): 633–53.

Neft, N. and A.D. Levine. (1997). *Where Women Stand: An International Report on the Status of Women in 140 Countries*. New York: Random House.

The Times of India News Network. (2006). Mumbai, 2 May.

Tsui, A.S. and B.A. Gutek. (1984). 'A Role-set analysis of gender differences in performance, affective relationships and career success of industrial middle managers', *Academy of Management Journal*, 27(3): 619–35.

2

Gender Research: Different Perspectives and Impact on Women Managers

GENDER DISCRIMINATION AND DIFFERENT EXPERIENCES OF WOMEN MANAGERS

Research studies in the west document the many negative facets of women managers' experiences in the workplace, like career immobility, recruitment and evaluation differences, power differences, differences in training and developmental opportunities, feedback differences and job segregation.

There is a great deal of research evidence in the western context (Adams and Yoder 1985; Nieva and Gutek 1980; Olson et al. 1985; Powell 1987; Remus and Kelley 1983; Stewart and Gudykunst 1982; Taylor and Ilgen 1981) to show that female executives experience greater obstacles than their male counterparts in entering organizations; are given less favourable evaluations after entrance; are promoted at a slower rate and there is an invisible ceiling for promotions; they are paid lower salaries and are given less challenging positions.

The Glass Ceiling

Several authors have suggested in the past decade that overt or covert sex discrimination or differential treatment of women and men because of their gender is a major reason that women's experiences in organizations differ from those of men and is an explanation for the glass ceiling (Gutek et al. 1991; Heilman 1995; Morrison 1992; Powell and Mainiero 1992). The underlying cause of sex discrimination is thought to be the inaccuracies in widely shared beliefs about the attributes of men and women (Heilman 1983; Ruble et al. 1984).

Symphony orchestras, for example, were long made up exclusively of men. When orchestras eliminated discrimination in hiring by holding auditions behind a screen, the representation of women increased dramatically. As the percentage of women rose above token levels and neared half of the orchestra, musicians of both genders reported better interpersonal relations, job security, orchestra structure and organizational stability (Golin and Rouse 1997).

Biased Evaluation/Appraisals

Another cause of concern is that women's achievements tend to be devalued or attributed to luck or effort rather than ability or skill (Deaux 1976; Nieva and Gutek 1980) which may reduce the organizational rewards they receive.

It has been observed that academic works produced by men may be valued more highly than those by women (Lott 1985). A female student may have to outperform her male peers to be taken seriously by her professors. This general tendency to devalue women and their work is illustrated by Nieva and Gutek's study (Nieva and Gutek 1980), in which two groups were asked to evaluate articles, paintings, resumes and other similar products. The name on each item was clearly masculine or feminine. The sex of the originator of each item was switched for the second group of evaluators. Regardless of the type of item evaluated, those ascribed to a male were rated higher than those ascribed to a female. In all trials, female evaluators were as likely as male evaluators to downgrade the items ascribed to women.

Research also shows that managers more frequently rank women below men when evaluating the performance of identical subjects in controlled experiments (Pazy 1986). Such stereotyping creates and sustains glass ceilings that keeps women away from senior, policy-making posts (Adler 1994).

For example, Greenhaus and Parasuraman (1993) had supervisors rate managers' performance and attributions for their performance in 1993. They learned that (for high performing employees) men's high performance was attributed more to their high ability than women's high performance was. In general, those studies that examined evaluation found that men and women are evaluated differently. Competent males are perceived more favourably than competent females.

Most organizations use performance evaluation in one way or another to decide salary increases and promotions to be given to employees. Much research has been done on understanding the factors that influence fairness and accuracy of performance evaluations. Some studies have shown that males tend to be evaluated more favourably than females, especially when the job is traditionally male dominated (Kaolin and Hodgins 1984).

Fewer Developmental Opportunities/ Poor Career Advancement

One consequence of inaccurate gender stereotyping is that women are less likely to be chosen or recruited for traditionally male positions, such as those in senior management. This occurs because the perceived lack of congruence between the job requirements and the stereotypic attributes ascribed to women leads to expectations that they will fail (Heilman 1983).

Women, therefore, receive fewer developmental opportunities than men. Research has indicated that managerial development results from job characteristics associated with higher-level positions, such as high stakes, opportunities to manage diverse businesses and external pressure, as well as from opportunities to work in unfamiliar areas of the business (McCauley et al. 1994). Perhaps because of the expectations that they will fail, women are less likely to be chosen for assignments involving risk or working in unfamiliar areas of the business (Ruderman and Ohlott 1992; Van Velsor and Hughes 1990).

Difficult Leadership Experiences

Leadership research (Eagly and Jonhson 1990; Terborg 1977) has shown that employees are often reluctant to have a female supervisor, resulting in a less supportive environment for female managers. Structural research on skewed sex ratios has shown that when only a small number of women are included in a job category such as senior management, they encounter obstacles such as being excluded from information networks and not being recognized for their achievements (Freedman and Phillips 1988; Mainiero 1986; Tsui and Gutek 1984). Whereas Kanter suggested that these outcomes could occur for either gender when they were a minority group, later research and reviews (Konrad and Gutek 1987; Ragins and Cotton 1996; Yoder 1991) have indicated that these outcomes occur only for women in predominantly male occupations.

Job Segregation

Gender stereotyping also confines many women to separate and unequal 'women's work' (Manley 1995). Further, when work is performed mostly by women, employees earn lower salaries than when the work is performed mostly by men (Huffman and Valasco 1997). The nursing profession in India is a case in point. Thus, stereotyping also helps ensure that equal pay for equal work remains a distant goal.

THE INDIAN SCENARIO

In the Indian context, there is scant research which is as pervasive as the ones conducted in the west. However, in our everyday life, in reported and unreported news, in our women managers' and management students' experiences, gender discrimination is rampant. A news item in one of the leading dailies of the financial capital of India is reproduced here as a case in the point:

In IAS, gender may be a glass ceiling

Chitkala Zhutshi, Sharwaree Gokhale and Chandra Iyengar may have shattered the glass ceiling by rising to top posts in the male dominated world of babudom. However, far from basking in the glory of being role models for women in governance, these IAS officials complain of gender bias and denial of equal opportunity.

Unwilling to endure discrimination, they openly blame their male colleagues of sexism in the workplace. Sixteen such women IAS officials, who work in the Mantralaya, meet every Friday for lunch and discuss, among other matters, gender discrimination. Once a taboo in formal circles, the issue threatens to snowball into a controversy that would leave the Democratic Front (DF) coalition red-faced.

'All that we are asking for is to do away with this gender-role stereotype. The bias is apparent as women IAS officials in Mantralaya are being rotated around in some select posts. How come key posts like municipal commissioner of Mumbai or Thane are never assigned to a woman IAS officer? If Jayalalitha can appoint a woman IPS officer police commissioner of Chennai, and UP can have a woman home secretary, Maharashtra seems to have a long way to go,' said Iyengar, who is principal secretary in the home department. The 1973 batch IAS officer reports to additional chief secretary AP Sinha, three years her senior.

In the case of Gokhale, secretary, environment and the first woman collector of Maharashtra, she has seen the bias being perpetrated for over two decades. Gokhale became collector of Kolhapur in 1981. 'Until then women were not considered for the post. It was only after we jointly protested that the government relented,' the 1974-batch IAS officer said. While the women are clear in their determination to battle such prejudices, their male counterparts are quite skeptical about the issue. 'What bias? It does not exist. Is this an attempt to seek gender-based reservations in postings?' asked a senior IAS official.

Unwilling to go on record, the bureaucrat said that complaints of discrimination were unfounded. 'Most ministers are reluctant to have a woman as secretary of his department, for their own reasons. We cannot impose a lady officer against the will of the minister. Moreover, barring a few exceptions like Zutshi or Gokhale, most women officers breeze in and out of their office at will and rarely stay beyond 5.30 pm. Agreed they have a family and other priorities to tackle, but office work is always the first casualty', he said.

Another male IAS official alleged that most women officials feel key postings are a matter of right. 'Somehow they feel, once you are on the bandwagon you are sure to reach a destination, irrespective of your work,' he said.

The women are able to counter such charges about the IAS being a meritocracy by pointing out that many men have benefited by cosying up to politicians.

The Times of India News Network, Mumbai, Tuesday, 2 May 2006

In a study of Indian firms (Nath 2000) where performance management and reward structures were mostly considered gender-free, women managers still reported the extra hard work required from them to prove their worth. They attributed their success accomplished so far to their personal drive and their ability to adapt to the environment and stay focused.

Numerous other instances can also be cited in India. For example, the nursing profession, which is strongly women-dominated, is one of the lowest-paid professions in India, despite the necessity of professional certification to enter the profession. It has been such an underpaid profession traditionally that the domestic nursing pool is losing its better-qualified members, almost all women, to a better-paid and better-respected reality in the US and other developed countries.

Women like Kiran Mazumdar Shaw, who leads Biocon; Kiran Bedi, Indian Police Service and recipient of the Magsaysay award; Naina Lal Kidwai, top boss of the largest private bank in India, are the rare exceptions to a prevailing trend where women are found to be underrepresented in Indian corporates and the Indian administration due to the phenomenon of glass ceiling.

One look at the percentage of women management stu-dents in the top management institutes of the country would give us an idea about the status of women in management. Women represent 10 to 15 per cent of the total number of management students. If at the level of fresh graduates from the top management institutes, we have approximately 17 women managers for every 100 men managers graduating every year, is it a surprise then that the total number of women managers per 100 men managers (quoted in Chapter 1) is 2 in India as compared to 67 in the USA?

Even if one looks at management teachers in the top institutes in India, it tells us a consistent story of skewed numbers and area segregation. A look at the composition of the faculty members in any top management institute would give us an optimistic maximum of 10 per cent women as compared to 90 per cent men. More so, this 10 per cent of the faculty members would be found to belong to the traditionally 'soft areas' like Human Resource Management (HRM), Organizational Behaviour (OB) and Communication. The 'traditionally male' areas of Production and Operations Management, Finance, Quantitative Methods and Strategy are dominated almost entirely by men. Maybe the traditional notion in India, portrayed by the prevalent saying,'Girls are weak in mathematics,' has something to do with this phenomenon.

In the Indian society, where we still have many pockets where female foeticide is rampant, where child marriages are a way of the world, where we still need government-sponsored advertisements to end gender discrimination against the girl child, where we still need legislation offering free education to the single girl child, basic social equality is still a far cry. Constitutionally, however, India provides a level playing field to its women citizens in all aspects of life.

In modern India, the hype surrounding the emergence of the new working woman is a phenomenon restricted mostly to the lower levels of the service industry in an urban setting, especially the IT and ITES industries. Once again, it shouldn't come as a surprise that the status of women in management—a field widely perceived by most as the gateway to wealth and power—is still a far cry from what exists in the developed west.

So, if western research over the past two decades has shown us the various facets of gender discrimination against women managers, we can safely say—in spite of scant indigenous research—that the plight of Indian women managers would be the same, if not worse, especially since the number of women managers were 2 and 67 per 100 men managers in India and the US, respectively, in 1997. These numbers have been revised to a range of 3 per cent to 6 per cent (the percentage of women represented in the Indian urban management workforce) in the Indian management scenario in 2002–03 (Kulkarni 2002; Singh 2003) and even then, we are referring to the organized urban management workforce.

That brings us to some fundamental questions. Why are there so few women in the top tiers of organizations? Do a woman's gender and position in the organizational hierarchy determine the way she is treated? How can 'perceived' womens' behaviour and the differential treatment they receive in organizations be explained? These are some of the commonly researched questions in the field of 'women in management' and researchers in the west have been trying to find answers to them for about four decades now.

THE DIFFERENT PERSPECTIVES IN GENDER LITERATURE

Five theoretical perspectives have been advanced in gender literature to answer the above questions: the *person-or-gender-centred* perspective, the *situation-centred* or the *organization-structure* (or the *organization-centred*) perspective, the *gender-organization* perspective, the *gender-organization-system* perspective and the *gender-context* perspective.

The Gender-centred Perspective

The first perspective, the person-or-gender-centred view was first advocated by Horner (1968) in a 1968 study of low achievement among women and in Hennig and Jardim's book (Hennig and Jardim 1976) on successful women in management. According to this perspective, the attributes individuals perceive they possess vary according to their sex (Betz and Fitzergald 1987; Horner 1972; Loden 1985). Men perceive themselves as possessing masculine characteristics (they see themselves as aggressive, forceful, strong, rational, self-confident, competitive and independent), while women perceive themselves as possessing feminine characteristics (they see themselves as and therefore are warm, kind, emotional, gentle, understanding, aware of others' feelings and helpful to others—Schein 1972; Putnam and Heinen 1976; Feather 1984). And since it is traditionally the masculine characteristics that help people succeed in the competitive corporate world, women have been left behind. Evidently, this perspective blames women's limited corporate progress to factors that are internal to women. Hence gender-centred theorists (Riger and Galligan 1980) have promoted that women's biological and socialization patterns have prompted them to exhibit traits and behaviours that are not conducive to their becoming successful and potentially promotable managers. Not only the gender theorists, most of us still subscribe to this perspective when we express opinions like 'Girls are weak in mathematics', or 'The corporate world is a man's world' or 'She has succeeded because she is not really a "woman" in the traditional sense'.

Traditionally, a vast amount of gender research in management has revolved around the gender-centred perspective. Most of the researchers (Beutel and Brenner 1986; Chusmir 1985; Dobbins and Platz 1986; Powell 1988; Powell et al. 1984) primarily pointed to gender differences while explaining differences in a number of variables like motivation to manage, management style, leadership, values, decision-making, and so on. In other words, women were found to score low on managerial characteristics thought to be necessary for success, like confidence, dominance and the like.

A closer look at the gender-perspective research revealed studies (McCarty 1986) which used students from non-managerial fields as subjects and tried to generalize the findings to managers and in which women exhibit lower self-confidence, lower dominance, etc. However, other studies (Foster and Kolinko 1979), which used MBA students as their samples, usually had results far more similar to those using managers. According to a study (Steinberg and Shapiro 1982) of MBA students, women fitted the image inherent in managerial ideology more closely than their male counterparts. That was somewhat inexplicable under the premises of the first perspective.

Moreover, it was also found that studies (Freedman and Phillips 1988; Mainiero 1986; Tsui and Gutek 1984) following the first perspective, which did not incorporate situational variables, were open to alternative interpretation. On the other hand, studies which did incorporate a situational viewpoint (Brenner 1982; Donnell and Hall 1980; Harlan and Weiss 1982) found that gender differences in personality traits like achievement, dominance, responsibility and self-assurance could be explained by controlling education and level in the organization, that differences in work attitudes could be explained by organizational level (Brief and Oliver 1976), that differences in influencing strategies used by different genders could be explained by job dependency, and so on.

Therefore, conclusive interpretations could not be arrived at in such studies by considering gender differences only. Evidently, the first perspective left studies open to alternative interpretations and appeared to be deficient in explaining differences.

The Situation-centred Perspective

The second perspective, the situation-centred or organization-structure perspective, was advocated by Kanter (Kanter 1977a; 1977b) in 1977 and was further promoted by other researchers like Mainiero (1986) and Fagenson(1986). According to Kanter, an individuals' position in the organizational power hierarchy shapes their perceptions, attributes, traits and behaviour. According to this perspective, there are two types of situations in organizations: advantageous and disadvantageous. Advantageous situations are located in the upper corporate levels and offer power to their occupants. In organizations, the key form of power is access to important people and resources. Disadvantageous positions are located at the lower levels of the organization and offer little power to their occupants. Kanter asserted that situations that give individuals power also give them the ability to satisfy their own needs and desires within a given work situation. In contrast, work situations lacking in power inhibit individuals from acting on their own behalf. As a result, individuals in the lower positions in the hierarchy are more dependent on others to meet their needs than are individuals situated in the higher positions. This encourages lower level individuals to perceive themselves as being more 'feminine' (understanding, aware of others' feelings and helpful to others) or 'other focused' (Spence and Helmreich 1978) than upper level individuals. In contrast, upper level individuals will think of themselves as more instrumental or masculine as they can depend on themselves rather than others to satisfy their needs.

Women have traditionally been placed in lower level positions while men occupy the majority of jobs in the upper levels of the power hierarchy in organizations. Thus, women are feminine and develop feminine traits in response to being in low-level positions.

Therefore, according to the second perspective, men's perceived masculine characteristics and women's perceived feminine characteristics are believed to be associated with their organizational·level and not with their sex.

Now, if the situation-centred perspective is a good predictor of behaviour and traits of men and women, then, men, who have been placed in low organizational positions, would exhibit feminine behaviours and traits. However, this view, when applied to men in lower positions, was not corroborated by Fagenson's extensive study in 1990 (Fagenson 1990). In this study, being located in lower levels in the organizational hierarchy did not promote a feminine identity for men, as suggested by the *situation-centred* approach.

On the other hand, according to this perspective, if women were situated in high-level positions they would exhibit the 'masculine' behaviours and traits that men exhibited in these positions. In this case, however, the study found support for this view regarding women in upper levels of the hierarchy.

Though the second perspective mitigated the anomaly of the first perspective, it was deficient in explaining differences, especially when switching levels between men and women.

The Gender-organization and the Gender-organization-system Perspectives

The third and fourth perspectives make use of a combination of the two above-mentioned perspectives to advance their viewpoint. They suggest that individuals' perceptions of their characteristics are influenced both by their level in the organizational power hierarchy and their sex (Powell et al. 1984; Schneer 1985; Terborg 1977). The third perspective, that is, the gender-organization perspective suggests that an individual's gender and level make independent and linear contributions to the attributes that individuals perceive they possess. Thus it agrees with both the former perspectives, while predicting an additive relationship (Terborg 1981) and may be statistically termed an additive model.

The fourth perspective, that is, the gender-organization-system, also suggests that individual's perceptions of their characteristics are influenced by both their level in the organizational power hierarchy and their sex. However, it suggests that individuals' sex and level make non-independent, non-linear contributions to their attributes (Martin et al. 1983) and predicts a non-additive interaction and may be termed statistically as focusing on the multiplicative relationship or interaction between the variables.

Fagenson (1990) examined all four perspectives in one extensive study in 1990 and found minimal support for both the gender-centred hypothesis as well as the organization-structure perspective. She, however, found no support for the third and fourth perspectives. Evidently another theory or perspective with much broader implications was the key to explaining the differences in men and women managers' behaviours and experiences.

The Gender-context Perspective

Another perspective, gender-context, is influenced by three streams of research: *gender stereotyping, gender numerical proportions* and *gender-ascribed social status* (Falkenberg and Rychel 1985; Marshall 1984). Schneer (1985) conceptually combined these three streams into one perspective and labelled it 'gender context'.

According to these streams of research, it is not only a proportion of a certain gender present in a situational context (the proportion determines the dominant majority group in that situation) that is important in determining differences, but also the ascribed social status of that group. As stated under this perspective, women are perceived as possessing traits associated with a homemaker, which has created the second perception that women do not have the necessary traits to enter perceived masculine and/or high status occupations.

Compounding this perception is the perceived higher value of men and masculine traits over women and feminine traits (Powell and Butterfield 1979). This perception in itself prevents women from entering occupations on an equal footing with men and thus modifies the applicability of Kanter's situation-centred perspective.

This difference in ascribed social status between the genders has been an explanatory variable in explaining relationships between men and women (Spence and Helmreich 1978). People who are high in the power hierarchy are evaluated positively and highly valued. Men are dominant in the upper levels of not only organizations but also society and are therefore more highly valued than women. The gender context perspective also helps in explaining the findings of a study concerning the higher status of token males than of token females (Fairhurst and Snavaley 1983).

According to this perspective, the dominant majority has two concerns: of maintaining its position of power in the system and keeping the sub-dominant group in place by labelling this group substandard in a variety of ways and ascribing to members of this latter group appropriate social roles. The sub-dominant group thus becomes preoccupied with basic survival and copes by accommodation or adjustment. In addition, because the cultural, social and political systems are controlled by the dominant group, the members of the sub-dominant group define their aspirations in terms of dominant group goals. In order to avoid sanctions, the sub-dominant group must be continually sensitive to the dominant group's needs and play down its own. Thus, understanding the world around them becomes a major priority and listening is cultivated as a basic skill in these group members.

In management, women, being lower status members, are expected to provide support and encouragement while men, who already have high status, have more opportunities to make task contributions, have more influence, are allowed to demonstrate competence and receive more expressions of acceptance. Women have to work much harder to be accepted in the organization. They have to prove that they are both competent and well-intentioned. This probably explains why some women who are competitive and hard-driving at work are viewed with a negative connotation of being aggressive, while the same behaviour by men is not viewed negatively. But it is because these women assimilate the traits and behaviours of the dominant majority, that they find success and rise in organizations.

The gender-context perspective can be extended to analyzing ethnic and racial minorities in management positions and through this theory, the position of various minorities in management can be compared and contrasted.

One conclusion from the cited studies indicates the importance of 'perception' as compared to 'actual behaviour'. It has been found that women do possess the personality traits and the motivation to manage and that they also have the leadership skills and other qualities required to be successful managers. However, the perception still exists that women do not possess these personality attributes or leadership skills (Gregory 1990).

Attention should therefore be directed away from gender differences in management, as significant differences do not exist among managers when age, education and level of organization are controlled. Instead, if one has to improve upon differences in the situations of women and men in management, one should work on the perceptions that are prevalent about women managers.

Thus, research which probes perceptions, rather than that which probes gender differences, would be far more useful in explaining how such perceptions could be changed. The gender-context approach is far more useful in this regard than any of the other four perspectives outlined earlier. Gregory (1990) calls for a more holistic and action-oriented research for probing perceptions and what could be done on both personal and organizational levels to change the perceptions towards women managers.

This perceptual problem, which has antecedents in ascribed social status and numerical proportions, is what the gender-context perspective refers to as the phenomenon of 'gender stereotyping'. Stereotyping is a common phenomenon in all contexts and humans are known for their dependence upon stereotypes to reduce information processing demands. Unfortunately, it is this dependence that manifests itself in the form of inaccurate stereotypes which create major barriers in the advancement of minority status individuals like women managers (Van Fleet and Saurage 1984). We have already seen the various consequences of negative and inaccurate gender stereotypes in organizations.

Stereotypes, however, cannot be eliminated, therefore making it imperative for organizational behaviour researchers to identify conditions that propagate more accurate stereotypes. To understand how inaccurate stereotypes develop and how to reduce (if possible) such inaccuracies, we will first have to understand the process behind the formation and maintenance of stereotypes. This forms the basis for our next chapter which deals with stereotypes, their inaccuracies, ways of reducing such inaccuracies and the contribution of social psychology research to the entire process.

REFERENCES

Adams, J. and J.D. Yoder. (1985). 'When Sex roles and work roles conflict: A critical look at standards of evaluation'. Paper presented at Academy of Management, San Diego.

Adler, M.A. (1994). 'Male-Female Power Differences at Work: A Comparison of Supervisors and Policymakers', *Social Inquiry*, 37: 45–49.

Betz, N.E. and L.F. Fitzergald. (1987). *The Career Psychology of Women*. Orlando, FL: Academic Press.

Beutel, N.J. and O.C. Brenner. (1986). 'Sex differences in work variability', *Journal of Vocational Behavior*, 28: 29–41.

Brenner, O.C. (1982). 'Relationship of education to sex, managerial status, and the managerial stereotype', *Journal of Applied Psychology*, 67: 380–83.

Brief, A.P. and R.L. Oliver. (1976). 'Male-female differences in work attitudes among retail sales managers', *Journal of Applied Psychology*, 61: 526–28.

Chusmir, L.H. (1985). 'Motivation of managers: Is gender a factor'?, *Psychology of Women Quarterly*, 9: 153–59.

Deaux, K. (1976). 'Sex: A perspective on the attribution process', in J. Harvey, W.J. Ickes and R.F. Kidd (eds), *New Directions in Attribution Research*, Vol. 1, pp. 335–52. Hillsdale NJ: Erlbaum.

Dobbins, G.H. and S.J. Platz. (1986). 'Sex differences in leadership: How real are they?', *Academy of Management Review*, 11: 118–27.

Donnell, S.M. and J. Hall. (1980). 'Men and women as managers: A significant case of no significant difference', *Organizational Dynamics*, 11: 60–77.

Eagly, A. and B.T. Jonhson. (1990). 'Gender and leadership style: A meta-analysis', *Psychological Bullettin*, 108: 233–56.

Fagenson, E.A. (1986). 'Women's work orientation: Something old, something new', *Group and Organization Studies*, 11: 75–100.

———. (1990). 'Perceived masculine and feminine attributes examined as a function of individuals' sex and level in the organizational power hierarchy: A test of four theoretical perspectives', *Journal of Applied Psychology*, 75: 204–21.

Fairhurst, G.T. and B.K. Snavaley. (1983). 'A test of the social isolation of male tokens', *Academy of Management Journal*, 26: 353–61.

Falkenberg, L. and C. Rychel. (1985). 'Gender Stereotypes in the Workplace'. Concordia University Faculty of Commerce and Administration Working Paper Series, Montreal: Quebec. (pp. 85–123).

Feather, N.T. (1984). 'Masculinity, femininity, psychological androgyny and the structure of values', *Journal of Personality and Social Psychology*, 47: 604–21.

Foster, L.W. and T. Kolinko. (1979). 'Changes to be a managerial woman: An examination of individual variables and career choice', *Sex Roles*, 5: 627–34.

Freedman, S.M. and J.S. Phillips. (1988). 'The changing nature of research on women at work', *Journal of Management*, 14: 231–51.

Golin, C. and C. Rouse. (1997). 'Orchestrating Impartiality: The Impact of "Blind" Auditions on Female Musicians'. Working Paper No. 376, Industrial Relations Section, Princeton University.

Greenhaus, J.H. and Parasuraman. (1993). 'Job performance attributions and career advancement prospects: An examination of gender and race effects', *Organizational Behavior and Human Decision Processes*, 55: 273–97.

Gregory, A. (1990). 'Are women different and why women are thought to be different: Theoretical and methodological perspectives', *Journal of Business Ethics*, 9: 257–66.

Gutek, B.A., S. Searle and L. Klepa. (1991). 'Rational vs. Gender-role explanations for work-family conflict', *Journal of Applied Psychology*, 76: 560–68.

Harlan, A. and C.L. Weiss. (1982). 'Sex differences in factors affecting managerial career advances', in Phylis A. Wallace (ed.), *Women in the Workplace*, pp. 59–100. Boston: Auburn House.

Heilman, M.E. (1983). 'Sex bias in work settings: The lack of fit model', in B.M. Staw and L.I. Cumings (eds), *Research in Organizational Behaviour*, Vol. 5, pp. 269–98. Greenwich, CT: JAI Press.

———. (1995). 'Sex stereotypes and their effects in the workplace: What we know and what we don't know', *Journal of Social Behavior and Personality*, 10: 3–26.

Hennig, M. and A. Jardim. (1976). *The Managerial Woman*. Anchor Press: New York.

Horner, M.S. (1968). 'Sex differences in achievement motivation and performance in competitive and non-competitive situations'. Doctoral Dissertation, University of Michigan. University Microfilms, Ann Arbor.

———. (1972). 'Towards an understanding of achievement related conflicts in women', *Journal of Social Issues*, 28: 157–76.

Huffman, M.L. and S.C. Valasco. (1997). 'When more is less: Sex composition, organizations, and earnings in U.S. firms', *Work & Occupations*, 39: 214–38.

Kanter, R.M. (1977a). *Men and Women of the Corporation*. New York: Basic Books.

———. (1977b). 'Some effects of proportions on group life: Skewed sex ratios and responses to token women', *American Journal of Sociology*, 82: 965–90.

Kaolin, R. and D.C. Hodgins. (1984). 'Sex bias and occupational suitability', *Canadian Journal of Behavioral Science*, 16: 311–25.

Konrad, A.M. and B.A. Gutek. (1987). 'Theory and research on group composition: Applications to the status of women and minorities', in S. Oskamp and S. Spacapan (eds), *Interpersonal Processes: The Claremont Symposium on Applied Social Psychology*, pp. 85–121. Newbury Park, CA: Sage.

Kulkarni, S.S. (2002). 'Women and professional competency—a survey report', *Indian Journal of Training and Development*, XXXII(2): 72–83.

Loden, M. (1985). *Feminine Leadership or How to Succeed in Business without Being One of the Boys*. New York: Times Books.

Lott, B. (1985). 'The devaluation of women's competence', *Journal of Social Issues*, 41: 43–60.

Mainiero, L. (1986). 'Coping with powerlessness: The relationship of gender and job dependency to empowerment strategy usage', *Administrative Science Quarterly*, 31: 633–53.

Manley, J.E. (1995). 'Sex-segregated work in the system of professions: The development and stratification of nursing', *Social Quarterly*, 36: 297–308.

Marshall, J. (1984). *Women Managers: Travellers in a Male World*. Chichester, UK: John Wiley & Sons.

Martin, Y.M., D. Harrison and D. Dinitto. (1983). 'Advancement for women in hierarchical organizations: A multi-level analysis for advancements and prospects', *Journal of Applied Behavioral Science*, 19: 19–33.

McCarty, P.A. (1986). 'Effects of feedback on the self confidence of men and women', *Academy of Management Journal*, 29: 840–47.

McCauley, C.D., M.N. Ruderman, P.J. Ohlott and J.E. Morrow. (1994). 'Assessing the developmental components of managerial jobs', *Journal of Applied Psychology*, 79: 544–60.

Morrison, A.M. (1992). *The New Leaders Guidelines on Leadership Diversity*. San Francisco: Jossey Bass.

Nath, G. (2000). 'Gently shattering the glass ceiling: Experiences of Indian women managers', *Women in Management Review*, 15(1): 44–52.

Nieva, V.F. and B.A. Gutek. (1980). 'Sex effects on evaluation', *Academy of Management Review*, 5: 267–76.

Olson, J.E., D.C. Good and I.H. Frieze. (1985). 'Income differentials of male and female MBAs: The effects of job type and industry'. Paper presented at Academy of Management, San Diego.

Pazy, A. (1986). 'Persistence of pro-male bias despite identical information regarding causes of success', *Organizational Behavior & Human Decision Processes*, 38: 366–73.

Powell, G.N. (1987). 'The effects of sex and gender on recruitment', *Academy of Management Review*, 12: 731–43.

———. (1988). *Women and Men in Management*. Beverly Hills, CA: Sage.

Powell, G.N. and A. Butterfield. (1979). 'The "good manager": Masculine or androgynous?', *Academy of Management Journal*, 22: 345–403.

Powell, G.N., B.Z. Posner and W.H. Schmidt. (1984). 'Sex effects in managerial value systems', *Human Relations*, 37: 909–21.

Powell, G.N. and L.A. Mainiero. (1992). 'Cross currents in the river of time: Conceptualizing the complexities of women's careers', *Journal of Management*, 18: 215–37.

Putnam, L. and S.J. Heinen. (1976). 'Women in management: The fallacy of the trait approach', *MSU Business Topics*, 24(3): 47–53.

Ragins, B.R. and J. Cotton. (April 1996). 'The influence of gender ratios on organizational attitudes and outcomes'. Poster session presented at the 11th Annual Conference for the Society for Industrial and Organizational Psychology. San Diego, CA.

Remus, W.L. and L. Kelley. (1983). 'Evidence of sex discrimination: In similar populations man are paid better than women', *American Journal of Economics and Sociology*, 42: 149–52.

Riger, S. and P. Galligan. (1980). 'Women in management: An exploration of competing paradigms', *American Psychologist*, 35: 902–10.

Ruble, T.N., R. Cohen and D.M. Ruble. (1984). 'Sex stereotypes: Occupational barriers for women', *American Behavioral Scientist*, 27: 339–56.

Ruderman, M.N. and P.J. Ohlott. (August 1992). 'Managerial promotions as a diversity practice'. Paper presented at the 52nd annual meeting of the Academy of Management, Las Vegas.

Schein, V.E. (1972). 'Fair employment of women through personnel research', *Personnel Research*, 51: 330–35.

Schneer, J.A. (1985). 'Gender Context: An alternative perspective on sex differences in organization'. Paper presented at the Academy of Management, San Diego.

Singh, K. (2003). 'Women managers: Perception vs. performance analysis', *Journal of Management Research*, 3(1): 31–42.

Spence, J.T. and R.L. Helmreich. (1978). *Masculinity and Femininity: Their Psychologican Dimensions, Correlates and Antecedents*. Austin: University of Texas Press.

Steinberg, R. and S. Shapiro. (1982). 'Sex differences in personality traits of female and male MBA students', *Journal of Applied Psychology*, 67: 306–10.

Stewart, L. P. and W. B. Gudykunst (1982). 'Differential factors influencing the hierarchical level and numbers of promotions of males and females within the organization', *Academy of Management Journal*, 25: 587–97.

Strober, M.H. (1982). 'The MBA: Same passport to success for men and women?', in Phylis, A. Wallace (ed.), *Women in the Workplace*, pp. 25–58. Boston: Auburn House.

Taylor, M.S. and D.R. Ilgen. (1981). 'Sex discrimination against women in initial placement decisions: A laboratory investigation', *Academy of Management Journal*, 24: 859–65.

Terborg, J.R. (1977). 'Women in management: A research review', *Journal of Applied Psychology*, 62: 647–64.

———. (1981). 'Interactional psychology and research in human behavior in organizations', *Academy of Management Review*, 6: 569–76.

The Times of India News Network. 2006. Mumbai. 2 May.

Tsui, A.S. and B.A. Gutek. (1984). 'A Role analysis of gender difference in performance affective relationships and career success of industrial middle managers', *Academy of Management Journal*, 27: 619–35.

Van Fleet, D.D. and J.G. Saurage. (1984). 'Recent Research on women in management', *Akron Business and Economic Review*, 15(2): 15–24.

Van Velsor, E. and M.W. Hughes. (1990). *Gender differences in the development of managers: How women managers learn from experience*. (Technical Representation 145). Greensboro, NC: Center for Creative Leadership.

Yoder, J.D. (1991). 'Rethinking tokenism: Looking beyond numbers', *Gender and Society*, 5(2): 178–92.

3

Formation and Maintenance of Stereotypes: The Role of Contact

WHAT ARE STEREOTYPES?

All the people like us are we,
And everyone else is they
......Kipling.

The topic of human differences, real or alleged, and responses to them, has been studied over ages. Social psychologists tend to discuss it in terms of 'stereotypes'. Stereotyping is the process by which people use social categories (for example, race, sex) in acquiring, processing and recalling information about others. Walter Lippmann (1922) introduced the term 'stereotype' to represent the typical mental picture associated with a particular social group. Stereotypes are the traits and roles associated with certain groups or categories (Dovidio et al. 1996).

Within a social cognition framework (Christensen and Rosenthal 1982; McCauley et al. 1980), stereotypes function to reduce and simplify information processing demands, define group membership and predict behaviour based on group membership. Stereotyping has a negative connotation because it is often a source or excuse for injustice, is based on relatively little information, is resistant to change even with the availability of new information and is rarely accurately applied to specific individuals.

However, stereotyping is not in itself a negative process; rather it is a neutral subconscious cognitive process that increases the efficiency of interpreting environmental information. We use stereotypes all the time without knowing it.

HOW ARE STEREOTYPES
FORMED AND MAINTAINED?

Stereotyping begins with the classification of individuals into groups according to diffuse, visible criteria (for example, gender, race, etc). As group members are observed in particular activities, the traits and behaviours related to those activities become a component of the stereotype. That is, the abilities and personality attributes connected with the observed activities of certain individuals are considered typical of all members of a group (Eagly and Steffen 1984). It is inaccurate generalization that gives rise to inaccurate stereotypes, which easily crowd out any possibility of focusing on individual traits or characteristics. Instead, it is the membership of an individual to a certain category or group that acts foremost in the mind when forming opinions about that individual.

This initial classification affects the social structure of groups. Individuals with desired attributes and characteristics similar to the perceiver are identified as 'in-group' members and are assigned a higher status than 'out-group' members. The pervasiveness of this structuring is noted in the relatively small amount of information needed to produce a division of in and out-group members and assignment of status. Within controlled experiments, social structuring and status assignment occur even when the only information about other individuals is verbally provided and there is no personal contact between the in- and out-group members (Hamilton 1979).

Compounding the impact of this social structuring are the divergent performance expectations for individuals of different status. High status members are expected to organize and direct tasks but low status members are expected to complete assigned tasks and support group activities. The acceptance of a low status member's contribution to the group's activities is again dependent on the perceived motive of the low status member. If an out-group member is considered to be competitive (as is the case with most women who are competitive and perform well), his/her contribution is considered to be an attempt at increasing status and therefore ignored. If the person is considered to be cooperative and working for the best interests of the group, the contribution is accepted (Meeker and Weitzel-O-Neill 1977). This explains why competitive performance by women (out-group members) is acknowledged and evaluated positively only if she meets the criterion of being a cooperative and feminine individual supporting the majority group's interests.

Once stereotypes are formed with whatever diffuse visible criteria that are observed to be common to a number of members of the group, inaccuracies build up through one or all the following processes:

1. Focussing on information that corresponds to current stereotypes: Valid stereotypes require accurate estimation of past behaviour and performance levels. Unfortunately, we humans overestimate the occurrence of expected behaviour rather than actual behaviour. In short, stereotypes are maintained because information that does not fit current perceptions is ignored, more so, because a few deviations from stereotypic behaviour do not lead to reasonable revisions of assumptions (Cantor and Mischel 1979).

2. Attributing deviant behaviours to the situation rather than the person (Kelly 1972): Attribution also perpetuates stereotypical thinking by associating expected behaviours with internal qualities and identifying behaviour inconsistent with expectations with external or situational

factors. Attribution has specific implications for success-ful and poor performance. Success in tasks requiring atypical behaviour is related to situational rather than personal attributes; thus the achievement is never ex-pected again. Poor performance, on the other hand, is associated with internal qualities and reinforces current stereotypes.

3. Increasing perceptual barriers when minority or out-group members are perceived as a threat (Blalock 1967): Simply increasing the number of women managers in the workplace might not help reduce inaccurate stereotypes. Perceptual barriers can be heightened as the number of out-group members increases and the in-group members feel threatened, thereby enhancing perceived differences between in-group and out-group members.

From an understanding of what stereotypes are, how they are formed and how inaccuracies are built-up and maintained, some essential points that need to be kept in mind when attempting to reduce inaccurate stereotypes are:

1. A stereotype can be labelled as a characteristic in which a significant difference exists when comparing in-group and out-group members.

2. A stereotype can be either positive or negative, depending on the context in which such a characteristic is either deemed desirable or undesirable.

3. Ascription of in-group or out-group status, which forms the basis of stereotypes, is usually based on very little information.

4. Once such ascription has occurred, the status differences are highlighted in future instances.

5. Such ascribed status differences tend to develop negative ideas about the out-group, like expectations of failure from out-group members.

6. Stereotyping is a natural and supposedly neutral phenomenon.

7. Inaccurate generalization is what makes stereotypes inaccurate. Maintenance of inaccuracy follows one or all of three processes:

- Unstereotypic behaviour, if encountered in a few instances, or from a few members of the out-group, is ignored.

- Different attribution mechanisms start operating for stereotype-consistent outcomes and stereotype-inconsistent outcomes. Success, which is a stereotype-deviant outcome, is attributed to situational factors, rather than the person. Similarly, failure, which is stereotype-consistent behaviour, is attributed internally to the person.

- If the presence of out-group members is perceived as a threat, it can heighten perceived differences between in-group and out-group members, leading to stronger mental blockage towards any revision of inaccuracy.

HOW DO WE REDUCE INACCURATE STEREOTYPES?

Inaccurate gender stereotyping has been established to have negative effects on a variety of outcomes for women managers. There are ways and means suggested in research, which can reduce such inaccuracies in stereotyping. The most widely offered suggestion in gender literature involves increasing gender diversity in the workplace.

It has been said that gender diversity in the workforce helps reduce stereotyping and promotes understanding of individual talents and abilities. Inaccurate stereotyping decreases in diverse work environments as people learn to appreciate their co-workers' similarities and differences (Locksley et al. 1980).

However, by hiring only 'token' numbers of women, many employers perpetuate gender stereotyping. For example, research (Sackett et al. 1991) shows that when women are a small minority in the workforce, their performance ratings are consistently lower than those of their male counterparts, even after controlling for education, experience and ability.

Therefore, simply increasing gender diversity in the workplace might not help in reducing inaccurate managerial gender stereotypes. Instead, it might increase perceptual barriers and have an opposite effect. Maybe that explains why, despite so many organizations following gender diversity policies, stereotypic inaccuracies have seldom seen revision in the managerial sphere.

This point is illustrated by one study in the Indian context (Bhatnagar and Swamy 1995). The study explores the relationship between 'exposure' or 'interaction' with women managers (in terms of number and frequency of such interactions) and 'the attitudes toward women managers', the sample being male bank managers. Results show little relation between 'the extent of interaction' and 'attitudes towards women managers'. However, a separate variable, 'satisfaction with interaction with women managers' shows significant positive relation with attitudes toward women managers. The very fact that just the number and frequency of interactions with women managers are not significantly related to attitudes, leads one to believe that such interaction could have more to it than meets the eye. Maybe, the 'quality' of such interaction, if measured, could lead to better explanations of the study.

However, rarely have studies been conducted in gender literature in the Indian context which have tried to measure the pattern of managerial gender stereotypes in India and neither does any study address the measurement of the inaccuracy of such stereotypes, or for that matter, how to help reduce it.

The Role of Quality Interaction

Interaction plays an important role both in the formation of and reduction of inaccuracy in stereotyping as it has been amply established that inaccurate stereotypes, especially negative stereotypes, are formed with very little information about the out-group. Logically, increased contact provides enough information about the out-group and makes way for forming positive and accurate stereotypes about the out-group and also paves the way for a separate, alternate category of stereotyping (for example, that which is based on occupational segregation, rather than segregation based on gender). Increasing interaction through change in the structure of workgroups is one of the easier and more powerful methods to help in the revision of inaccurate stereotypes.

This interaction, could be divided into two components: *quantity of interaction* and *quality of interaction*. In increasing the quantity of interaction (gender diversity and frequency), we re-sort to increasing the number of out-group members, that is, women in organizations.

Gender Diversity: As more women enter male-dominated professions, the number of professional interactions between genders increases (Kanter 1977). This reduces the visibility of mistakes and poor performance and leads to performance expectations based on individual rather than group traits. Also, as more women enter male-dominated occupations, it is expected that gender will lose its representation of social roles and prediction of status, which classifies them as an out-group. (Deaux 1984; Eagly and Steffen 1984)

Frequency of Interaction: We have seen that a few instances of unstereotypic behaviour coming from a few members of the stereotyped group are usually ignored. Thus, we need to not only increase the number of women managers, but also increase instances of unstereotypic behaviour. Gender diversity coupled with increased frequency of interaction with women managers helps in this respect.

Also, the tendency of people to focus on stereotype-consistent behaviour makes it necessary to ensure that information pertaining to stereotype-inconsistent behaviour is not neglected or overlooked. Repeated contact situations ensure that overlooking stereotype-inconsistent behaviour becomes an effort.

However, in this context, we also need to remember that the more the number of minority members in a group, the more threatened the majority group members feel and the more the enhancement of negative stereotypes (Blalock 1967). As the proportion of women increases in managerial ranks, their presence is more likely to be seen as a threat, with women competing for and receiving jobs that normally would have gone to men. Stereotypes and sexist behaviour would be reactivated by male managers as a means of coping with frustration and fear, and the presence of women would be justified as being a result of external pressure and not because they are competent.

Both the theories combined suggest that increasing the number of women in groups will take either a positive or negative direction depending on the opportunity provided for personal interaction with women and the rationale for including women in the group. Thus, interaction between men and women has to be of a desired *quality* to help in reducing inaccurate stereotypes.

Ascribing positive or negative status has been found to be a predominant factor in the phenomenon of stereotyping and its effects on accepting an out-group member's contributions. Gender categories are directly related to the assignment of status. The perceived lower status of women in organizations may be partially explained by the in/out-group orientation. Men, as the majority members, categorize women as 'outsiders', who do not have traits similar to themselves. As out-group members, women are consequently assigned lower status.

If perceived and visible status is controlled, this categorization may be reduced and the effects of stereotyping arising from such categorization could therefore be reduced. It could then be assumed that 'gender' as a diffuse characteristic is not strong enough to affect stereotyping in the presence of more specific status characteristics like job-related expertise or job titles, which are usually more salient in organizations (Eagly 1983). Or, in other words, ascribing equal status to both in-group and out-group members (that is, men and women), might help in removing or at least decreasing inaccuracies in stereotyping. Equal status in the organizational context means the same job title, job-related expertise, same importance of job, etc.

FORMATION AND MAINTENANCE OF STEREOTYPES

Evidently, ascription of equal status in a task situation has to be done with the full support of external authority. Thus, such ascription should have the implicit/explicit support of the organization in evident ways.

We have also seen that if an out-group member is perceived as being competitive in an attempt towards status improvement, his/her contribution and unstereotypic behaviour are ignored. To eliminate this perception of competition between men and women, the task situation should involve all group members working together towards some common goal. A common goal would improve the quality of interaction by removing the element of competition from the situation.

Just working towards a common goal and ascribing equal status to both men and women in the task situation might result in the majority group members, that is, men, ignoring and overlooking the task requirement and contribution that comes from the women in the task group. Thus, interdependence among the members of the task group is also a prerequisite for quality interaction to take place. Reciprocal interdependencies require mutual adjustment among group members to establish coordination and involve all members in decision-making. Mutual adjustment requires recognition of specific member skills and expertise rather than working from stereotypes based on diffuse criteria. Coordinating through mutual adjustment also requires more flexible orientation and attitudes, making it harder to work from inaccurate stereotypes. Thus, the presence of reciprocal interdependencies among men and women in the task situation is required to make any progress towards revision of stereotypes.

However, even after coming to work together with equal status, with approval and support from authority figures, and interdependently working towards a common goal, the quality of such interaction might still be compromised as the men and women involved might be so aloof from each other that increased interpersonal interactions (through which additional information about the individuals of the out-group is supposed to be solicited) do not happen. Thus, another condition that is required for the quality of interaction to be fruitful enough for reducing inaccuracies of gender stereotypes is the potential for interpersonal interaction.

This is where the contribution of social psychology and its focus on social stereotypes comes in. An array of social cognitive approaches (Brewer 1991; Hewstone and Brown 1986) examines the utility of stereotyping and its basis in our tendency to categorize people into social groups, leading to prejudicial attitudes and discriminatory behaviour. The social cognitive approaches are also concerned with the conditions under which people are likely to stereotype others, as well as with how to design interactions to promote better inter-group relations and better forms of stereotyping (Gaertner et al. 1989).

Most of the social psychologists who subscribe to cognitive perspectives hold that increasing contact between individual members of different groups promotes more accurate beliefs by each about the other and under proper conditions, may promote better relations between them. This view has come to be associated with Allport's classic Contact Hypothesis (Allport 1979).

The conditions for the 'quality' interaction, outlined above, as potentially contributing to reducing the inaccuracy of managerial gender stereotypes, have already been found to be instrumental in reducing the inaccuracies of racial stereotypes. All these conditions, put together under the head of 'contact', comprise the 'Contact Hypothesis' as purported by Allport and later promoted and advanced by other researchers (Cook 1985; Pettigrew 1998).

The Contact Hypothesis

Allport holds that the positive effects of inter-group contact occur only in situations marked by four key conditions:

1. Equal group status within the situation;
2. Common goals;
3. Inter-group cooperation; and
4. The support of authorities, law, or custom.

Equal Status

Allport stressed equal group status within the situation of contact. It is important that both groups expect and perceive equal status in the situation (Cohen 1982; Cohen and Lotan 1995). The outcome of a contact situation might not be positive if there is perceived inequality in the situation of contact. This perception of equality therefore, is necessary, irrespective of the status that group members enjoy outside the contact situation. Thus, we find some studies (Jackman and Crane 1986) showing negative effects from contact with out-group members of perceived lower status within the situation of contact.

Common Goals

Prejudice reduction through contact requires an active, common goal-oriented effort. Athletic teams furnish a prime example (Chu and Griffey 1985; Patchen 1982). In striving to win, inter-racial teams need each other to achieve their goal.

Inter-group Cooperation

Attainment of common goals must be an interdependent effort without inter-group competition (Bettencourt et al. 1992). Inter-group cooperation in schools provides the strongest evidence (Desforges et al. 1991). This technique has led to positive results for a variety of children: Australians (Walker and Crogan 1997), Germans, Japanese and Mexican Americans.

Support of Authorities, Law, or Custom

The final condition concerns the contact's auspices. With explicit social sanction, inter-group contact is more readily accepted and has more positive effects. Authority support establishes the norms of acceptance. Field research underscores its importance in military (Landis et al. 1984; Miller and Brewer 1984), business (Morrison and Herlihy 1992) and religious institutions.

Allport formulated his hypothesis after extensive field research and his formulation continues to receive support across situations and groups. Some research studies, while not providing the key conditions, have uncovered negative effects (Brooks 1975; Zuel and Humphrey 1971). In these studies, the key conditions are not met and yet some writers have mistakenly concluded that their studies have falsified the Contact Hypothesis. The erroneous notion that inter-group contact 'will of itself produce better relations between... groups' still persists.

However, many studies have reported positive contact effects, even in situations lacking key conditions. The contact literature ranges from inter-racial workers in South Africa to German and Turkish school children and Americans getting to know Southeast Asian immigrants (Riordan 1987). It involves attitudes towards a wide range of targets beyond ethnic groups—the elderly (Drew 1988), the mentally ill (Desforges et al. 1991), disabled persons (Anderson 1995) and victims of AIDS (Werth and Lord 1992). In addition, diverse research methods yield supporting results—field (Ohm 1988), archival (Fine 1979), survey (Sigelman and Welch 1993) and laboratory (Desforges et al. 1991).

Acquaintance or Friendship Potential

Pettigrew (1998) identified a fifth condition necessary to facilitate the reduction of negative stereotyping. He stated that the power of cross-group friendship to reduce prejudice and generalize the beneficial effects to other out-groups demands the addition of a fifth condition to the original Contact Hypothesis. He postulated that the contact situation must provide the participants with the opportunity to become friends, as such an opportunity implies close interaction that would make self-disclosure mechanisms possible. It also implies the potential for extensive and repeated contact in a variety of social contexts. Allport alluded to this point when he favoured 'intimate' to 'trivial' contact; Cook (1985) called it 'acquaintance potential'. Pettigrew (Pettigrew 1998) suggested that 'friendship potential' is an essential, not merely facilitating, condition for positive inter-group contact effects that generalize. He further suggested that Allport's conditions were important in part because they provide the setting that encourages inter-group friendship.

Pettigrew further stated that the thrust of the time dimension in his reformulation of Allport's original contact hypothesis is to underline the need for research 'over a period of time' in inter-group contact. Though 'repeated contact exposure' is rare in the literature reviewed by him, his reformulated theory holds that such research designs are necessary for further progress.

Apart from this fifth condition of potential for friendship, personal differences resulting from prior experience and attitudes of contact with the out-group member, as well as social conditions (whether there are explicit or implicit norms which support or deter such contact situations) structure the form and effects of contact situations (Kinloch 1981). One study (Sagiv and Schwartz 1995) found that value differences shaped the differential readiness for inter-group contact among both Israeli Arabs and Jews. Also, the quantity and quality of contact that a person may have had in the past with the out-group members may shape the effects of any conditioned contact in future and his/her readiness to accept the contact situation favourably or unfavourably. Further, the society which one hails from and the implicit and explicit norms followed in that society as regards general ideas about the out-group as well as about the sanctioning of such prior contact might also affect the future attempts through optimal contact.

An analysis of how inaccurate stereotypes are formed and maintained gave us certain conditions of interaction which would help reduce stereotypic inaccuracies. Social psychology corroborates the necessity of the same conditions for reducing inaccuracies in racial stereotypes. If we project the conditions for reduction in inaccuracies to managerial gender stereotypes, we find a potential situation for predicting not only the major antecedents of inaccurate managerial gender stereotypes, but also how to reduce them in future. 'Contact' with women managers, should therefore, determine to a great extent the accuracy or inaccuracy of gender stereotyping of women managers.

HYPOTHESES

From the foregoing review of literature, I predicted the effects of prior contact and the optimal conditions of such contact in shaping and reducing inaccurate and negative stereotypes of women managers, the overriding hypothesis being, the greater the contact, the lesser the inaccuracies of managerial gender stereotypes.

Hypothesis 1

Quantity (in terms of number and frequency) of prior (to the point of study) contact with women managers would determine the inaccuracies of already formed stereotypes of women managers. The more the quantity of prior contact with women managers, the less the inaccuracy of managerial gender stereotypes.

Hypothesis 2

Quality of prior contact with women in professional situations in groups will shape the inaccuracies of existing stereotypes of women managers.

1. The more the perceived equality of status in such prior situations of contact, the less the inaccuracy of managerial gender stereotypes.
2. The more the commonality of goal(s) in such prior contact situations, the less the inaccuracy of managerial gender stereotypes.
3. The more the interdependent cooperation in such prior contact situations, the less the inaccuracy of managerial gender stereotypes.

4. The more the perceived support from the concerned authorities for such prior contact, the less the inaccuracy of managerial gender stereotypes.
5. The more the perceived potential for friendship/acquaintance in such prior contact situations, the less the inaccuracy of managerial gender stereotypes.

Hypothesis 3

Gender stereotyping of women managers is amenable to change through 'simulated' contact. Increasing the quantity of contact with women, that is, an increase in the number of women in a group and the frequency of contact in a given task situation, would reduce the inaccuracy of managerial gender stereotypes at the end of such task situation(s).

Hypothesis 4

Simulating the quality of contact in the task situation would help reduce inaccuracies of stereotypes of women managers:

1. The more the equality of status of men and women in the group in the contact situation, the more likely is a reduction of inaccuracy of managerial gender stereotypes.
2. The more the cooperation between men and women managers towards a common goal of the group, the more likely is a reduction of inaccuracy of managerial gender stereotypes.
3. The more the reciprocal interdependence between men and women in the group in the contact situation, the more likely is a reduction of inaccuracy of managerial gender stereotypes.

4. The more the support from authorities in the contact situation, the more likely is a reduction of inaccuracy of managerial gender stereotypes.

5. The more the potential for friendship/acquaintance between men and women in the contact situation, the more likely is a reduction of inaccuracy of managerial gender stereotypes.

While the first two hypotheses are easily tested using survey techniques, it is the latter two which pose a challenge. The latter two would require an elaborate experimental set-up to verify their predictions in detail. When operationalizing the studies, I did maintain a combination of a survey-questionnaire and an experimental approach, but the experimental approach was modified for simplicity. The modification was also aimed at testing the basic premise on which hypotheses 3 and 4 are based. A better explanation is provided in the chapter covering the experiment and its results.

Before verification of the hypotheses, it became necessary to not only explore existing Indian managerial gender stereotypes, but also fix the measures of such existing stereotypes and their inaccuracies. The next chapter deals with explaining the different measures and variables involved in understanding the concepts behind the hypotheses.

REFERENCES

Allport, G.W. (1979). *The Nature of Prejudice*. Reading, MA: Addison-Wesley. (Originally published in 1954).

Anderson, L.S. (1995). 'Outdoor adventure recreation and social integration: A social-psychological perspective'. PhD thesis. University of Minnesota, Minneapolis, MN.

Bettencourt, B.A., M.B. Brewer, M.R. Rogers-Croak and N. Miller. (1992). 'Cooperation and the reduction of intergroup bias: The role of reward structure and social orientation', *Journal of Experimental & Social Psychology*, 28: 301–19.

Bhatnagar, D. and R. Swamy. (1995). 'Attitudes toward women as managers: Does Interaction make a difference?', *Human Relations*, 48(11): 1285–1307.

Blalock, H.M. (1967). *Toward a Theory of Minority Group Relationships*. New York: John Wiley & Sons.

Bornman, E. and J.C. Mynhardt. (1991). 'Social identification and intergroup contact in South Africa with specific reference to the work situation', *Genet. Sociology and General Psychological Monographs*, 117: 437–62.

Brewer, M.B. (1991). 'The social self: On being the same and different at the same time', *Personality and Social Psychology Bulletin*, 84: 888–914.

Brooks, D. (1975). *Race and Labour in London Transport*. London: Oxford University Press.

Cantor, N. and W. Mischel. (1979). 'Prototypes in person perception', in L. Berkowitz (ed.), *Advances in Experimental Social Psychology*, pp. 12, 4–52. New York: Academic Press.

Christensen, D. and R. Rosenthal. (1982). 'Gender and nonverbal encoding skill as determinants of interpersonal expectancy effects', *Journal of Personality and Social Psychology*, 42: 75–87.

Chu, D. and D. Griffey. (1985). 'The contact theory of racial integration: The case of sport', *Sociology in Sport Journal*, 2: 323–33.

Cohen, E.G. (1982). 'Expectation states and interracial interaction in school settings', *Annual Review of Sociology*, 8: 209–35.

Cohen, E.G. and R.A. Lotan. (1995). 'Producing equal-status interaction in the heterogeneous classroom', *American Educational Research Journal*, 32: 99–120.

Cook, S.W. (1985). 'Experimenting on social issues: The case of school desegregation', *American Psychologist*, 40: 452–60.

Deaux, K. (1984). 'From individual differences to social categories: Analysis of a decade's research on gender', *American Psychologist*, 39: 105–16.

Desforges, D.M., C.G. Lord, S.L. Ramsey, J.A. Mason, M.D. Van Leeuwen, S.C. West and M.R. Lepper. (1991). 'Effects of structured cooperative contact on changing negative attitudes toward stigmatized social groups', *Journal of Personality and Social Psychology*, 60: 531–44.

Dovidio, J.F., J.C. Brigham, B.T. Johnson and S.L. Gaertner. (1996). 'Stereotyping, prejudice, and discrimination: Another look', in N. Macrae, C. Stangor and M. Hewstone (eds), *Foundations of Stereotypes and Stereotyping*, pp. 276–322. New York: Guilford.

Drew, B. (1988). 'Intergenerational contact in the workplace: An anthropological study of relationships in the secondary labor market'. Ph.D. thesis. Rutgers University: New Brunswick, NJ.

Eagly, A.H. (1983). 'Gender and social influence: A social psychological analysis', *American Psychologist*, 21(September): 971–81.

Eagly, A.H. and V.J. Steffen. (1984). 'Gender stereotypes stem from the distribution of women and men into social roles', *Journal of Personality and Social Psychology*, 46: 735–54.

Fine, G.A. (1979). 'The Pinkston settlement: An historical and social psychological investigation of the contact hypothesis', *Phylon*, 40: 229–42.

Gaertner, S., J. Mann, A. Murrell and J. Dovidio. (1989). 'Reducing intergroup bias: The benefits of recategorization', *Journal of Personality and Social Psychology*, 57: 239–49.

Hamilton, D.L. (1979). 'A cognitive-attributional analysis of stereotyping', in L. Berkowitz (ed.), *Advances in Experimental Social Psychology*, pp. 3–84. New York: Academic Press.

Hewstone, M. and R. Brown (eds). (1986). *Contact and Conflict in Intergroup Encounters*. Oxford: Blackwell.

Jackman, M.R. and M. Crane. (1986). '"Some of my best friends are black...": Interracial friendship and whites' racial attitudes', *Public Opinion Quarterly*, 50: 459–86.

Kanter, R.M. (1977). 'Some effects of proportions on group life: Skewed sex ratios and responses to token women', *American Journal of Sociology*, 82: 965–90.

Kelly, H.H. (1972). 'Attribution in social interaction', in E.E. Jones, D.E. Kanouse, H.H. Kelley, R.E. Nisbett, S. Valins and B. Weiner (eds), *Attribution: Perceiving the Causes of Behaviour*, pp. 1–26. Morristown, NJ: General Learning Press.

Kelly, R.E. Nisbett, S. Valens and B. Weiner (eds). (1972). *Attribution: Perceiving the Causes of Behaviour*, pp. 1–26. Morristown, NJ: General Learning Press.

Kinloch, G.C. (1981). 'Comparative race and ethnic relations', *International Journal of Comparative Sociology*, 22: 257–71.

Landis, D., R.O. Hope and H.R. Day. (1984). 'Training for desegregation in the military', in N. Miller and M.B. Brewer (eds), *Groups in Contact: The Psychology of Desegregation*, pp. 257–78. Orlando, FL: Academic Press.

Lippmann, W. (1922). *Public Opinion*. New York: Harcourt, Brace.

Locksley A., E. Bongrida, N. Brekke and C. Hepburn. (1980). 'Sex Stereotypes and Social Judgment', *Journal of Personality & Social Psychology*, 39: 821–30.

McCauley, C., C.L. Stitt and M. Segal. (1980). 'Stereotyping: From prejudice to prediction', *Psychological Bulletin*, 87: 195–208.

McGarty, C. and A.M. de la Haye. (1997). 'Stereotype formation: Beyond illusory correlation', in R. Spears, P.J.Oakes, N. Ellemers and S.A. Haslam (eds), *The Social Psychology of Stereotyping and Group Life*, pp. 144–70. Oxford: Blackwell.

Meeker, B.F. and P.A. Weitzel-O-Neill. (1977). 'Sex roles and interpersonal behavior in task-oriented groups', *American Sociological Review*, 42: 91–105.

Miller, N. and M.B. Brewer (eds). (1984). *Groups in Contact: The Psychology of Desegregation,* 316 pp. Orlando, FL: Academic.

Morrison,E.W. and J.M. Herlihy. (1992). 'Becoming the best place to work: Managing diversity at American Express Travel related services', in S.E. Jackson (ed.), *Diversity in the Workplace*, pp. 203–26. New York: Guilford.

Ohm, R.M. (1988). 'Constructing and reconstructing social distance attitudes'. PhD thesis, pp. 316. Arizona State University. Tempe.

Patchen, M. (1982). *Black-White Contact in Schools: Its Social and Academic Effects*. West Lafayette, IN: Purdue University Press.

Pettigrew, T.F. (1998). 'Intergroup Contact Theory',*Annual Review of Psychology*, 49: 65–85.

Riordan, C. (1987). 'Intergroup contact in small cities', *International Journal of Intercultural Relations*, 11: 143–54.

Sackett, P.R., C.L.Z. Dubois and A.W. Noe. (1991). 'Tokenism in performance evaluation: The effects of work group representation on male-female and white-black differences in performance ratings', *Journal of Applied Psychology*, 76: 263–67.

Sagiv, L. and S.H. Schwartz. (1995). 'Value priorities and readiness for out-group social contact', *Journal of Personality and Social Psychology*, 69: 437–48.

Sigelman, L. and S. Welch. (1993). 'The contact hypothesis revisited: black-white interaction and positive racial attitudes', *Social Forces*, 71: 781–95.

Spears, R., P.J. Oakes,. N. Ellemers and S.A. Haslam (eds). (1997). *The Social Psychology of Stereotyping and Group Life*. Oxford, UK: Blackwell.

Wagner, U., M. Hewstone and U. Machleit. (1989). 'Contact and prejudice between Germans and Turks', *Human Relations*, 42: 561–74.

Walker, I. and M. Crogan. (1997). 'Academic performance, prejudice, and the jigsaw classroom: new pieces to the puzzle'. Presented at Annual Meeting of Social Psychology, 3rd, Wollongong.

Werth, J.L. and C.G. Lord. (1992). 'Previous conceptions of the typical group member and the contact hypothesis', *Basic and Applied Social Psychology*, 13: 351–69.

Zuel, C.R. and C.R. Humphrey. (1971). 'The integration of black residents in suburban neighborhoods', *Social Problems*, 18: 462–74.

4

Exploring Indian
Managerial Gender
Stereotypes

E ven before recommending gender diversity benefits to counter the negative effects of gender stereotypes, we need to assess what they are. Stereotypes held of women managers have often been measured in the western cultural context. Stereotypes have also been measured internationally after extending the research done in the United States to countries like the United Kingdom, Germany, China and Japan and attempts have been made to distill an international managerial stereotype (Schein 2001). There being a dearth of such stereotype-assessment studies in the Indian context, this study was long overdue.

As explained before, stereotypes have been simplistically defined as those characteristics which differentiate one group from the others. In this study, we are dealing with groups of men managers and women managers. Gender stereotypes 'in general' have been found to be different from the managerial subset of gender stereotypes. So, in this case, managerial gender stereotypes would be those characteristics on which a distinct differentiation can be made between men and women managers, and not between men in general and women in general.

However, a managerial characteristic on which a simple differentiation is made between men and women managers, is not what concerns us here. As we have seen, when such a differentiation is made on characteristics which are considered necessary for success, we have stereotypes which are debilitating in nature. Therefore, in this study, we are also concerned with those traits which are associated with success in the workplace. A precondition of 'associations with success' would therefore become necessary for any stereotype to be of consequence to this study and its objectives.

The tables in this chapter refer to data generated as part of the study covered in the chapter.

Since men managers and women managers are mutually exclusive gender-groups within the universal set of managers, managerial gender stereotypes would be those characteristics on which (i) there is a significant perceived difference between men managers and women managers, and (ii) on which there is a close association of either group with managerial success.

A managerial gender stereotype is therefore a managerial characteristic on which a significant 'perceived' difference is found, coupled with a significant association with managerial success. The word 'perceived' needs explanation. Whose perception are we talking about here?

Gender stereotypes are held by both men managers and women managers. Since Indian organizations are mostly male-dominated and since men managers mostly occupy positions of power, and since it the decisions of these men managers which perpetuate discriminatory practices against women managers, our primary concern is the perception of Indian men managers.

That, of course, does not exclude the need for assessing gender stereotypes held by women managers themselves, as women are increasingly occupying important positions in organizations and will equally share employee assessment and recruitment functions with men managers in the not so distant future. Therefore the respondent sample for the first study has both men and women managers.

To illustrate further, let us consider a managerial trait like 'analytical ability'. For analytical ability to be considered a managerial gender stereotype, respondents would have to first associate analytical ability with managerial success and then again would have to make a significant difference while rating men and women managers on the trait of analytical ability.

So, on the same scale pertaining to analytical ability, if they rate successful managers and men managers high while rating women managers low, analytical ability would be considered a managerial gender stereotype.

This stereotype-assessment issue in the Indian context was addressed in part by an Indian study (Bhatnagar and Swamy 1995), in which researchers explored the relationship between 'interaction with women managers' and 'attitudes towards women managers' as measured by a 22-item WAMS (Women as Managers Scale which measures attitudes towards women in management positions) instrument. The 22 items in the modified WAMS instrument, however, did not seem enough to capture the entire stereotypical picture of women managers in the Indian context. A more comprehensive and exhaustive list of managerial characteristics was needed. The BSRI (Bem's Sex Roles Inventory) was also considered but rejected, as the characteristics (items in the instrument) were found to be too general in applicability and not as managerially-oriented in nature as was necessary for this study. Literature also revealed Schein's Descriptive Index (henceforth referred to as SDI) (Schein 1973), which fitted the requirements of this study better. Formulated and tested by Schein, the SDI has been comprehensively used in the western context and other countries to measure managerial gender stereotypic patterns. The SDI is a list of 92 managerial characteristics.

There are four reasons for choosing SDI for this study, despite contentious issues of cross-cultural applicability. First, the formulation of the SDI was an exhaustive process culminating in an exhaustive list of 92 managerial characteristics normally displayed at the workplace. Therefore, SDI, by its very nature, helped look at the managerial subset of gender stereotypes of women, rather than the overall social stereotypes of women in general. The assumption here of course was that social stereotypes would be different from managerial stereotypes. The managerial setting was assumed to overshadow the social setting in this case.

Second, even though Indian managers are a different lot when compared with western managers socially, Indian organizations (barring the old-world family-owned business houses), their management philosophy and their systems and structures in today's world are very strongly influenced by western management philosophy.

Third, the process of stereotype-pattern identification used by the SDI is very close to the thought process I have followed so far in exploring and understanding Indian managerial gender stereotypes.

Finally, using the SDI provided an opportunity for interesting comparisons with outcomes in the western and international context.

The SDI is a list of 92 managerial characteristics on which respondents rate either of the three groups/sets: men managers, women managers and successful middle managers. Stereotypes would be those characteristics on which there is a significant difference in ratings among the three sets/groups. Out of the 92 managerial traits, only those were selected on which a significant difference was found after conducting an analysis of variance (ANOVA). From this list, again, only those traits that had a significant association with success were finally considered as stereotypes in this study.

A question might arise here regarding why one set of respondents are asked in the SDI to rate 'successful middle managers' rather than simply rating 'successful managers'. The explanation follows.

Towards the end of the period 1987–1996, the ratio of men to women in all managerial positions in the USA was 1.4 to 1. At the very top level of salary, however, the ratio of men to women (Daily and Trevis 1999) was 20 to 1. A survey (Catalyst 2003) in 2003 revealed that women held only 7.9 per cent of the highest titles of the Fortune 500 companies. In the Indian context, the absence of such studies leaves little room for factual verification of the same phenomenon. Only six Indian companies appear on the Fortune 500 list. Even without equivalent data for the top 50 companies in India, one can safely conclude that the percentage of women at the very top would not be high.

Also, given that the management schools across India are churning out fresh women managers who represent about 7–10 per cent of the total fresh graduate managers at the junior organizational levels, it cannot be expected that the percentage of women managers in the top tiers in India would reach any significant number. Evidently, more women enter the managerial workforce at the junior levels. It is at the middle managerial level that they stagnate, resulting in a dismal number graduating from the middle to the top. Therefore, it was perfectly acceptable that the third set in the SDI solicited ratings of 'successful middle managers', the other two sets referring to 'men managers' and 'women managers'.

STUDY 1: THE METHOD

Participants in the study were 198 practicing managers in total, with 105 male managers and 93 female managers, from three levels of management (junior, middle and senior) located mostly in the major metropolitan cities of India. Their ages ranged from 22 to 57 years (mean = 31.95 years, median = 30 years). Managerial experience ranged from 'less than one year' to 36 years (mean = 7.25 years, median = 6 years). The demographic statistics were quite comparable to a western study (Heilman et al. 1989), with which an overall comparison is made to understand the difference in cultural and chronological context. Very unlike the western study, the present sample comprised individuals from all over India and from a variety of divisions and a variety of industries like engineering, banking, media, FMCG, pharmaceuticals, food, automobiles, power, software, etc. Keeping in mind the need for inclusion of perceptions of women managers too, the total sample contained 93 women managers, who comprised 46.9 per cent of the total sample.

Respondents in this study were randomly assigned to either of the three target groups and received one of the three versions of the SDI, in which they were asked to rate either successful middle managers, men managers or women managers on each of the 92 characteristics, using a five-point rating scale (ranging from 1 = not characteristic, to 5 = characteristic) to score their ratings. The ratings on these three different sets (men managers, women managers and successful middle managers) were then compared and correlated for various insights.

OVERALL RESULTS

In keeping with the objectives of the study which focuses on stereotypes held of women managers by men managers, findings based on the exclusively male sample and the exclusively female sample have been reported separately.

Men-managers' Sample

For the exclusive male sample, the respondents' ages ranged from 22 to 57 years (mean = 33.86 years, median = 30 years). Managerial experience ranged from 'less than 1 year' to 36 years (mean = 8.84 years, median = 6 years). This was quite comparable to a western study (Heilman et al. 1989) in which the age range was from 24 to 63 years, and managerial experience ranged from 'less than 1 year' to 42 years (median = 6 years). The sample comprised of 28.57 per cent junior, 41.9 per cent middle and 29.53 per cent senior level managers.

Intra-class Correlation Coefficients

To determine the degree of correspondence between ratings of successful middle managers and men managers, and that between successful middle managers and women managers, two intra-class coefficients (ICCs) were computed. This was done to compare the similarity of respondents' ratings of successful middle managers and women managers and successful middle managers and men managers. Thus, a high ICC would reflect a similar description of each set of descriptors (successful middle managers and men managers or successful middle managers and women managers) and a low ICC would reflect a difference or dissimilarity in the descriptions of each set.

The intra-class correlation coefficients in this study showed a large and significant relationship between ratings of successful middle managers and men managers, but no significant relationship between ratings of successful middle managers and women managers. Table 4.1 presents the ICCs for successful middle managers and men managers, and for successful middle managers and women managers, for the present study as well as for

Table 4.1
ICC and PPMC Values for Male Managerial Sample

Intra-class Correlation Coefficients for Male Managers' Sample		
Group	Heilman et al. (1989)	Present study
Men managers and successful middle managers	0.86**	0.75**
Women managers and successful middle managers	0.58**	0.38††

Pearson Product-Moment Correlation Coefficients for Male Managers' Sample		
Men managers and successful middle managers	0.90**	0.84**
Women managers and successful middle managers	0.73**	0.44††

Notes: ** $p < 0.001$
†† implies significant difference between the two groups [(M & SM) vs. (W & SM)] at $p = 0.01$

an earlier study (Heilman et al. 1989). Even though we have provided comparisons with an earlier study in the US, there have been replications in other countries like UK, Germany, China and Japan and the results for the male samples (these replication studies used management students instead of a managerial sample) bear equally strong resemblance to the studies conducted so far in the US.

Pearson Product-Moment Correlations

Pearson Product-Moment Correlations (PPMC) were computed to determine the linear relationships between the descriptions of successful middle managers and men managers and of successful middle managers and women managers. The use of

Pearson correlations enabled investigations into the presence of any inverse relationships in characteristics of women managers and successful middle managers, whereas ICCs investigated the absence of direct relationships.

Table 4.1 also presents the PPMCs for successful middle managers and men managers, and for successful middle managers and women managers, for the present study and for the earlier study.

As the numbers indicate, both the correlations for successful managers and men and for successful managers and women show a decrease in value between studies. While the decrease in value for the PPMC between successful managers and men managers is not so significant (from 0.90 to 0.84), the value for the PPMC between successful managers and women managers shows quite a significant decrease (from 0.73 to 0.44).

When compared to the coefficients derived from the western study (Heilman et al. 1989) the results arrived at in this study indicate a difference for the worse when the cultural context of the study is changed. In other words, Indian male managers as respondents closely associate successful managers with men and make much lesser associations between women and successful managers.

Women Managers' Sample

For the exclusively female sample, the women respondents' ($n = 93$) ages ranged from 22 to 46 years (mean = 29.78 years, median = 29 years). Managerial experience ranged from 'less than 1 year' to 15 years (mean = 5.46 years, median = 5 years). This was somewhat similar to another comparable western study (Schein 1975), in which the age range was from 24 to 64 years; and managerial experience ranged from 1 to 40 years. As mentioned earlier, the respondents were practicing managers from three levels of management (junior, middle and senior) in different industries and from all over India. The sample comprised 49.46 per cent junior, 45.16 per cent middle and 5.38 per cent senior level managers.

Unlike the results from the male managerial sample, the intra-class correlation coefficients for the female sample (Table 4.2) show a strong relationship between ratings of successful middle managers and men managers, and *an equally strong relationship between ratings of successful middle managers and women managers*. When compared to the Intra-class Correlation coefficients and the PPMC coefficients derived from a western study (Schein 1975) in the 1970s and then again in the late 1980s,

Table 4.2
ICC and PPMC Values for Female Managerial Sample

Intra-class Correlation Coefficients for Female Managers' Sample			
Group	Schein (1975)	Schein (1989)	Present study
Men managers and successful middle managers	0.54*	0.59*	0.75**
Women managers and successful middle managers	0.30*†	0.52*	0.64**

Pearson Product-Moment Correlation Coefficients for Female Managers' Sample			
Men managers and successful middle managers	0.70*	0.63*	0.77**
Women managers and successful middle managers	0.40*†	0.62*	0.66**

Notes: * $p < 0.01$, ** $p < 0.001$.
† implies significant difference between the two groups [(M & SM) vs. (W & SM)] at $p = 0.05$.

the results indicate a difference for the better, even with a change in the cultural context of the study.

DISCUSSION

For the men managers' sample, the results make it clear that the descriptions of women managers are still far less congruent with descriptions of successful managers than are descriptions of men managers. Not only has there been little change across cultures in the pattern of these differential descriptions over the last decade or so, but there has also been a change for the worse in the Indian context. In other words, Indian male managers make even lower associations between women managers and managerial success than the male managers in the west did more than a decade ago (which itself was found to be very low).

The findings are in accordance with the international trend that has been revealed in international replications of the original Schein studies. In countries like Germany, the UK, China and Japan, male business management students have consistently rated women managers lower on their associations with managerial success, while at the same time making very strong associations with men managers and managerial success. Thus the Indian male managerial sample not only subscribes to the international perception of 'think manager–think male' but does it with even more élan than his male counterparts in the US or in other countries of the world.

This can be looked upon as an expected outcome, given the long history of a traditionally male-dominated society in India. Moreover, it is a psychological phenomenon that has been observed in many countries across the world. Even in countries in which the studies have not been conducted, maybe with the exception of the Scandinavian countries, my hunch is that the same trend will be replicated. India is no exception, more so, given its cultural and historical roots in which masculinity has been considered a prerequisite for success at most activities including business. Moreover, given that the trend of inducting women managers in corporate India has been very recent, this attitudinal outcome is an expected one.

Table 4.1 shows that though the ICC values for associations between men managers and successful managers are comparable to those obtained in the previous study (Heilman et al. 1989), when it comes to ICC values for associations between women managers and successful managers, our sample falls far short of the values derived from a similar sample more than a decade ago in a different cultural context. The same can be said for PPMC coefficient values.

One encouraging finding is that women respondents have portrayed women managers to be as representative of successful managers as men managers, as is evident from both the ICC and PPMC coefficient values in Table 4.2 (there is no significant difference between the ICC and PPMC values between groups).

This is indeed an interesting finding. Using a similar sample consisting exclusively of women managers in the US, Schein (1975) had concluded that there was no difference in the way women managers associated 'women in general' with 'successful managers' and the way in which men managers associated 'women in general' with 'successful managers'. In her exclusively female sample, the ICC and PPMC coefficient values were comparable to those in her original study conducted with an exclusively male sample. However, almost a decade and a half later, Schein studied a similar female managerial sample

(Brenner et al. 1989) and found that women's perceptions of women managers had indeed changed over time (even though men's perceptions had not). The international replications, however, showed that female samples (management students) very strongly stereotyped the successful manager's role and found little association with women managers. In other words, in most of the countries studied except the US, women were also strong believers in the 'think manager–think male' perception. The explanation that was provided for the very different outcome in the US was the introduction of affirmative action laws and judicial interventions over the span of a decade and a half, after which the results showed a significant positive difference for the female managerial and student sample.

So, while women negatively stereotyped women extensively in many countries of the world including developed countries, Indian women managers did not seem to follow that trend. The encouraging results for the exclusively female sample bring out some interesting insights. In India, there is a common saying that women are their own greatest enemies. Clearly, this expectation does not translate into reality for women managers as a separate class. They think highly of themselves. What is very encouraging is that women managers' perceptions of themselves in India did not need laws and affirmative action on the part of the legislature to ensure that women managers thought highly of themselves.

However, caution needs to be exercised before drawing sweeping conclusions. This phenomenon can also be partly attributed to the fact that most women managers in the sample belonged to industries like the IT and ITES sectors, where women have already been in the fray for a relatively long time, thus positively affecting their perceptions of women managers.

In India, therefore, the focus clearly shifts to men managers and their perceptions about women managers in the workplace, the effect of which can be seen in the abysmally low numbers of women managers in the managerial workforce in India. Also, since India has traditionally been as male-dominated in nature (if not more) as the west, the effects of this male domination can be gauged from this study in the twenty-first century.

RESULTS RELATED TO STEREOTYPES

Stereotypes with negative connotations which perceptually hamper the progress of women managers would be those on which successful managers are rated closer to men managers than to women managers. The positive stereotypes held of women managers would be those characteristics on which successful managers were rated closer to women managers than men managers.

However, any stereotypical characteristic would not hold much interest in this study if it isn't associated closely with success. Thus, for a stereotype to be considered important for further studies, two things have been considered:

1. Managerial characteristics which are considered necessary for managerial success and are also associated more with men managers than with women managers. These would be 'masculine-positive' stereotypes.
2. Managerial characteristics which are considered necessary for managerial success and are also associated more with women managers than with men managers. These would be 'feminine-positive' stereotypes.

Male Managerial Sample

As explained before, to separate those managerial characteristics on which a significant difference existed between men and women managers, an analysis of variance (ANOVA) was conducted. On this list of separated characteristics, another test (Duncan's Multiple Range Test) was conducted to determine the specific associations between the three sets.

A series of one-way ANOVAs was conducted, with an overall alpha level of $p < 0.05$, on each of the 92 Descriptive Index items from the male respondents' sample, to determine the ones whose ratings were significantly different, across the three sets/groups: women managers, men managers and successful middle managers. A significant effect was found for 35 items.

To identify the specific items that were seen as more descriptive of successful middle managers and men managers and those that were seen as more descriptive of successful middle managers and women managers, a Duncan's multiple range was done on each of the 35 items for which significant effects were found in the ANOVA analysis.

Out of the 35 significant characteristics illustrated in Table 4.3, for 18 items, ratings of successful middle managers were more similar to men managers than to women managers (Table 4.3b) and for 2 items, ratings of successful middle managers were more similar to women managers than men managers (Table 4.3a). There were 15 items (Table 4.3c) on which no significant differential associations were made with successful managers.

It is disheartening to note that none of the two items on which women managers have been rated closer to successful managers are actually thought of as 'required' for success.

Table 4.3
Male Sample—35 Significant Items after ANOVA and Duncan's Multiple Range Test

4.3a. Items on which Successful Managers Rated More Similarly to Women Managers

Values pleasant surroundings	Vulgar (less)

4.3b. Items on which Successful Managers Rated More Similarly to Men Managers

Not uncomfortable about being aggressive	Sympathetic (less)
High need for power	Kind (less)
Vigorous	Sentimental (less)
Adventurous	Timid (less)
Skilled in business matters	Humanitarian values (less)
Aggressive	Shy (less)
Analytical ability	Interested in own appearance (less)
Strong need for achievement	Submissive (less)
Not conceited about appearance	Talkative (less)

4.3c. Items without Significant Differential Associations with Successful Managers

Decisive	Wavering in decision
Well-informed	Easily influenced
Persistent	Quarrelsome
Objective	Passive
Self-controlled	Uncertain
Creative	Nervous
Leadership Ability	Strong need for security
Speedy recovery from emotional disturbances	

In other words these two characteristics (as opposed to characteristics like 'analytical ability' and 'skilled in business matters') are not usually thought necessary in hard performance terms.

When compared to the international stereotypes (Schein 2001) held by male managers and male business-management students in six countries in the world, we see quite an overlap between the masculine stereotypes held by Indian male managers and those held internationally. Some characteristics which were perceived to be important to successful managers across cultures were leadership ability, desire for responsibility, skill in business matters and analytical ability. Out of these, analytical ability and skill in business matters were found to be common to the Indian male managerial sample. Leadership ability figures in the list of characteristics (Table 4.3c) where no distinction was made between men managers and women managers and their associations with successful managers. The other internationally found stereotype of 'desires responsibility' was not found to be rated significantly different at all.

The exclusion of leadership ability from the masculine list can be attributed to the history of strong women leaders (especially in politics) in the Indian sub-continent and their influence on managerial perceptions. However, hard performance-related stereotypes like being 'skilled in business matters' and having 'analytical ability' still remain on the list. The overall message still remains: business is better handled by men and analytical ability being one of the prerequisites to succeeding in the business arena, women (even as managers) are not thought of as possessing it.

Before proceeding to the next table of items, it is necessary to explain the inclusion of the word 'less' in Table 4.3. The rating scale of the SDI is a five-point scale, as illustrated further. There is a neutral point 3 in the scale, which represents 'neither characteristic nor uncharacteristic'.

5 – Characteristic
4 – Somewhat characteristic

3 – Neither characteristic nor uncharacteristic
2 – Somewhat uncharacteristic
1 – Not characteristic

After performing the Duncan's multiple range test for the characteristic of 'vulgar', a close look at the three means (from the three different sets...women managers, successful managers and men managers) reveals that though both successful managers and women managers have been rated closely, but on the lower side of 3, that is, towards 1, while men managers have been rated highly, that is, towards 5. Please refer Table 4.4 for a detailed understanding.

Table 4.4
Mean Ratings for Three Sets of Managers for the Characteristic 'Vulgar'

Groups	Women managers	Successful managers	Men managers
Mean ratings	1.3429	1.5714	3.4571

Thus, to describe a feminine characteristic, an additional word 'less', has been included to indicate that successful managers and women managers together are considered to be 'less' vulgar. The same nomenclature was used for describing the masculine and feminine stereotypes derived from previous western studies (Heilman et al. 1989).

Therefore, a stereotypic characteristic is determined by two criteria. One is the association with successful managers, or success itself and the other is the direction of ratings of means for that particular characteristic. The former is determined by the closeness of mean ratings between either group (men or women managers) and successful managers, while the latter is determined by which side of the neutral point 3 do the closely associated means for that particular characteristic lie.

In the case of 'Vulgar', (Table 4.4) though the association between women managers and successful managers is high, denoting it as a 'positive' feminine stereotype, the direction of ratings of both successful managers and women managers dictated the need for an additional adjective to portray the complete picture. Notwithstanding its explanatory power, this additional adjective of 'less' might give rise to ambiguity in future studies. This problem will be addressed in further discussions.

It is, however, heartening to note that the usual masculine stereotypes of leadership ability, decisiveness, self-control etc., (previous studies) and also the traditional feminine stereotypes of passivity, being quarrelsome, etc. (previous studies) have moved out of the traditional masculine/feminine sphere and have been designated separately. Men managers and women managers have been rated close enough on these traditionally masculine/feminine parameters to indicate that some perceptions have changed for the better.

Female Managerial Sample

Analysis of variance (ANOVA) for an exclusive female sample ($n = 93$) distilled 41 significant items (Table 4.5) out of which, for 18 items, successful managers were considered to be similar to men managers (Table 4.5b), for 6 items, successful managers were considered similar to women managers (Table 4.5a) and 17 items on which no significant differential associations were made with successful managers (Table 4.5c).

A scrutiny of the 18 + 6 items leaves no doubt that when the sample was composed of women managers only, the nature of the items, which were similarly rated for successful managers and women managers, shows quite a positive change.

Table 4.5

Female Sample—41 Significant Items after ANOVA and Duncan's Multiple Range Test

4.5a. Items on which Successful Managers Rated More Similarly to Women Managers

High need for power (less)	Intelligent
Vulgar (less)	Persistent
Modest	Competent

4.5b. Items on which Successful Managers Rated More Similarly to Men Managers

Not uncomfortable about being aggressive	*Sympathetic (less)*
Logical	Reserved (less)
Strong need for monetary rewards	*Kind (less)*
Forceful	Sophisticated (less)
Devious	Strong need for security (less)
Aggressive	*Interested in own appearance (less)*
Knows the ways of the world	Grateful (less)
Well-informed	*Sentimental (less)*
Feelings not easily hurt	Helpful (less)

4.5c. Items without Significant Differential Associations with Successful Managers

Self-confident	Consistent
Leadership ability	Dawdler and Procrastinator
Skilled in business matters	Wavering in decision
Analytical ability	Obedient
Intuitive	Values pleasant surroundings
Humanitarian Values	Neat
Understanding	Creative
Sociable	Courteous
Aware of feelings of others	

The addition of important characteristics (like 'intelligent' and 'competent') to the women respondents' list of feminine stereotypes goes on to show that there has been some contextual change in women's stereotypes held by themselves. Moreover, contrary to the international common list from female samples across countries, the only characteristic that made it to the list of masculine stereotypes for the Indian women managers was 'well-informed'. The other characteristics held by female respondents in other countries included 'self-confident', 'leadership ability', 'skilled in business matters', 'prompt' and 'desires responsibility'. The first three characteristics have been rated no differently across men as well as women managers by the Indian women managers. This is in accordance with the encouraging correlation values.

Only 6 out of the 18 masculine items in Table 4.5b are in common with the masculine stereotypes derived from the exclusively male sample (the ones in common are in italics) in this study, implying that women managers have a different set of perceptions as compared to the perceptions held by men managers. The right column in Table 4.5b contains items which are mostly negative in nature, like 'less helpful' or 'less grateful'. This shows that women managers have a negative evaluation of men managers and the characteristics that they exhibit in the workplace to be successful, and that women respondents also relate these negative characteristics to success.

As noted, many of the items in Table 4.5c like analytical ability, skill in business matters, etc., were traditional masculine items in previous studies and also in the results of the male respondents' sample in this study. It is a positive change that women respondents rated men managers and women managers no differently on these performance related characteristics.

By the nature of the 41 significant items and the ICC and PPMC coefficient values for the female sample, it is evident that women are far more progressive in thought, especially when it comes to comparisons between men managers and women managers. They do not make the usual differentiation that men make, either in favour of men managers or against women managers.

This outlook is a better-balanced outlook, as there is no distinction made between successful middle managers and men managers or women managers for even traditionally masculine items like 'leadership ability', or 'business skills'. Also, traditionally masculine items like 'intelligent' or 'competent' are thought to be exhibited more by women managers for success. This brings out insights into the minds of women managers and how they are reacting perceptually to their new-found independence and success in corporate India.

In stark contrast, the findings of the male sample (even when compared to the male samples in previous studies) seem to imply that Indian male managers need reforms in their perceptions of association between managerial characteristics of women and managerial success.

FURTHER DISCUSSION

According to the interpretation based on previous studies, 2 'feminine' and 18 'masculine' stereotypic characteristics have been found to be held by the exclusively male sample. Given the encouraging correlation coefficient values obtained from the female sample, I restricted the scope of this study to address managerial gender stereotypes held by men managers only.

A stereotype (feminine or masculine) is interpreted when there is a significant difference in rating either women managers or men managers and successful managers. There are two components of this stereotypic measure: one is the association with success and the other is the direction of rating. The example of the 'feminine' stereotype of 'vulgar (less)' will illustrate this further.

This characteristic has been labelled a stereotype because women managers and successful managers have been rated closely on this characteristic while men managers have been rated differently. However the adjective 'less' had to be included in the stereotype as the direction of rating (as discussed earlier, see Table 4.4) made its inclusion imperative. The inclusion of the adjective 'less' in the stereotype, however, has its own implications for the future usage of these stereotypes derived from this study.

When a respondent is asked to rate a characteristic like 'less' vulgar [or vulgar (less)], on whatever scale or for whatever purpose, the introduction of the word 'less' brings with it a lot of ambiguity in interpretation. 'Less' to one respondent might not mean the same as it means to another. A large amount of relativity is associated with such adjectives, which in turn might allow ambiguity of interpretation to creep in while responding to or interpreting these stereotypes.

Thus, it would not be advisable to have the adjective 'less' associated with the stereotypes selected from Duncan's multiple range test results. It would be advisable to strive for a better interpretation of the 18 + 2 stereotypes that have been interpreted as masculine and feminine using the nomenclature used in earlier studies.

Coming back to the item 'less vulgar', from the means of the three sets in Table 4.4 and the pattern of rating by the respondents, it is evident that men managers are perceived as 'vulgar' (mean = 3.46 and greater than the neutral point = 3), whereas women managers are not thought of as vulgar. Neither are successful managers. Thus, the trait of 'vulgar' is uncharacteristic of women managers as well as successful managers. Therefore, it can be said that absence of 'vulgarity' in the managerial context is associated positively with success, which in turn means that 'not being vulgar' or being 'less vulgar' is a positive stereotype (related to or associated with success) and since women managers are associated more with such success, 'less vulgar' is a 'positive' and 'feminine' stereotype.

The fact that the descriptor 'vulgar' is a stereotype remains unchanged, as there have been significant differences in rating the three sets (men managers, women managers and successful managers) on that descriptor. However, we can also interpret the characteristic of vulgar in another way, in which the adjective of 'less' or 'not being' vulgar can be done away with. Being vulgar is associated with men managers (mean > 3) and is not associated with success. It can therefore be said that 'vulgar' is a masculine stereotype (men managers are perceived to possess this trait significantly differently from women managers and successful managers as well) and is also 'negative' in nature as 'being vulgar' is not associated with successful managers.

Thus, though 'less vulgar' or 'not vulgar' is interpreted as a 'feminine' stereotype according to earlier nomenclature, this interpretation offers a look at the same in a different light, without contradicting the original assumptions. Just reversing the direction of interpretation leads to a better position and avoids ambiguity in stereotypes that could help further stereotype-related studies. Based on the above, the 'less-added', 'positive', 'feminine' stereotype of 'less vulgar' is converted to a 'negative', 'masculine' stereotype of 'vulgar'.

Applying the same logic, the nine 'less-added', 'positive', 'masculine' stereotypes (right column in Table 4.3b) can be converted into nine 'negative' 'feminine' stereotypes. This exercise produces (9+1) masculine stereotypes and (1+9) feminine stereotypes (one negative masculine stereotype and nine negative feminine stereotypes). The 20 stereotypes based on the foregoing discussion are illustrated in Table 4.6.

Table 4.6
Redistributed List of Managerial Gender Stereotypes in India

Feminine stereotypes	Masculine stereotypes
Values Pleasant surroundings (+)	Adventurous
Sympathetic	Vigorous
Timid	Not uncomfortable about being aggressive
Talkative	Not conceited about appearance
Submissive	High need for power
Interested in own appearance	Strong need for achievement
Shy	Skilled in business matters
Humanitarian Values	Analytical ability
Sentimental	Aggressive
Kind	Vulgar (−)

The redistribution of the list of items in Table 4.6 has been based on some deeper insights into the pattern of responses and keeping in mind how gender stereotypes that affect women managers' progress in organizations have been defined. This further interpretation has been done to ensure that researchers pursuing further studies face no sense of ambiguity about the managerial gender stereotypes in the Indian context. It also ensures a smooth transition from Study 1 to Study 2, where these same stereotypes were used for exploring the relationship between inaccurate stereotypes and quality contact.

LIMITATIONS

The SDI used in this study, though comprehensive, has its own limitations when looked upon in context. The adaptation of the 92 SDI managerial descriptors, page to page, to the Indian context might have led to oversight with regard to some specific traits endemic to India as a country. However, though apparently the cross-cultural adaptability of the SDI to the Indian context can be contentious, we also need to keep in mind that most of our management philosophy has been a derived version of western management philosophy. Our pioneering management education institutes, which again are the sources of managerial excellence, had started out with the help and hand-holding of established management schools in the US. Therefore, while admitting to a cultural difference socially, we can say that the same cultural difference might not be as relevant managerially in corporate India.

IMPLICATIONS FOR FURTHER RESEARCH

Gender stereotypes and their inaccuracies in the Indian context have not been measured before. Studies like Bhatnagar and Swamy (1995) have tried to link 'interaction' with 'attitudes towards women managers', but specifically gender stereotype-related studies have not been done so far. This study therefore achieves a pioneering position paving the first step in the quest for revising inaccurate gender stereotypes in the Indian context. It delineates the stereotypes and the inaccuracies which might need revision in future. Inaccurate stereotypes have been seen to have a host of negative consequences for women managers. The number of women managers in Indian organizations is also not a figure which gives us something to rejoice about. Thus, these managerial gender stereotypes held by men managers give further research in this book and outside a base to start with.

This study also points out the positive difference between the international context and the Indian context in managerial gender stereotypes held by women managers themselves. In India, stereotypes held by women managers of themselves are not a matter of concern, but the stereotypes held by men managers of women managers are. The latter have been found to be much more prejudiced than the stereotypes held in the west. The Indian male manager seems to believe in the 'think manager–think male' phenomenon even more strongly than his counterparts in countries across the world.

REFERENCES

Bhatnagar, D. and R. Swamy. (1995). 'Attitudes toward women as managers: does Interaction make a difference?', *Human Relations*, 48(11): 1285–1307.

Brenner, O.C., V.E. Schein and J. Tomkiewicz. (1989). 'The relationship between sex role stereotypes and requisite management characteristics revisited', *Academy of Management Journal*, 32(3): 662–69.

Catalyst. (2003). 'Women and men in U.S. corporate leadership: Same workplace, different realities?', http://www.catalystwomen.org/bookstore/files/exe/wmicl4executivesummary.pdf (Accessed on 10 July 2007).

Daily, C. and C. Trevis. (1999). 'A decade of corporate women: Some progress in the boardroom, none in the executive suit', *Strategic Management Journal*, 20(1): 93–9.

Heilman, M., C. Block, R. Martell and M. Simon. (1989). 'Has anything changed? Current characterisations of men, women and managers', *Journal of Applied Psychology*, 74: 935–42.

Schein, V.E. (1973). 'The relationship between sex role stereotypes and requisite management characteristics', *Journal of Applied Psychology*, 57: 95–100.

———. (1975). 'Relations between sex role stereotypes and requisite management characteristics among female managers', *Journal of Applied Psychology*, 60: 340–44.

———. (2001). 'A Global look at psychological barriers to women's progress in management', *Journal of Social Issues*, 57(4): 675–88.

5

**Measures of
Inaccuracy in
Stereotypes**

Efforts to measure stereotypes and their accuracy/inaccuracy have been on since the 'checklist measure' (Katz and Braly 1933) was first introduced. In the checklist type of measure, which contains a given list of traits, respondents check a number of traits which they consider 'most typical' of a particular group. A stereotype exists to the extent to which respondents agree on the choice of the 'most typical' traits. The checklist measure is a 'social' or 'cultural' stereotype, because it is a group measure, defined by the extent of agreement across respondents. With a few exceptions (Spence and Helmreich 1978; Spence et al. 1974), most studies initially investigated 'social' or 'cultural' stereotypes of men and women (Broverman et al. 1972; Heilbrun 1976; Williams and Bennett 1975).

Despite the popularity of the checklist approach, the method was found to be limited in that it could not easily measure individual differences in degree of stereotyping, or identify the particular items that define a single individual's stereotype (Ashmore and Del Boca 1979). Individuals hold stereotypes, but the checklist could measure only a kind of group average. It was felt that an ideal assessment should not only be able to measure 'social' or 'cultural' stereotypes, but also individual stereotypes and individual differences in stereotyping.

To overcome the limitations of the checklist measure and to provide a better measure of stereotypes, another measure was suggested (Brigham 1971): the percentage of a stereotyped group thought to have any trait or characteristic. In this measure, respondents were asked to estimate the percentage of members of a target group with a particular characteristic. Researchers used this percentage measure in some later studies (Brigham 1973; 1974) and observed some interesting results. In many

---

The tables in this chapter refer to data generated as part of the study covered in the chapter.

cases the 'typical' traits, as chosen using the checklist measure, were depicted as being characteristic of less than half of the members of the stereotyped group. These results were somewhat surprising and raised the possibility that the percentage measure might have tapped something different from what the checklist did.

To refine the 'percentage measure' and to make it more representative of the definition of stereotypes, a 'ratio measure' was formulated (McCauley and Stitt 1978) and was called the Diagnostic Ratio (or the Likelihood Ratio). The premise on which the 'ratio measure' was formulated was that stereotypes are formed by those characteristics which distinguish one group from the population in general. The Diagnostic ratio of a trait, therefore, is the estimated incidence of that trait in the target group, divided by the estimated base rate (the estimated incidence of that trait in the whole population). The extent to which a characteristic's ratio differs from 1.0 indicates the extent to which that characteristic is believed to distinguish the group. It was found that the Diagnostic Ratio did better than the within-group 'percentage measure' in distinguishing known stereotype traits.

To further refine the 'ratio measure' so that researchers could investigate and compare stereotypes of two mutually exclusive groups such as men and women, a second form of the Diagnostic Ratio (McCauley et al. 1980) was recommended, in which the two groups were compared directly rather than one group being compared with the population in general. The utility of this measure was demonstrated in a later study (Martin 1987). This study measured accuracy of stereotypes by calculating a Diagnostic Ratio by dividing the percentage estimate p (trait/men) by the percentage estimate p (trait/women) and a Criterion Ratio (CR) by dividing the proportion of men by the proportion of women who actually endorsed the trait, and comparing the two for accuracy.

The advantages of using the above measure were manifold. Both 'social' or group stereotypes and individual stereotypes were measurable with this refined ratio measure. 'Cultural' or 'social' stereotypes were assessed by averaging the ratio scores of an attribute or a range of attributes across respondents. The items with a mean ratio score significantly above or below 1.0 constituted a consensual stereotype. Individual stereotypes typical to an individual were measurable by indicating those characteristics for a single respondent, for which significantly different (from 1.0) mean ratio scores were observed. Also, individual differences in stereotyping (the degree of stereotyping) were measurable by an index arrived at by averaging an individual's ratio scores across a set or domain of items. This index indicated the extent to which the individual perceived that the two groups were different (or one group was different from the population).

Only a small number of studies have directly assessed the accuracy of stereotypes and the results have been mixed. In some cases, stereotypes have been found to be similar to the actual group characteristics (Schuman 1966), whereas, in other cases, stereotypes have been found to be quite dissimilar to group characteristics (Abate and Berrien 1967).

We have already seen in Chapter 3 how stereotypic inaccuracies are formed and maintained over time. As social perceivers, we make judgments about traits and behaviours associated with members of a particular group. As has been mentioned before, while making such judgments, we over-estimate the occurrence of expected behaviour rather than actual behaviour. Systematic errors in these estimates are referred to as illusory correlations (Hamilton and Rose 1980). Studies on illusory correlations indicate that perceivers overestimate the frequency of occurrence of expected information as compared to unexpected information.

Thus, it is expected that reliance on such perceptions would lead perceivers towards exaggeration errors, such that judgments of the incidence of occurrence of stereotype-consistent infor-mation, (for example, percentage of men who are dominant) would be overestimated when compared to judgments of the incidence of occurrence of stereotype-inconsistent information (for example, the percentage of women who are dominant). Thus, the diagnostic ratio ('estimate of percentage of men man-agers possessing a particular trait' divided by 'estimate of per-centage of women managers possessing that particular trait') for a masculine stereotype would be greater than 1, while the diag-nostic ratio for a feminine stereotype would be lesser than 1.

Following the refined 'ratio measure', the inaccuracy of gender stereotypes in this study was measured by comparing (estimated) diagnostic ratios on a number of characteristics with actual self-reports of respondents on the same characteristics (as measured by criterion ratios). The inaccuracy of stereotypes was measured in two parts, one relating to the individual degree of traditional stereotyping and the other relating to the estimation errors measured through the difference between estimated ratios and actual ratios on selected stereotypes.

The individual degree of traditional stereotyping is meas-ured as the difference between the mean diagnostic score on masculine stereotypes and the mean diagnostic score on feminine stereotypes. The more traditional the degree of individual stereotyping, the more the respondent differentiates between men and women in a traditional way.

The estimation errors (illusionary correlations) are measured by comparing the diagnostic ratio for a particular trait with the criterion ratio of that trait. This is done by comparing the ratios of men to women estimated to have various traits, with the actual ratios of men to women who endorse the same traits. If a particular gender stereotype is relatively accurate, the diagnostic (estimated) ratio should not differ significantly in magnitude from the criterion (actual) ratio. If gender stereotypes are exaggerations of gender differences, the estimated ratio should be more extreme in the stereotypic direction than the actual ratio. Thus, a measure of the inaccuracy would be the absolute value of the difference between the diagnostic ratio of a stereotype and the criterion ratio of that same stereotype.

For checking inaccuracies in 'group' stereotypes for each trait, a one-sample *t*-test would verify whether the difference between the criterion ratio and the mean diagnostic ratio is significant or not, that is, whether significant inaccuracies exist in that stereotype or not.

CONCEPTS AND MEASUREMENT OF VARIABLES FOR STUDY 2

Women managers: Managers here included officers and executives, as many organizations use such designations for their management cadre employees.

Independent Variables

Seven independent variables in total—two relating to 'quantity of contact' from gender literature and five relating to 'quality of contact' from social psychology literature. The variables have been explained as follows:

'Contact' in a professional situation refers to situations where the respondent has worked with women managers in a task or job situation(s) (as in a temporary/permanent job or project) where the outcomes of the task/job are measurable.

Quantity of Contact

Here, the first part is the *number* of women managers on an average that a respondent has come in contact with in a professional situation and the second part is the *frequency* at which (again on an average) this contact has taken place in the work experience of the respondent till date.

Quality of Contact—Five Conditions

1. **Equal status of contact:** A task situation in which the importance of the respondent and the woman manager(s) in contributing towards the task is equal and the task expertise required and task description(s) are the same.

2. **Common goal:** A task situation in which the goals of both the genders would be as similar and as important as the common goal(s) for the task, that is, competition between members of both genders for the goal(s) is absent.

3. **Interdependent cooperation:** A task situation in which cooperation would require both genders to be dependent equally on each other's contribution to reach the goal(s) of the task.

4. **Support from authorities:** A task situation where there would be explicit support from the authorities for informal interpersonal interactions with member(s) of the other gender.

5. **Potential for friendship:** A task situation in which the environment would provide the opportunity to know the member(s) of the other gender informally through interpersonal interaction.

Dependent Variables

We have *n* dependent variables related to 'estimation errors' and one dependent variable related to 'individual degree of traditional stereotyping'. To generalize the outcomes of this study, *n* variables are mentioned, because the value of *n* (the number of dependent variables) is dependant on the outcome of Study-1. The value of *n* after the Study 1 in this book was 20. To arrive at the dependent variables, we would need to go into the details of Diagnostic Ratios and Criterion Ratios (explained in the preceding section on measurement of stereotypes).

Inaccurate Estimation Errors

At the end of Study 1, we arrived at 20 stereotypes. These 20 stereotypes included ten masculine and ten feminine stereotypes. My questionnaire asked respondents to 'estimate' the percentage of men managers and women managers who exhibit the 20 characteristics. So, for each stereotype, we had two percentage estimates—percentage of men managers estimated to have that trait and percentage of women managers estimated to have that trait. Therefore, for each stereotype and each respondent, it was possible to calculate the diagnostic ratio (DR), that is, the ratio of the estimated percentage of men managers to the estimated percentage of women managers.

Since the same questionnaire also asked respondents to indicate whether they themselves endorsed those 20 characteristics, a true percentage of men managers and women managers in the sample who endorsed each characteristic could be calculated. The ratio of these actual percentages of men managers and women managers was the CR for each trait.

A note on the calculation of the CR is necessary here. In the previous studies, the true percentage of men and women who endorsed the traits was measured by asking respondents to make a choice between True and False. However, the list of stereotypes distilled from the first study reveal some socially undesirable traits like 'vulgar'. A true/false format inherently increases the chances of erroneous endorsement percentages. This is because the true/false format with its binary choice-set induces errors arising from 'social desirability bias'. To overcome this bias in responses, the format for endorsement of stereotypes in the questionnaire was changed to a six-point scale. This point is elaborated in more detail in Chapter 6 on Study 2.

Now, for each respondent and each stereotype, we therefore had a value of the difference between the diagnostic ratio and the CR. This difference represented the inaccuracy in that particular gender stereotype and was indicative of the amount of 'illusory correlation' or 'estimation exaggerations' present in the mind of the respondent.

In this study, for each respondent, we had 20 such 'differences' (between the DR and the CR), representing the inaccuracies of stereotypes held of women managers. These formed the 20 dependent variables or DVs for the analysis.

Individual Degree of Traditional Stereotyping

As mentioned above, the 20 stereotypes had a mix of masculine stereotypic traits and feminine stereotypic traits. To determine an individual's degree of traditional stereotyping, we averaged the diagnostic scores on the feminine stereotypes and subtracted the same from the averaged diagnostic scores for the masculine stereotypes. This gave us a parameter called TSI (total stereotyping index), which measured the individual degree of traditional stereotyping and also took into account the direction of the measure.

A short numerical example is explained in Table 5.1 to illustrate the measures of Diagnostic Ratios (DR) and Criterion Ratios (CR).

With an accurate idea about the variables and their measurements, the questionnaire, derived from the results of Study 1, was pilot-tested on 42 respondents. The respondents were first-year MBA students in a renowned management institute in India. Their ages ranged from 21 to 31 years (mean and median = 24 years.) They were erstwhile practicing managers and their managerial experience ranged from less than 1 year to 9 years (mean = 2.12 years, median = 1.79 years). The respondents came from all over India from a variety of industries like banking, engineering, FMCG, automobiles, shipping, etc. Analyzing the inputs from the pilot study, the instrument was found to be highly reliable. Cronbach Alpha value was 0.9. Validity of the instrument was also measured. Apart from multi-collinearity among the seven independent variables, overall correlations showed significantly high values to establish high instrument validity.

Apart from validity and reliability measures, the pilot study results also validated the process of selection of masculine

Table 5.1

An Example Illustrating Measures of Stereotypic Inaccuracies

	% men managers estimated		
Stereotypes	R1	R2	R3
1 Analytical Ability	75	60	80
2 Skilled in Business Matters	70	75	70
3 Aggressive	80	90	75
4 Sentimental	50	40	40
5 Timid	40	30	30
6 Submissive	30	20	50

Six stereotypes (3 masculine + 3 feminine) and three respondents (R1, R2 & R3)

The first three stereotypes are masculine and the last three are feminine in nature

	% women managers estimated		
Stereotypes	R1	R2	R3
1 Analytical Ability	25	40	60
2 Skilled in Business Matters	35	65	65
3 Aggressive	60	60	65
4 Sentimental	70	60	50
5 Timid	60	60	40
6 Submissive	60	40	55

	Diagnostic Ratios (DR)		
Stereotypes	R1	R2	R3
1 Analytical Ability	3	1.5	1.3
2 Skilled in Business Matters	2	1.2	1.1
3 Aggressive	1.33	1.5	1.2
4 Sentimental	0.71	0.7	0.8
5 Timid	0.67	0.5	0.8
6 Submissive	0.5	0.5	0.9

(Table 5.1 continued)

(*Table 5.1 continued*)

Total Masculine Index (TMI) is the mean DR across the three masculine stereotypes

Total Feminine Index (TFI) is the mean DR across the three feminine stereotypes

Individual degree of traditional stereotyping (TSI = TMI − TFI)	1.48	0.83	0.37

Evidently, degree of traditional stereotyping decreases from R1 to R2 to R3

Now, suppose out of 10 men and 10 women manager respondents, the actual endorsements for each stereotype are as below

Stereotypes	Men	Women	CR
1 Analytical Ability	9	8	1.1
2 Skilled in Business Matters	9	9	1
3 Aggressive	10	9	1.1
4 *Sentimental*	5	5	1
5 *Timid*	3	4	0.8
6 *Submissive*	5	5	1

Estimation Inaccuracies for each stereotype for each respondent would be the difference between the Diagnostic Ratio (DR) and the Criterion Ratio (CR)

and feminine stereotypes. All masculine stereotypes had DR values significantly greater than 1.0 and all feminine stereotypes had DR values significantly lesser than 1.0. Unfortunately, since women could not be included in the pilot sample of 42 respondents, CR values could not be calculated.

The other measure of inaccuracy, however, was measured. The TSI (total stereotypic index), as explained before, was calculated and correlated with the independent variables. All seven correlation values turned out to be negative, but not significant. This lack of significance was attributed to the small sample size and also to the observed trend in the pilot study of extreme responses on some stereotypes like submissive, shy and vulgar.

Overall, the pilot study and its results signalled the way towards Study 2, which is described in detail in Chapter 6.

REFERENCES

Abate, M. and F.K. Berrien. (1967). 'Validation of stereotypes—Japanese versus American students', *Journal of Personality and Social Psychology*, 7: 435–38.

Ashmore, R.D. and F.K. Del Boca. (1979). 'Sex stereotypes and implicit personality theory: Toward a cognitive-social psychological conceptualization', *Sex Roles*, 5: 219–48.

Brigham, J.C. (1971). 'Ethnic Stereotypes', *Psychological Bulletin*, 76: 15–38.

———. (1973). 'Ethnic stereotypes and attitudes: A different mode of analysis', *Journal of Personality*, 41: 206–23.

———. (1974). 'Views of black and white children concerning the distribution of personality characteristics', *Journal of Personality*, 42: 144–58.

Broverman, I.K., S.R. Vogel, D.M. Broverman, F.E. Clarkson and P.S. Rosenkratz. (1972). 'Sex Roles Stereotypes: A Current Appraisal', *Journal of Social Issues*, 28: 59–79.

Hamilton, D.L. and T. Rose. (1980). 'Illusory correlation and the maintenance of stereotypic beliefs', *Journal of Personality and Social Psychology*, 39: 832–45.

Heilbrun, A.B. (1976). 'Measurement of masculine and feminine sex role identities as independent dimensions', *Journal of Consulting and Clinical Psychology*, 44: 183–90.

Katz, D. and K.W. Braly. (1933). 'Racial stereotypes of one hundred college students', *Journal of Abnormal and Social Psychology*, 28: 280–90.

Martin, C.L. (1987). 'A ratio measure of sex stereotyping', *Journal of Personality and Social Psychology*, 52: 489–99.

McCauley, C. and C.L. Stitt. (1978). 'An individual and quantitative measure of stereotypes', *Journal of Personality and Social Psychology*, 36: 929–40.

McCauley, C., C.L. Stitt and M. Segal. (1980). 'Stereotyping: From prejudice to prediction', *Psychological Bulletin*, 87: 195–208.

Schuman, H. (1966). 'Social change and the validity of regional stereotypes in East Pakistan', *Sociometry*, 29: 428–40.

Spence, J.T. and R.L. Helmreich. (1978). *Masculinity and Femininity: Their Psychologican Dimensions, Correlates and Antecedents*. Austin: University of Texas Press.

Spence, J.T., R. Helmreich and J. Stapp. (1974). 'The personal attributes questionnaire: A measure of sex role stereotypes and masculinity-femininity', *Journal of Supplemental Abstract Service Catalog of Selected Documents in Psychology*, 4: 43–5.

Williams, J.E. and S.M. Bennett. (1975). 'The definition of sex stereotypes via the Adjective Checklist', *Sex Roles*, 1: 327–37.

6

Exploring Relationships between Contact and Inaccurate Stereotypes

P ast contact with women managers was hypothesized to have a significantly inverse relationship with inaccuracies in managerial gender stereotypes. What is different about this is the inclusion of 'quality of contact' conditions in the ambit of 'contact'.

As we have seen in Chapter 2, the predominant method suggested over time to counter negative gender stereotypes has been to increase gender diversity. Gender diversity implies increasing the number of women in organizational ranks and increasing interaction with them over time. While intuitively this sounds fine and seems to make sense, research, however, has provided mixed results. Most research works have been unable to verify that simply increasing interaction with women leads to better inter-gender relations and lesser inaccuracies of gender stereotypes. There have been studies in the west which have not been able to significantly relate diversity to stereotypic inaccuracies. Studies in the Indian context, like the Bhatnagar and Swamy study (1995), tried relating quantity of contact with 'attitude towards women managers' and found no significant relationship.

If we closely study the mechanism behind the formation and maintenance of stereotypes in general as illustrated in Chapter 3, it becomes clear why simply increasing the number of women in organizations might not suffice. Just as 'quality interaction' has been found to improve racial inter-group relations in social situations, it was hypothesized that it would take 'quality' interaction between men and women managers to help reduce inaccuracies in managerial gender stereotypes.

Therefore, the overall proposition was that 'contact' with women managers is significantly inversely related to inaccurate managerial gender stereotypes. This 'contact', however, included

---

The tables and figures in this chapter refer to data generated as part of the study covered in the chapter.

the concept of 'quality of contact' over and above quantity (number of women managers and frequency of interaction). In other words, if I hold certain significantly inaccurate managerial gender stereotypes, those inaccuracies would be significantly inversely related to not only the number of women managers I have interacted with in the past, but also dependent on the conditions under which such interaction occurred.

So, while traditionally gender literature has suggested more interaction with women managers to reduce negative gender stereotyping, I extended this concept of interaction by drawing heavily from social psychology and proposed that the quality of the interaction will also significantly influence stereotypic inaccuracy.

This chapter therefore deals with the second phase of the study, the attempt being to verify the first two hypotheses arrived at in Chapter 3. Study 2 addressed the following broad objectives:

1. Verifying whether quantity of past contact (number of women and frequency of contact) with women managers is inversely related to stereotypic inaccuracies, as predominantly predicted by gender literature.
2. Verifying whether the 'quality of contact' conditions are inversely related to inaccuracies in managerial gender stereotypes as well.
3. Exploring the extent or degree to which managerial gender stereotypic inaccuracies can be traced back to a composite of quantity and quality of contact.

Towards this goal, Chapter 4 gave us 20 gender stereotypes held by men managers in Indian corporates, while Chapter 5 gave us measures of inaccuracies of those 20 gender stereotypes and the seven independent variables, which together make up the composite of 'quantity and quality' contact. These together helped frame the questionnaire, which, after pretesting, was administered to a separate Indian managerial sample. The process is explained in some detail here.

STUDY 2—THE METHOD

The final questionnaire (refer Annexure A), improved after minor modifications from the results of the pretest, was administered to 191 practising managers from a variety of organizations from the major metropolitan cities of India. Out of these 191 managers, 157 were men managers, while 34 were women managers (see Figure 6.1).

Figure 6.1
Sample Gender Break-up

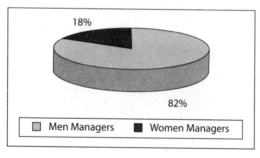

A few points regarding the sample need mention here. As explained before, this study was an exploration of the stereotypes held by men managers about women managers in work settings. Even though the women managers' perceptions of themselves were somewhat explored in Chapter 4, this study restricted itself to the exploration of managerial gender stereotypes held by men managers. So, even though we needed women managers for calculating self-perception ratios, the effective sample size for further exploration and analysis was 157.

The sample comprised managers from all over India and from a variety of industries like software, heavy engineering, banking, automobiles, power, petroleum, cement, etc. These industries could be classified into three wide categories; services, manufacturing and infrastructure. Services comprised 46 per cent of the sample and included industries like software, consulting, media, telecom, etc. Manufacturing comprised 35 per cent of the sample and included industries like heavy engineering, construction, cement, steel, etc. Infrastructure comprised 19 per cent of the sample and included industries like power, utilities, oil, etc (see Figure 6.2).

Figure 6.2
Industry Break-up of Sample

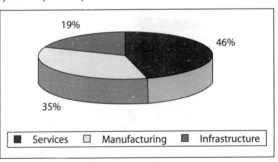

The managers hailed from all three levels of management (junior, middle and senior), 32 per cent of the sample belonged to the junior level of management, 45 per cent belonged to the middle level of management and 23 per cent belonged to the senior level of management (see Figure 6.3).

Figure 6.3
Management Level of Sample

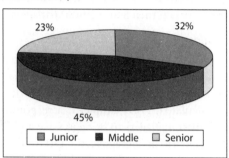

Their educational backgrounds varied from commerce graduates to chartered accountants and from engineers to MBAs. The ages of the participants ranged from 23.5 to 59 years (mean = 37.02 years, median = 34 years). Managerial experience ranged from 1 year to 39 years (mean = 13.61 years, median = 10.25 years). On an average, the respondents had contact with approximately 8 women managers in their work experience (the median being 5 women managers).

STUDY 2—RESULTS

Apart from the seven independent variables (related to contact with women), the data from the questionnaire[a] gave 20

[a] Overall Cronbach Alpha value was found to be 0.8752, which denoted high reliability.

Dependent Variables (DVs) related to *inaccuracy of estimates* which in other words meant the collective extent to which the individual respondent's estimates would differ from reality and one DV related to *traditional degree of individual stereotyping* which in other words meant the extent to which an individual differentiated between men and women managers.

Diagnostic Ratios

The calculation of DVs has been explained in Chapter 5. A quick recap of the method once again might help. For each respondent, for each stereotype, a diagnostic ratio (henceforth referred to as DR) was calculated. For example, if a respondent judged 75 per cent of men managers to be aggressive and 25 per cent of women managers to be aggressive, the DR for the stereotype of 'aggressive' for that respondent would be 75/25, that is, 3.0. Thus for each respondent, we arrived at 20 DR values for the 20 stereotypes. The difference between the mean masculine DR and the mean feminine DR gave us a measure on how much an individual respondent differentiated between the genders. This measure was termed Total Stereotypic Index (henceforth referred to as TSI). The difference between the 20 Criterion Ratios (CR), which are the actual endorsed ratios, and these 20 DR denoted the estimated inaccuracies of stereotypes held (henceforth referred to as DV[b]).

---

[b] The inaccuracies of gender stereotypes, for each respondent on each of the 20 stereotypes were calculated by substracting the transformed CR from the transformed DR, and then taking the absolute value of the difference between the two. Thus we get 20 absolute values of DV for the 7 IVs for each respondent.

Criterion Ratios

The percentage of men managers (male respondents) and the percentage of women managers (female respondents) who endorsed each stereotype were calculated from the self-ratings for each stereotype. CR value for a stereotype was calculated by dividing the percentage of men managers who endorsed that stereotype by the percentage of women managers who endorsed the same stereotype. Thus we had 20 CR values, or 'actual' percentage values for each stereotype.

To get self-rating responses, a 6-point scale (–3 to +3) was used, where a positive score of any value implied endorsement, while a negative score of any value implied non-endorsement. This 6-point scale was used in place of a True-False format (Martin 1987), as it was suspected that for stereotypes like 'vulgar', if a True-False format were provided, not too many respondents would be ready to admit that they were 'vulgar' and thus we could end up with a false outcome of 100 per cent non-endorsement. A break in the degree of endorsement through the 6-point polarized scale provided a tool for tapping the actual endorsement frequencies for stereotypes like 'vulgar'. This method however did not ensure that social desirability bias was eliminated completely and left some of the CR values, especially for sensitive stereotypes like 'vulgar', open to the effects of social desirability bias.

Validating Prior Assumptions

Criterion Ratios

The prediction was that the CR values of all 20 stereotypes would be close enough to the value of 1.0 (as men managers and women managers supposedly do not possess very different managerial traits). CR values for the 20 stereotypes are appended in Table 6.1.

While hovering around the value of 1.0, most of the masculine stereotypes were found to follow a trend of having values slightly greater than 1.0, while most of the feminine stereotypes were found to follow a trend of having values slightly less than 1.0.

Among the 10 masculine stereotypes, the exception to the trend was the stereotype of 'adventurous', on which the CR value did not follow the trend (CR value for *adventurous* turned out to be 0.956, which is less than 1.0). This meant that more women than men endorsed themselves as being 'adventurous' in managerial matters. This could be because of different perspectives of what one perceives as 'adventure'. For men

Table 6.1
CR Values for the 10 Masculine and 10 Feminine Stereotypes

Masculine traits	CR	Feminine traits	CR
Adventurous #	0.95	Values pleasant surroundings	0.97
Vigorous	**1.13**	Sympathetic	0.91
Not uncomfortable about aggressive	**1.09**	Timid	0.94
Not conceited about appearance	**1.03**	Talkative	0.74
High need for power	**1.06**	Submissive	0.99
Strong need for achievement	**1.02**	Interested in own appearance #	**1.16**
Skilled in business matters	**1.02**	Shy #	**1.04**
Analytical ability	**1.00**	Humanitarian values	0.94
Aggressive	**1.08**	Sentimental	0.78
Vulgar	**2.68**	Kind	0.92

Note: # implies for that stereotype, the CR value did not follow the trend.

managers, the threshold at which they would perceive themselves as adventurous might be higher than that for women managers, resulting in more women endorsing 'adventurous' in managerial matters than men.

Among the feminine stereotypes, the exceptions to the trend were the stereotypes of 'shy' and 'interested in own appearance', for which the CR values did not follow the trend (CR values for 'shy' and 'interested in own appearance' turned out to be 1.04 and 1.17 (which are greater than 1.0). This meant that more men than women endorsed themselves as 'shy' and 'interested in own appearance'. While from a social angle, one could attribute the exception for the stereotype of 'interested in own appearance' to the rise of the metrosexual male in urban India (where the sample was drawn from), who does not find it unconventional to be 'shy' or 'interested in his appearance', there could be another explanation as well. Looking at it the other way, one could conclude that among managers, lesser women managers endorsed or accepted themselves as 'shy' or 'interested in own appearance', a trait which, according to popular workplace perceptions, might be looked upon as too feminine and therefore unacceptable in a professional manager. A third explanation concerns that of relative perceptions about the self. The threshold of being interested in one's own appearance for a woman might be higher than that for a man, which in turn might have affected the endorsement ratios.

The other factor of course is the understanding of the word 'shy' in India. It arises from the issues of cross-cultural applicability of traits and their understanding in this country. Even the urban citizen of India might incorrectly understand the implications of the word 'shy', which in other words might mean bashful and modest to the average Indian male. The opposite of 'shy' in India would suggest bold and brash. Now, India being a relatively high-context, collectivist and long-term oriented culture (in contrast to the west), Indians might have a tendency of renouncing traits associated with being bold and brash, whereas to an average Indian woman, the concept of 'shy' would usually mean 'ill at ease' or 'introvert' or 'demure', which again, would not be expected from a professional manager in a working context. Therefore, fewer women than men might have endorsed themselves as being 'shy'.

From the CR values for the 20 stereotypes provided in Table 6.1, it is evident that most of the CR values were moderate in nature, i.e., never extremely divergent from the central neutral value of 1.0. Exceptions included the CR value for the masculine stereotype of 'vulgar' which was much higher than 1.0, implying that the social desirability bias might have affected the CR value for this stereotype. Apart from social desirability bias, in general, vulgarity, as a trait, might be more acceptable to men than to women. It results not only from the upbringing but also from the process of socialization of women in India. Therefore, it just might be true that more men than women (even in a managerial context) would accept and therefore endorse themselves as vulgar.

Also, the masculine stereotype of 'vigorous' had a CR value (value = 1.13) somewhat divergent from 1.0. This too, could be attributed to the understanding of the word 'vigorous' in India and its implications in the socialization and upbringing of women in India. Women in India, as opposed to men, are brought up to be more or less calm and composed, while the word 'vigorous' would imply just the opposite—full of activity, which is not what too many women would perceive themselves to be.

Similarly, among the feminine stereotypes, the CR values for 'talkative' and 'sentimental' (values of 0.74 and 0.78 respectively), are widely divergent from 1.0, implying a possible effect of social desirability bias. In India (and even in the western context) men are brought up to believe that expressing sentiments is not a 'manly' quality in any context whatsoever but women are not. Indian men are simply not supposed to be 'sentimental'. That, coupled with the fact that in managerial settings, being sentimental is considered taboo, more women than men might have endorsed themselves to be sentimental. The same logic applies for the trait of 'talkative', which in India is traditionally attributed to women in almost all contexts.

Confirmation of Choice of Masculine and Feminine Stereotypes

Mean Diagnostic Ratios

Diagnostic ratios were averaged across respondents to arrive at a mean DR score for each stereotype. The mean DR values for the 20 stereotypic items validated the choice of stereotypic traits (masculine and feminine).

Table 6.2 explains this, as the DR values for all masculine traits have been found to be significantly greater than 1 and those for feminine traits have been found to be significantly less than 1.

A one-sample t-test was performed on each mean DR, to test whether the value differed significantly from the value of 1.0. For both masculine and feminine stereotypes, the difference between DR values and 1.0 was significant at $p < 0.05$, two-tailed. This implied that respondents attributed masculine stereotypes more to men than to women. It also implied that respondents attributed feminine stereotypes more to women than men.

Table 6.2
Mean DR Values for 10 Masculine and 10 Feminine Traits

Masculine traits	Mean DR	Feminine traits	Mean DR
Adventurous	2.19	Values pleasant surroundings	0.63
Vigorous	1.61	Sympathetic	0.60
Not uncomfortable about aggressive	1.58	Timid	0.56
Not conceited about appearance	2.04	Talkative	0.65
High need for power	1.46	Submissive	0.68
Strong need for achievement	1.19	Interested in own appearance	0.40
Skilled in business matters	1.43	Shy	0.55
Analytical ability	1.53	Humanitarian values	0.74
Aggressive	1.62	Sentimental	0.53
Vulgar	6.13	Kind	0.68

Checking for Significant Inaccuracies

Knowing that the stereotypes chosen as masculine and feminine were correct, the next step was to ascertain whether the differences between estimated DRs and actual CRs ratios were indeed significant enough to warrant further exploration. To check for significant inaccuracies in the stereotypes, the estimated values were compared to the actual values for each stereotype. We compared the mean DR values with the CR values for each stereotype. A one-sample *t*-test was performed once again to test whether the differences between the DR and the CR values for the 20 stereotypes were significant or not. This was done by subtracting the transformed[c] criterion

[c] To equate the ratio scores lying in the range of 0 to 1.0, with the ratio scores lying in the range of 1.0 and above, diagnostic ratios were tansformed prior to obtaining mean ratios. For DR values > or = 1.0, the transofrmed DR

ratio from the transformed mean diagnostic ratio and the result divided by the standard error of the diagnostic ratio. A significant difference would imply the presence of significant inaccuracies in gender stereotyping. The results are presented in Tables 6.3a and 6.3b.

On almost all the stereotypes, both masculine and feminine, the difference between the mean DR and the CR was found to be significantly different at $p < 0.05$, two-tailed. The exceptions were the feminine stereotypes of 'talkative' and 'interested in own appearance' and the masculine stereotype of 'vulgar' which were significant only at $p < 0.10$, two-tailed. These differences could be attributed to a comparatively large standard deviation for the DRs of these stereotypes, resulting

Table 6.3a
Comparison between Mean DR and CR Values for Masculine Stereotypes

Masculine traits	CR	Mean DR
Adventurous	0.95	2.19
Vigorous	1.13	1.60
Not uncomfortable about aggressive	1.09	1.58
Not conceited about appearance	1.03	2.04
High need for power	1.06	1.46
Strong need for achievement	1.02	1.19
Skilled in business matters	1.02	1.43
Analytical ability	1.00	1.53
Aggressive	1.08	1.62
Vulgar*	2.68	6.13

Note: * implies that the difference between the mean DR and the CR value was significant at $p < 0.10$.

was calculated by subtracting 1.0 from the original DR. For dignostic ratios < 1.0, the transformed DR was calculated by subtracting the inverse of the DR from 1.0. Transformed diagnostic ratios were untransformed for presentation purposes (Martin 1987).

Table 6.3b
Comparison between Mean DR and CR Values for Feminine Stereotypes

Feminine traits	CR	Mean DR
Values pleasant surroundings	0.97	0.63
Sympathetic	0.91	0.60
Timid	0.94	0.56
Talkative*	0.74	0.65
Submissive	0.99	0.68
Interested in own appearance*	**1.16**	0.40
Shy	**1.04**	0.55
Humanitarian values	0.94	0.74
Sentimental	0.78	0.53
Kind	0.92	0.68

Note: * implies that the difference between the mean DR and the CR value was significant at $p < 0.10$.

from extreme responses from outliers. On the whole, the conclusion, however, was that significant inaccuracies did exist in managerial gender stereotypes held by men managers.

Now that it was established that gender stereotypes of women managers were significantly inaccurate, the next step was to determine how these significant inaccuracies were related to and whether they could be explained by the quantity and quality of prior contact with women managers.

Data Cleaning

Before proceeding further with our analysis, we looked at the dependent variable (TSI) plot (Figure 6.1) to determine whether extreme outliers existed or not. As explained before, the dependent variable, denoted by TSI = TMI – TFI, where TMI represents Total Masculine Index and TFI represents Total Feminine Index (TMI = mean of all diagnostic ratios on the 10 masculine items and TFI = the mean of all diagnostic ratios on the 10 feminine items). Their difference, as explained, gave us an idea about the degree to which a respondent would be traditionally stereotyped.

There are many possible methods for determining if a value is an outlier. If we knew the maximum TSI values, then the obtained TSI values could be compared to these maximum values, but unfortunately this information was not available. The other methods to identify outliers involve observing the distribution of obtained values of TSI. If the values are normally distributed, then one can identify outliers using a number of statistical procedures. If the values have an unknown or non-standard distribution, then there exist no standard statistical procedures for identifying outliers. Nevertheless, people can observe a distribution and usually say with different degrees of confidence whether some value is an extreme outlier.

In this case, cluster analysis was used as a tool for cleaning the data as the existence of quite a few outliers is evident from visual inspection of the TSI chart in Figure 6.4. The majority of the calculated TSI values lay close to each other within a range of +/– 20, while the outliers lay in the range of 1000.

Cluster analysis was performed on two measures of the dependent variable, that is, the value of TSI and the mean of the DV values. Clustering was repeated by increasing the number of clusters with each step, until the number of cases in the dominant cluster stabilized. It was found that the dominant cluster stabilized at 113 cases and despite increasing the number of clusters for more than 3 steps, the number of cases in the dominant cluster and the corresponding cluster membership did not change. This provided enough ground to stop clustering further and clean the data based on the membership of the dominant cluster. The above exercise left us with 44 outliers and further analysis was carried out with the cleaned 113 data points. The TSI plot for the cleaned 113 data points is appended as Figure 6.5 for quick perusal.

Figure 6.4
TSI Plot for Overall Dependent Variable Data

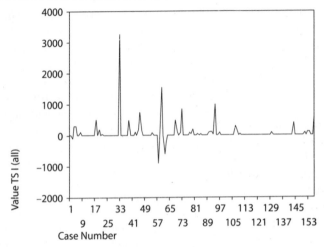

Figure 6.5
TSI Plot for Cleaned Dependent Variable Data

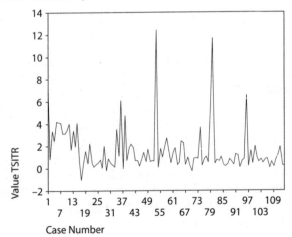

Correlation Analysis for Determining Relationships

Exploring the relationship and validating our hypotheses about how prior contact was related to managerial gender stereotypic inaccuracies required segregating the analysis of the two measures of inaccuracies. The two different measures of inaccuracy needed two different sets of analysis to determine the relationship between inaccuracies and contact.

For each respondent, we had one measure of TSI and seven measures of contact. Therefore, for the *traditional degree of individual stereotyping*, a simple correlational analysis provided the relationships between the measures of contact and that of TSI, the direction of the correlations and their significance. So did a multiple regression analysis, which helped determine the extent to which inaccuracies could be explained by the various measures of contact.

Table 6.4 refers to the correlation coefficients between the *traditional degree of individual stereotyping* (TSI).

As predicted, the independent variables of contact were found to be negatively correlated with the dependent variable measure of inaccuracy, TSI. Moreover, as predicted, all values of correlation were significant except those between 'frequency' and 'authority support' and TSI. What is worth noting is the high values of correlation between the independent variables of contact.

It would be too premature to try and seek explanation at this stage regarding why the correlation coefficients between TSI and 'frequency of contact with women managers', and between TSI and 'authority support' were not found to be significant. Instead, regressing the dependent variable with the seven measures of 'contact' and then trying to explain the phenomenon makes more sense.

Table 6.4
Correlation Coefficient Values

Pearson Correlation Coefficients

	TSI	IV1	IV2	IV3	IV4	IV5	IV6
No. of women managers	-0.191*	1.000					
Frequency of contact	-0.134	0.462**	1.000				
Equal Status	-0.227*	0.458**	0.786**	1.000			
Common Goal	-0.295**	0.472**	0.771**	0.844**	1.000		
Interdependent Cooperation	-0.299**	0.472**	0.708**	0.804**	0.812**	1.000	
Authority Support	-0.164	0.445**	0.739**	0.818**	0.779**	0.811**	1.000
Friendship Potential	-0.229*	0.457**	0.774**	0.854**	0.782**	0.745**	0.782**

Notes: ** Correlation is significant at the 0.01 level (2-tailed)
* Correlation is significant at the 0.05 level (2-tailed)

Regression for Further Explaining Relationships

A regression was done with the seven independent variables and TSI. The results are illustrated in Tables 6.5a, 6.5b and 6.5c.

From the regression results, we have a clear idea that 15.6 per cent of the variance in the dependent variable TSI was explained by the independent variables. The Beta coefficients were also found to follow the trend of the correlational analysis. What we need to keep in mind here is that the independent variables fed into the regression equation were strongly correlated with each other. While that is a positive sign indicating high validity for the instrument used, it also leads to multi-collinearity which in turn, might have affected the regression output. What that means for the study has been discussed in details in the 'Discussion' section of this chapter.

The next step was to try and determine what kind of relationship existed between the second measure of inaccuracy (estimation errors) and contact. However, in this case, for each respondent, we had 20 DVs and 7 IVs. Not only was a simple correlational analysis ruled out as a tool, so was multiple regression.

Since the original proposition was that all the estimation errors for all stereotypes would be predicted in totality by the seven measures of contact with women managers, the inaccuracies in stereotypes would be best represented by the additive composite of all the 20 DVs, while contact would be best represented by the additive composite of all the 7 IVs. A mean would average out many distinctive characteristics of the different stereotypes.

As noticed earlier in the table detailing the correlation coefficients between the IVs and TSI, a high multi-collinearity existed between the independent variables. This could lead to anomalous results in a regression analysis, which is sensitive to high multi-collinearity of the IVs fed into the regression equation.

Table 6.5
The Results of Regression for TSI vs. the IVs

Table 6.5a
Model Summary

Model	R	R square	Adjusted R square	Std. error of the estimate
1	.395	.156	.100	1.94553

Note: Predictors: (Constant), IV7, IV1, IV5, IV2, IV6, IV4, IV3.

Table 6.5b
ANOVA

Model		Sum of squares	df	Mean square	F	Sig.
1	Regression	73.652	7	10.522	2.780	.011
	Residual	397.435	105	3.785		
	Total	471.087	112			

Note: Predictors: (Constant), IV7, IV1, IV5, IV2, IV6, IV4, IV3; Dependent Variable: TSI.

Table 6.5c
Beta Coefficients

Coefficients

Model		Unstandardized coefficients		Standardized coefficients	T	Sig.
		B	Std. Error	Beta		
1	(Constant)	2.896	.508		5.697	.000
	IV1	-2.015E-02	.027	-.078	-.742	.460
	IV2	.250	.150	.268	1.660	.100
	IV3	5.926E-02	.267	.049	.222	.825
	IV4	-.410	.233	-.339	-1.763	.081
	IV5	-.375	.200	-.338	-1.873	.064
	IV6	.351	.218	.291	1.608	.111
	IV7	-.185	.225	-.154	-.821	.413

Note: Dependent Variable: TSI.

Moreover, when a composite independent variable predicts (contact with women managers) a composite dependent variable (estimation inaccuracies of gender stereotypes), we have techniques like canonical correlation to study the predictive relationship. We elaborate on canonical correlation in the next section.

Canonical Correlation

Canonical correlation is considered to be the general form on which multivariate techniques are based and it can use both metric and non-metric data for the dependent and independent variables. We can express the general form of canonical analysis as:

$$X_1 + X_2 + \cdots + X_n = Y_1 + Y_2 + \cdots + Y_n$$

Thus, by using canonical correlation we could predict the composite measure of stereotype inaccuracy, consisting of all 20 DVs, rather than having to compute separate multiple regression equations for each of the dependent variables. By applying a canonical correlation analysis we also could get a measure of the strength of the relationship between the two sets of multiple variables, which is expressed by the 'canonical correlation coefficient'. When squared, the canonical correlation represents the amount of variance in one (the dependent set) canonical variate that is accounted for by the other (independent set) canonical variate.

By applying canonical correlation we also derived a set of weights for each set of independent and dependent variables such that the linear combinations of the IVs and DVs themselves were maximally correlated. Moreover, we could also explain the nature of relationships between the sets of IVs and DVs by measuring the relative contribution of each variable to the canonical functions extracted.

We get as many canonical functions as the lower of the number of variables in either of the independent or dependent sets of variable. Thus, in this case, since we had 7 IVs, we had seven canonical functions and therefore seven canonical correlation values. The canonical correlation values are provided in Table 6.6a.

From Table 6.6a we see that though the canonical correlation value for function 2 is comparatively high enough (0.643) to be considered for interpretation, its statistical significance (value = 0.42) does not seem to suggest so. It is usually suggested that significance values of 0.05 and below should be considered for interpretation. Thus, given the level of significance and the magnitude taken together in choosing the canonical function which is to be accepted and interpreted, we found the first function (out of the seven functions derived) to be the one which should be interpreted. Thus we concerned ourselves with Function 1 only.

Table 6.6a
Canonical Correlation Values

	Canonical correlations	Tests that remaining correlations are zero:			
		Wilk's	Chi-SQ	DF	Sig.
1	**.680**	.164	177.208	140.00	**.018**
2	.643	.305	116.393	114.00	.420
3	.442	.519	64.211	90.00	.982
4	.384	.645	42.955	68.00	.992
5	.366	.757	27.278	48.00	.993
6	.296	.874	13.210	30.00	.997
7	.205	.958	4.208	14.00	.994

Table 6.7a

Factor Loadings and Variable Distribution for DV Set

Rotated Component Matrix

Sl No.	Item	1	2	3	4	5	6
	Factor 1						
9	Submissive	**0.763**	0.188	0.251	0.003	0.002	0.012
19	Kind	**0.756**	0.112	−0.043	0.132	0.036	0.025
3	Sympathetic	**0.744**	0.129	0.014	0.096	0.122	0.360
15	Humanitarian values	**0.574**	0.060	0.417	−0.042	−0.030	0.037
5	Timid	**0.540**	0.300	−0.327	0.024	0.101	0.432
1	Values Pleasant Surroundings	**0.507**	0.050	0.157	−0.141	0.125	0.462
	Factor 2						
10	High need for power	0.180	**0.774**	−0.012	0.136	0.041	0.104
6	Not uncomf. about being aggressive	0.058	**0.772**	0.356	0.100	0.141	0.032
18	Aggressive	−0.054	**0.625**	0.612	0.150	0.186	0.221
12	Strong need for achievement	0.099	**0.591**	0.077	−0.058	−0.144	−0.060
16	Analytical ability	0.131	**0.540**	−0.018	−0.017	0.052	0.020
	Factor 3						
4	Vigorous	0.290	0.177	**0.827**	−0.041	0.071	0.090
	Factor 4						
11	Interested in own appearance	0.001	−0.069	−0.002	**0.862**	0.053	−0.111
7	Talkative	−0.062	0.202	−0.002	**0.850**	0.001	0.039
17	Sentimental	0.421	0.020	0.021	**0.678**	−0.005	0.257
	Factor 5						
8	Not conceited about appearance	0.145	0.027	−0.167	0.102	**0.837**	0.058
20	Vulgar	−0.073	0.001	0.384	−0.054	**0.811**	−0.013
2	Adventurous	0.311	0.465	0.462	−0.029	**0.525**	−0.044
	Factor 6						
13	Shy	0.242	−0.037	0.060	0.039	−0.063	**0.845**
14	Skilled in business matters	−0.090	0.497	0.388	0.204	0.144	**0.516**

RELATIONSHIPS BETWEEN CONTACT AND INACCURATE STEREOTYPES

Table 6.7b
Variance Explained by DV Factors

Total Variance explained

	Initial eigenvalues		
Factor	Total	% of variance	Cumulative %
1	5.496	27.478	27.478
2	2.441	12.204	39.682
3	2.034	10.172	49.854
4	1.534	7.668	57.522
5	1.108	5.541	63.063
6	1.073	5.366	68.429

Table 6.7c
Factor Loadings for IV Set

Component Matrix

	Component
	1
IVZ1	0.589
IVZ2	0.874
IVZ3	0.933
IVZ4	0.913
IVZ5	0.894
IVZ6	0.900
IVZ7	0.903

We can also see that the single IV factor correlates significantly with three out of the six factors extracted. Out of the remaining three insignificantly correlated factors, two are negatively correlated while one is positively correlated.

Factor 4 which comprised three feminine stereotypes is negatively correlated, though not significantly. The explanation,

Table 6.7d
Correlation Values between DV and IV Factors

Correlations

	DV-FAC1	DV-FAC2	DV-FAC3	DV-FAC4	DV-FAC5	DV-FAC6
IV-fac1	−0.204*	*−0.302***	−0.102	−0.058	0.029	−0.208*

Notes: * Correlation significant at $p = 0.05$(2-tailed).
         ** Correlation significant at $p = 0.01$(2-tailed).

Factor and Variable Distribution

FAC1	Values pleasant surroundings, Sympathetic, Timid, Submissive, Humanitarian values, Kind
FAC2	Not uncomfortable about being aggressive, High need for power, Strong need for achievement, Aggressive, Analytical ability
FAC3	Vigorous
FAC4	Talkative, Interested in own appearance, Sentimental
FAC5	Adventurous, Not conceited about appearance, Vulgar
FAC6	Shy, Skilled in Business Matters

I guess, lies in the anomalous results for actual endorsement ratios for these stereotypes.

Factor 5 (masculine items), however, is positively, though not significantly correlated with the IV factor. Apart from a similar explanation about the anomalous results for actual endorsement ratios for these stereotypes, there are other contributors towards this unpredictable relationship between a dependent variable factor and the independent variable factor. As we have seen, of all the 20 stereotypes, the stereotype of 'vulgar' has most extremely responded to stereotype, resulting in a huge standard deviation as well as quite an extreme 'mean DR' value. The inclusion of the stereotype of 'vulgar' in Factor 5 can explain to a great extent the slight positive correlation between 'vulgar' and the fifth factor.

It is also noteworthy that the factors for which inverse correlation values were not found to be significant contained those variables for which CR values did not follow trends, or was significantly divergent from the value of 1.0. (for reasons discussed before).

DISCUSSION

India is different. While one side of the coin refers to a strong similarity between Indian managers and western managers because of the strong western management philosophical roots in the way our managers are educated and operate in the Indian organizations (especially the MNCs) of today, the other side refers to the equally strong Indian social and philosophical roots which our managers hail from. This dichotomy in philosophical undertones has been expressed in the managerial findings of this study.

The predictions were heavily drawn from western manage-ment principles, while the sample was Indian. The predictions were based on the very assumption that we can extrapolate a lot of western management principles to the Indian context of today. India prides itself in matching step to step with the world at large, yet there is another India which cannot deny its cultural roots of centuries.

The results of such a comparison have been very interesting indeed. While on one hand, a majority of our stereotype-related predictions held true for Indian corporates, the effect of the 'Indianness' was also evident in some of the findings.

Though it is said that general stereotypes (in a social context) are significantly different from managerial stereotypes, it seems that there exists an overlap which cannot be denied and which expressed itself when studying managerial stereotypes in a different social context. It seems like the latter is more of a subset of the former rather than being a different set altogether.

Let us start with the CR values which should denote actual endorsement ratios. Going by western principles of management, CR values should not be divergent from the central value of 1.0, as men managers and women managers have been found to demonstrate the same traits in a managerial context.

It is said that stereotypes are usually based on some aspect of reality. Inaccuracies creep in when stereotyping becomes far removed from reality. Therefore, it was also expected that for masculine stereotypes, the CR values would be slightly masculine in nature (as in being greater than 1.0 in value), while the CR values for the feminine items would be slightly feminine in nature (as in being less than 1.0 in value). As was evident from Table 6.1, a total of seven stereotypes did not follow trends or predictions of being close to a neutral value of 1.0.

Among the masculine stereotypes, the CR value for 'adventurous' was found to be slightly less than 1.0 while other CR values were greater than 1.0. The CR values for that of 'vigorous' and 'vulgar' were found to be widely divergent from the central value of 1.0 ('vulgar' being even more divergent than 'vigorous').

Among the feminine stereotypes, the CR values for 'interested in own appearance' and 'shy' were found to be slightly more than 1.0 while the other CR values were less than 1.0. The CR values for 'talkative' and 'sentimental' were found to be widely divergent from the central value of 1.0.

The implications of these anomalous findings have already been discussed in the corresponding section, social desirability and differing cultural ethos being some of the possible contributors. The effects of these anomalies were evident when a Factor Analysis was conducted to condense the 20 DVs and the 7 IVs for further correlation.

Having obtained the actual ratio measures (CR values) and the estimated ratio measures (DR values) of the 20 stereotypes, it was established that all the estimations (mean DR values) significantly differed from the actuals (the CR values). In other words, it meant that there existed significant inaccuracies in Indian managerial gender stereotypes.

The next step was trying to verify whether the relationship between contact and the inaccuracies was significantly negative in nature. It was also necessary to explore whether the measure of contact could explain a significant portion of these inaccuracies.

We had two types of inaccuracy measures: one, the TSI or the individual degree of traditional stereotyping and the other, the collective measure of 20 (DR-CR) values or the estimation errors (referred to as DVs).

The correlation coefficients between the IVs and the *traditional degree of traditional stereotyping* (denoted by TSI) followed predictions. For the inaccuracy measure of TSI, as hypothesized, all correlation values turned out to be negative in nature. The majority of the inter-variable correlation values were also significantly negative in nature, with the exception of the variables of 'frequency of contact' and 'authority support'.

The fact that it is mostly the 'quality of contact' that is significantly inversely correlated with the measure of stereotypic inaccuracy validates the extension from social psychology. Since 'quantity of contact' was not found to be a sufficient condition in explaining inaccurate stereotypes, the main emphasis of this piece of work was the inclusion of 'quality contact' as an explanatory measure of stereotypic inaccuracies.

One explanation that immediately comes to my mind when trying to explain the lack of significance in the negative relationship between 'frequency of contact' and the *traditional degree of individual stereotyping* (TSI) is the aegis under which contact would contribute to less differentiation between men and women managers. Until and unless the conditions under which a manager meets women managers change, how frequently he meets the women managers may not affect the way he differentiates between men and women. Therefore, while 'interdependent cooperation' and 'common goal' in the contact situation are maximally correlated with TSI, 'frequency of contact' isn't. This phenomenon has also been found in previous Indian studies (Bhatnagar and Swamy 1995).

The measure of 'authority support' not being significantly correlated with TSI deserves an explanation as well. The explanation also has to do with the gender context in a country like India. It is a recent phenomenon that women managers are being seen in better numbers in Indian corporates. Traditionally, for a very long time, corporates had been the forte of men managers. The advent of women managers was not without its own quirks and heartaches. When women managers started making their presence felt in Indian organizations, the natural explanation that men managers held close to their hearts was that the women were there because the authorities wanted them. Diversity being the buzzword, it seemed that the perceived 'authorities' had already made up their minds that they wanted more women managers and therefore, to start with, perceived 'authority support' for contact with women managers was already running high. Therefore, any wide variations in 'actual authority support' would have been reduced to minimal variations in 'perceived authority support'. This, in turn, would ensure that 'authority support' as perceived by men managers for quality contact would not be significantly related to inaccuracies in stereotypes.

Another finding from the correlation values was that all seven measures of contact were also highly correlated with each other. Thus, though such high correlation values implied high validity for the questionnaire, it also implied that multi-collinearity between the measures of contact (IVs) was surely a problem to reckon with in further analysis.

The results from the multiple regression indicated that only 15.6 per cent of the variance of the measure of inaccuracy (TSI) was explained by the contact measures. This was not an encouraging finding. According to predictions, the value of R^2 should have been much higher.

One plausible explanation of course is that the high multi-collinearity of the independent variables could have been responsible for dampening the value of R^2. However, a better explanation would be that the low variance explained by 'contact' can be traced back to the other individual-level factors like upbringing, past experiences etc., which we have not considered in our regression equation.

Thus, while we can say with confidence that contact is mostly inversely and significantly related to the *traditional degree of individual stereotyping*, we cannot say that it is only contact that explains the inaccuracies formed. In other words, the degree to which a manager differentiates between men and women managers is not a sole consequence of poor and scant contact with women managers in the past. While contact is definitely a factor which contributes to stereotypic inaccuracies, there could be other factors like social upbringing, family atmosphere, specific past experiences, etc., which could be equally responsible for inaccurate stereotypic perceptions, when it comes to differentiating between men and women managers.

When it came to estimation inaccuracies and contact and their relationship, things became a lot more complicated. A composite of 20 variables on the 'dependent' side and a composite of seven variables on the 'independent' side, it was not quite the elegant analysis and interpretation situation. On performing canonical correlation between the IV composite and the DV composite, the IV composite explained 46.24 per cent of the variance of the DV composite. It implied an important, though not significant contribution nonetheless. The cross loadings for the seven measures of contact corroborated the findings of the TSI correlation results. All the measures of contact were found to be negatively correlated with the DV composite. In other words, contact was negatively proportional to estimation inaccuracies in gender stereotypes. The explanation for only 46.24 per cent variance being explained by one composite of the other is similar to that of the TSI measure. While we can say that scant and low-quality contact is definitely a contributor towards stereotypic estimation errors, we cannot at the same time say that it is the sole contributor or a major contributor towards such inaccuracies. There just might exist other significant contributors which we have not dealt with in this study.

A factor analysis corroborated to a great extent our predictions that contact would be negatively and significantly correlated with stereotype inaccuracies. While the factors derived from the 20 DVs were mostly based on gender lines with masculine stereotypes and feminine stereotypes loading on separate factors (eleven stereotypes out of 20 followed predictions that they would separate into two distinct factors based on masculine and feminine leanings), the seven stereotypes on which CR values were found to be anomalous, separated out into factors, different from the majority.

The 11 stereotypes loaded on two very 'clean' factors, based very clearly on inaccuracies in masculine and feminine stereotypes and these two factors not only explained about 40 per cent of the total variance of the set, but also were negatively and significantly correlated with the single factor for 'contact'. This was, of course, yet another validation of the overall proposition.

We can say at the end of it all, that contact with women managers, or the lack of it, does make a difference in the formation of inaccurate managerial gender stereotypes. This contact naturally has more to it than just working with more number of women. The quality of contact makes more difference than just the quantity of contact. Thus, organizations which plan to follow a diversity policy should keep in mind that a contact situation with women managers which, for example, builds in 'interdependent cooperation' and 'common goals' and also has a good potential for 'friendship building' between genders (where there is a possibility of knowing the other gender personally through informal interpersonal interaction) would make the best situation for reducing inaccurate stereotypes of women managers. This is especially applicable to fresh managers for whom stereotypes about women managers would start building from the day they join the organization. Induction programmes in organizations could be so designed so that organizations create conducive quality of contact conditions which in turn, can help reduce inaccurate stereotyping.

Management educational institutes could also do well in appreciating that just ensuring the requisite numbers of women students will not be a good enough measure to counter the negative effects of gender stereotyping. If they take the first steps by catching them young and modifying the way men managers perceive women managers, organizations can rest easy in future when recruiting such managers.

This could also have a significant implication for training programmes, where managers from both the genders are trained. If it is possible to provide quality contact in such programmes through interactive tasks etc., there is a high possibility that gender stereotype formation would be more accurate.

While we have been quite prescriptive about whether past contact is inversely related to existing inaccuracies in managerial gender stereotypes, one question that might crop up, is a very basic one: Will the contact with women make a significant difference in reducing such inaccuracies? Whether the presence of women in such a contact situation in the Indian scenario actually leads to a reduction in inaccuracy or not is an interesting topic dealt with in the next chapter.

ANNEXURE

Contact and Estimates' Questionnaire

Please indicate below certain demographic details about yourself.

Sex: M/F   **Age:** .... (Yrs)   **Work Experience:** ....
(Yrs) .... (Months)
Level of management: Junior/Middle/Senior **Education:** ....
Industry your organization(s) belongs to: ....
(e.g., fmcg, hotel ....)

1. Please indicate below certain details of your **professional** interactions till date with **women managers** (managers include officers & executives) till date.

   > **contact in a professional situation:** where you have worked with women managers in a task or job situation(s) (as in a temporary/permanent job or project) where the outcomes of the task/job were measurable

1. (a) How many **women managers (approximately)** have you come in contact with **professionally,** in the entire span of your work experience ....

1. (b) How **frequent** has this professional contact with women managers been **on an average**? (Please **circle/tick**)

7	6	5	4	3	2	1
	Very		*Neither frequent*			
Always	*frequent*	*Frequent*	*nor rare*	*Rare*	*Very rare*	*Never*
More than 5 times a week	Twice/ Thrice a week	Once a week	Once a fortnight	Once in a month	Once in 3 or 4 months	Less than once a year

2. Please think about the **situation(s) of professional contact with women managers** (managers include officers & executives) that you have been in and indicate your **perception** about the following conditions of the contact **on an average**. Please refer to the definitions of terms given prior to questions 2(a) to 2(e), and mark your preference **(circle/tick)** on the 7-point scale below the question.

> **Equal Status of contact:** a task situation in which the importance of both you and the women manager(s) in contributing towards the task was equal, and/or task expertise required and/or task description(s) were the same.

2. (a) **How much of 'equal status' existed in the contact situation(s)?**

7	6	5	4	3	2	1
Extremely High	Very High	High	Neither High nor Low	Low	Very Low	Extremely Low

> **Common Goal:** a task situation in which the goals of both the genders are as similar and as important as the common goal(s) for the task, i.e., competition between members of both genders for the goal(s) is absent.

2. (b) **How common was/were the goal(s) in such situation(s)?**

7	6	5	4	3	2	1
Extremely High	Very High	High	Neither High nor Low	Low	Very Low	Extremely Low

> **Interdependent Cooperation:** a task situation in which cooperation required both genders to be dependent equally on each other's contribution to reach the goal(s) of the task(s).

2. (c) **How much 'interdependent cooperation' existed in the contact situation(s)?**

7	6	5	4	3	2	1
			Neither			
Extremely			High nor		Very	Extremely
High	Very High	High	Low	Low	Low	Low

Support from authorities: a task situation where there has been explicit support from the authorities for informal interpersonal interactions with member(s) of the other gender.

2. (d) **How much 'support from the authorities' existed in the contact situation(s)?**

7	6	5	4	3	2	1
			Neither			
Extremely			High nor			Extremely
High	Very High	High	Low	Low	Very Low	Low

Potential for friendship: a task situation in which the environment has provided the opportunity to know the member(s) of the other gender informally through interpersonal interaction.

2. (e) **How much potential for friendship did the situation(s) hold ?**

7	6	5	4	3	2	1
			Neither			
Extremely	Very		High nor			Extremely
High	High	High	Low	Low	Very Low	Low

3. *Based on your work experience* what **percentage of men managers** and **women managers** do you think exhibit the following characteristics? Please use your **own estimates** to answer this question and indicate them in the space provided.

Characteristic	% of men managers	% of women managers
1 Values Pleasant surroundings		
2 Adventurous		
3 Sympathetic		
4 Vigorous		
5 Timid		
6 Not uncomfortable about being aggressive		
7 Talkative		
8 Not conceited about appearance		
9 Submissive		
10 High need for power		
11 Interested in own appearance		
12 Strong need for achievement		
13 Shy		
14 Skilled in Business matters		
15 Humanitarian values		
16 Analytical Ability		
17 Sentimental		
18 Aggressive		
19 Kind		
20 Vulgar		

4. Please think about yourself *honestly in the context of professional situations*. **To what extent** the following characteristics are present **in you as a manager?** Please indicate your response by **circling/ticking** on the numbers on the 6-point scale provided.

The numbers in the scale represent:

+3 Strongly Characteristic
+2 Characteristic
+1 Slightly Characteristic
−1 Slightly Uncharacteristic
−2 Uncharacteristic
−3 Strongly Uncharacteristic

	Characteristic						
1	Values Pleasant surroundings	+3	+2	+1	−1	−2	−3
2	Adventurous	+3	+2	+1	−1	−2	−3
3	Sympathetic	+3	+2	+1	−1	−2	−3
4	Vigorous	+3	+2	+1	−1	−2	−3
5	Timid	+3	+2	+1	−1	−2	−3
6	Not uncomfortable about being aggressive	+3	+2	+1	−1	−2	−3
7	Talkative	+3	+2	+1	−1	−2	−3
8	Not conceited about appearance	+3	+2	+1	−1	−2	−3
9	Submissive	+3	+2	+1	−1	−2	−3
10	High need for power	+3	+2	+1	−1	−2	−3
11	Interested in own appearance	+3	+2	+1	−1	−2	−3
12	Strong need for achievement	+3	+2	+1	−1	−2	−3
13	Shy	+3	+2	+1	−1	−2	−3
14	Skilled in Business matters	+3	+2	+1	−1	−2	−3
15	Humanitarian values	+3	+2	+1	−1	−2	−3
16	Analytical Ability	+3	+2	+1	−1	−2	−3
17	Sentimental	+3	+2	+1	−1	−2	−3
18	Aggressive	+3	+2	+1	−1	−2	−3
19	Kind	+3	+2	+1	−1	−2	−3
20	Vulgar	+3	+2	+1	−1	−2	−3

Thank you for your participation and your time.

REFERENCES

Bhatnagar, D. and R. Swamy. (1995). 'Attitudes toward women as managers: Does interaction make a difference?', *Human Relations*, 48(11): 1285–1307.

Martin, C.L. (1987). 'A ratio measure of sex stereotyping', *Journal of Personality and Social Psychology*, 52: 489–99.

7

Does Contact Help Reduce Inaccurate Gender Stereotyping?

In the previous chapter we saw how inaccuracies in managerial gender stereotypes are inversely related to prior contact with women managers. If that is indeed the case, contact with women managers should help in reduction of such inaccuracies.

In a country like India, there is a substantial amount of skepticism about whether the presence of women in task situations helps or hinders outcomes. I thought it was high time we explored whether the presence or absence of women in task situations makes a difference in accuracies of stereotypes held so far. Sceptics would say it doesn't really matter. They would also say that the presence of women would actually perpetuate stereotypes. The findings of Study 2 seem to say just the opposite about past contact with women managers. It wouldn't therefore be too presumptuous to say that the presence of women managers in task situations might reduce inaccuracies of gender stereotypes. An experiment seemed the best way to explore the validity of such futuristic predictions.

In Chapter 3, we had mentioned that while the first two hypotheses were easily tested using survey techniques, the latter two would require an elaborate experimental set-up to verify their predictions in detail. While a combination of survey and experimental approach was maintained in this study, the experimental approach was modified for simplicity. The modification was aimed at testing the basic premise on which the third and fourth hypotheses were based.

In this context a word or two about the research support in a country like India is needed. Conducting an experiment in India is a daunting task, and that is an understatement. In general, awareness about research is low. Moreover, the support from organizational managerial ranks for research, especially experimental, is even lower. Therefore, given the unforeseen

---

The tables in this chapter refer to data generated as part of the study covered in the chapter.

situational constraints, only the basic premises of the third and fourth hypotheses were tested. In other words, what was tested was whether contact with women managers helped in reducing inaccuracies in managerial gender stereotypes in the first place.

As the requisite number of working managers/executives for conducting the experiment was not available, we made the best of the situation and conducted the experiment with MBA students. Research over time has used student samples and extrapolated results to the managerial population, sometimes accurately, sometimes inaccurately. Some studies have used non-MBA students as experimental samples and have anomalously tried extrapolating results to managers; some studies have resisted that temptation and have used management students as samples, and have extrapolated the results thus obtained, somewhat accurately, to a managerial population. This experiment followed the latter policy and utilized management students as experimental subjects. The modifications made, how the experiment was designed and carried out, the findings and their interpretation are explained in detail in the following sections.

STUDY 3—METHOD

Design

The original proposition was that varying the different conditions of contact would bring about a significant improvement in the inaccuracies of gender stereotypes. To test the original hypotheses, the required design would have necessarily been very elaborate. We would need to vary not only the quantity of female students in the experimental groups, but also the 'quality of contact' conditions across experimental and control groups. A research design incorporating all these conditions would require a very large number of experimental subjects, especially the rare breed of female management students, not to mention an immense amount of involvement from subjects and authorities alike. The number of subjects required to carry out that kind of elaborate design was unfortunately lacking.

Thus, though the original proposition and the original hypotheses were elaborate, as a first step in moving towards this ultimate design, we tried to establish whether the contact with women made a positive difference at all. Moreover, the total number of subjects ultimately available for the experiment compelled a change in the design to measure one single factor at one single level (50 per cent women in the experimental groups).

If the results of this short experiment, conducted as a first step to explore whether 'contact with women' indeed made a difference, turned out to be positive, then future research could be carried out taking into account the elaborate propositions put forth. The experiment was therefore kept short, the only factor that was varied between the experimental and the control groups being a '50 per cent strength' of women in the experimental groups. Both experimental and control groups were, however, exposed to a set of tasks, where the desired kind of interaction with or without women could occur. These interactional tasks were designed keeping the 'quality of contact' conditions in mind.

Sample

A between-subjects, single-factor experiment was conducted to study the effects of contact with women. Participants in the pre-test for the experiment were 74 MBA students (55 male and 19 female) from a school of business management in a western state-capital of India. They were a mix of first-year and second-year MBA students, most of whom did not have any previous work experience before joining the MBA programme. Approximately 61 per cent of the students belonged to the first year and 39 per cent belonged to the second year. Their ages ranged from 20 to 30 years (mean = 22.41 years, median = 22 years). Managerial experience ranged from 0 years to 2.92 years (mean = 0.952 years, median = 0.5 years).

The educational background of the pre-test sample was very similar—most of them came from a non-engineering educational background. A total of 35.12 per cent of the students came from a management background (BBA or MBA), 29.73 per cent came from an engineering background (BE or BTech), 16.22 per cent came from a commerce background and 10.82 per cent came from a science background (BSc or MSc). Only 9.46 per cent of the sample had a post-graduate degree.

Procedure

A slightly modified version of the questionnaire (please refer Annexure B) used in Study 2 was administered to students enrolled in both the years of the two-year MBA programme at a School of Management in a western state-capital in India, through personal administration in the classroom. The questionnaire measured the percentage estimates of male and female students who, the respondent thought, possessed the 20 managerial stereotypic traits.

The questionnaire was modified keeping in mind that if student respondents are asked to estimate the percentage of 'managers' who possess certain stereotypic traits, they could probably grossly overestimate or underestimate the percentages. Thus, the target group for the estimates was made relevant and the respondents were asked to estimate the percentage of students instead of estimating percentage of managers who possessed the managerial stereotypes identified in Study 1 and used in Study 2.

There were some other factors also that were kept in mind when administering the pre-test questionnaire. As suggested by experts in experimental design, we maintained a time lag between the pre-test and the post-test (or rather the actual experiment). This was done to avoid the occurrence of 're-tention' and 'sensitization' in the experimental measures. The time lag was approximately 10 days.

The next step was to calculate the sample size required to conduct a high-power experiment, whose results would hold their ground to scrutiny. Assuming a large (Cohen 1977) effect size (ω^2) of 0.15 as an outcome of the experiment, we did a power analysis to determine an adequate sample size. The calculations are shown in Table 7.1.

By research standards (Keppel 1991) a power of 0.7 and above is usually acceptable. Thus our sample size needed to be 24 or above to achieve a power greater than 0.7.

Table 7.1
Trial Sample Sizes for Experiment

(ω^2) Factor = $\omega^2/(1-\omega^2)$		Trial sample size (n)	ϕ^2 = Factor *n	ϕ df{den} = a(n-1)		df{num} = a-1	Power from P-H chart (alpha = 0.05)
0.15	0.1764	12	2.117	1.455	22	1	0.54
		14	2.470	1.571	26	1	0.60
		16	2.823	1.680	30	1	0.65
		20	3.529	1.878	38	1	0.70
		24	4.235	2.057	46	1	0.83

Given the time lag of 10 days between pre-testing and the actual experiment, even though the calculations said we needed at least 48 students, we were apprehensive about the actual turnout on the day of the experiment. Quite unlike many western countries, where students can earn course credits in lieu of participation in experiments, Indian students cannot be offered any such curriculum related incentives. Authority cooperation and support, and researcher requests are about all the tools that Indian researchers have at their disposal to ensure adequate participation in experiments.

As is evident from the research design, we needed an equal number of girls and boys for constituting the experimental groups which implied that the number of boys in the experimental group was dependent not only on the turnout of the number of male students on the day of the experiment, but more so on the turnout of the number of female students for the experiment.

Quite according to our expectations, the pre-test sample comprised more students than the post-test sample. The final number of students who finally participated in the experiment dwindled to about 65 per cent of the original number of students from the pre-test. We had 74 students in the pre-testing stage. We ultimately had a turnout of 11 female students and 38 male students (all pre-tested) in total for the experiment and therefore our male experimental sample size (number of male students) was restricted to 13. Thus the actual sample size for the experiment, including both the experimental and the control groups, was 48.

The 48 subjects were divided broadly into an experimental group (E-gr.) of 24 students and a control group (C-gr.) of 24 students. Each of the experimental and control groups were then subdivided into four groups of six members each. In the E sub-groups, out of six members, three were women (except for the last group, in which only two women were available). An example of an Experimental sub-group and a Control sub-group each is appended in Table 7.2.

Also, since the 'treatment' in the experiment was all about 'contact' with female students in the experimental time period and its effect on certain 'inaccuracy' related variables, we needed to ensure that the 'contact' during the experiment was as 'pure' as possible. If experimental contact occurred between groups who already had enough prior contact with each other, or knew each other well enough through prior interaction, the effect of the 'treatment' would be contaminated. It was therefore decided in the design stage itself that the experiment would be conducted either with students who had just joined a course (and therefore by extension did not know each other well), or came from different years in the post-graduate course.

Due to certain limitations we could not conduct the experiment with subjects who had just joined a course, but it was ensured that the subjects in the groups in the experiment belonged to different years of the post-graduate management course (as illustrated in Table 7.2). Apart from ensuring that the female students and the male students in the experimental groups belonged to different years, the assignment of students to groups was random in nature.

We had to ensure the quality of contact in the experimental tasks. This was done in a systematic manner. The total experiment lasted for 3 to 3.5 hours. The time span for the experiment was divided into tasks and interaction periods as illustrated in Table 7.3.

Table 7.2

Example of a Control and an Experimental Group

Group	Name	Year	Group	Name	Year
E1	Barkha Modi (Ms.)	1	C4	Faiyaz A, Ghumra	1
	Seena Menon (Ms.)	1		Mahebub Vahora	1
	Swati Aggarwal (Ms.)	1		Pradeep Ghoghara	1
	Kamal Kakkad	2		Sumit Gupta	2
	George Daniel	2		Chavda Darshan	2
	Abhinav Kaushik	2		Rushikesh Dhimar	2

Notes: E1-First experimental group.
C4- Fourth control group.

Table 7.3

Break-up of the Tasks for the Experiment

Time period	Task	Remark
15 min	Introduction of tasks and researchers and students themselves	Breaking Ice
30 min	Task-1 (Xerox Company Caselet)	Aronson technique
15 min	Break for informal interaction	
30 min	Task-2 (Detective Game)	= do =
15 min	Break for informal interaction	
30 min	Task-3 (Digital Company Caselet)	= do =
15 min	Break for informal interaction	
30 min	Traffic Jam exercise	Physical team exercise
30 min	Refreshments and prize distribution	

We designed the tasks and the interaction time spans to take into account the five 'quality of contact' factors, as explained in the following discussion.

'Equal status' and 'interdependent cooperation': Each of the first three tasks was designed so as to utilize Aronson's Jigsaw technique (Aronson et al. 1978). In this technique, used mostly with students, the study material is divided into separate exclusive parts which make up the whole study material. The number of parts is equal to the number of students in a group. Each student has her/his own part and the whole group is supposed to study or present the whole of the study material. This ensures that all members of the group are given equal importance in the task situation and are equally involved in the task so that when it comes to contribution, there is no difference between one member and another. The members have to depend on each other and contribute as a team, and would therefore compulsorily have to interact with each other, if the task is to be accomplished by the team together.

'Common goal': To ensure a common and tangible goal for each group (to suppress the perception of competition among boys and girls in a group), a cash prize was declared for the best performing group. The evaluation process for the cash prize was made transparent (one of the co-experimenters evaluated and explained the evaluation to them) to remove any doubts about bias, etc., and the prize declaration was done at the end of all activities and after gathering the post-test questionnaire responses to ensure that the declaration of the prize did not affect in any way the processes in the groups.

'Authority support' and 'potential for friendship': We had obtained explicit support from the school authorities before carrying out the experiment. Moreover, during the experiment, we (the experimenter and the co-experimenters) were considered to be the 'authority' in the situation. The interaction sessions and the refreshment sessions were included in the task-span so that there was enough scope for informal inter-personal interaction among the groups. The experimenter and the co-experimenter encouraged 'idle-talk', 'getting to know each other' and 'general bonhomie' explicitly among the sub-group members in the interaction sessions. For example, groups were told that they should know the names, hobbies, etc., of their group members by the time the tasks ended.

STUDY 3—RESULTS

The expectation, as in Study 2, was that the CR values of all 20 stereotypes would be close enough to the value of 1.0. Since men managers and women managers supposedly do not possess very different managerial traits and since MBA students are 'managers in the making', it was expected that this prior assumption should also hold for the CR values calculated from the student sample. The criterion ratios, calculated for the 20 stereotypic items, are appended in Table 7.4.

Table 7.4 brings out a trend similar to that in Study 2, where CR values of the majority of the masculine stereotypes are

Table 7.4
CR Values for the Masculine and Feminine Stereotypes

Masculine traits	CR	Feminine traits	CR
Adventurous	1.16	Values pleasant surroundings	1.00
Vigorous*	0.89	Sympathetic	1.00
Not uncomfortable about aggressive*	0.83	Timid	0.98
Not conceited about appearance	1.09	Talkative	0.78
High need for power	1.26	Submissive	0.96
Strong need for achievement	1.16	Interested in own appearance	0.95
Skilled in business matters	1.01	Shy*	1.53
Analytical ability	1.00	Humanitarian values	0.98
Aggressive	1.09	Sentimental	0.92
Vulgar	2.41	Kind	0.98

Notes: *Implies that for these stereotypes, CR values did not follow the expected trend.

marginally greater than 1.0, while the CR values of the majority of the feminine stereotypes are marginally less than 1.0.

Among the 10 masculine stereotypes, the exceptions to the trend were the stereotypes of 'vigorous' and 'not uncomfortable about being aggressive', on which the CR values did not follow the trend (CR value for *vigorous* turned out to be 0.89 and that for 'not uncomfortable about being aggressive' turned out to be 0.83, both of which were less than 1.0). This meant that more female students than male students endorsed themselves as being 'vigorous' and 'not uncomfortable about being aggressive'.

As before, this could be because of a very different understanding of what one perceives as 'vigorous'. We have already seen how the understanding of the word 'vigorous' was a problem point in the questionnaire in Study 2. With a nationally spread out sample in Study 2, the picture was different (CR value for 'vigorous' was much greater than 1.0), while when the sample was restricted to one single city in the western part of the country, the picture seemed to be even more different (CR value being less than 1.0).

The conjecture that it might have been the understanding of the word 'vigorous' that has resulted in this contradictory finding, is further confirmed by the other stereotype (not uncomfortable about being aggressive) whose CR value did not follow the trend. The use of the double negative in the stereotype of 'not uncomfortable about being aggressive' is something which most English language usage rejects in today's world. Double negatives were used to emphasize a statement and were expected to resolve to a positive. The reason why such usage has been abandoned is because of the confusion it creates in the minds of English language users who are not too comfortable with the language. In India, though most of management teaching is in English and the official language of most organizations is English, double negatives would still confuse many. My conjecture is that the double negative in the stereotype could have been the source of anomaly.

Among the feminine stereotypes, the exception to the trend was the stereotype of 'shy', for which the CR value did not follow the trend. Criterion Ratio values for 'shy' turned out to be 1.53 (which is greater than 1.0). This meant that more men than women endorsed themselves as 'shy'. This is very similar to the findings of Study 2. This being a sample of students from one part of the country, one could attribute the exception for the stereotype of 'shy' once again to the rise of the metrosexual male in young urban India, who of late does not find it unconventional to be 'shy'. This explanation is especially applicable to the student community which has led the transformation of the macho Indian male to the metrosexual Indian male.

Drawing from our previous assumptions, the expectation was that the CR values would not be too divergent from the central value of 1.0. From Table 7.4, it is evident that most of the CR values were moderate in nature, that is, never extremely divergent from the central neutral value of 1.0. Exceptions were, however, higher in number for the student sample (as compared to the managerial sample in Study 2). Exceptions once again included the CR value for the masculine stereotype of 'vulgar' which was much higher than 1.0, implying that the social desirability bias might have affected the CR value for this stereotype. Apart from social desirability bias in general, vulgarity as a trait might be more acceptable to male students than to female students.

Similarly, among the feminine stereotypes, the CR value for 'talkative' is widely divergent from 1.0, implying a possible effect of social desirability bias. In India the trait of 'talkative' is traditionally attributed to women in almost all contexts. This is very much a social perception, which again would be strongly affecting perceptions of students about themselves. Therefore, lesser male students than female students might have endorsed themselves as talkative.

ANOVA Results

A one-way ANOVA was performed on the experimental group and the control group, on two dependent variables, mean DV (explained in Chapter 6) and TSI (again explained in Chapter 6). We resorted to taking a mean of the DVs for the ANOVA, despite running the risk of averaging out many distinguishing characteristics, because over and above a comparison of the TSI (before and after the experiment), it was essential to also check if there was a significant reduction in the estimation errors as well.

ANOVA was performed on the two dependent variables both before and after the experiment. The one performed before the experiment helped in comparing the experimental and control group to find out if they had significant differences between them on the scores of the two variables of TSI and mean DV, before the experiment.

No significant difference between the two groups (experimental and control) was found on both variables. The results therefore confirmed that the experimental groups and the control groups were very similar in terms of their stereotypic inaccuracies before the experiment was conducted. The ANOVA results for before the experiment are appended in Table 7.5a and Table 7.5b.

Table 7.5a
Before Experiment ANOVA Results for Mean DV, Comparing Experimental
Group vs. Control Group

ANOVA-mean DV-EB vs. CB

	Sum of squares	Df	Mean square	F	Sig.
Between Groups	0.0074	1	0.0074	0.0002	0.987
Within Groups	1075.914	35	30.7408		
Total	1075.922	36			

Table 7.5b
Before Experiment ANOVA Results for TSI, Comparing Experimental Group
vs. Control Group

ANOVA-TSI-EB vs. CB

	Sum of squares	Df	Mean square	F	Sig.
Between Groups	271.117	1	271.117	2.287	0.1394
Within Groups	4149.211	35	118.548		
Total	4420.329	36			

When comparing the inaccuracy measures before and after the experiment according to our proposition, a significant difference in both inaccuracy measures should be found for the experimental group, while the difference should be non-significant when comparing the control group results. As an addendum to the ANOVA analysis, we also performed a post-test power analysis, where we calculated the effect size (ω^2) and the power of the test from the Pearson-Hartley charts (the $\propto$ level for interpreting the P-H charts was taken as 0.05). The experimental group results are appended in Table 7.6a and Table 7.6b, while the control group results are appended in Table 7.7a and Table 7.7b.

Table 7.6a

Experimental Group (TSI)—ANOVA for 'Before' and 'After' Experiment
ANOVA-TSI-EB vs. EA

	Sum of sq.	Mean sq.	F	Sig.	Power*	ω^2
Between Groups	258.204	258.204	3.979	**0.0575**	**0.67**	0.102
Within Groups	1557.361	64.890				
Total	1815.565					

Note: $*\propto = 0.05$ for interpreting Pearson-Hartley Chart.

Table 7.6b

Experimental Group (Mean DV)—ANOVA for 'Before' and 'After' Experiment
ANOVA-mean DV-EB vs. EA

	Sum of sq.	Mean sq.	F	Sig.	Power*	ω^2
Between Groups	67.718	67.718	4.202	0.051	0.72	0.109
Within Groups	386.752	16.114				
Total	454.471					

Note: $*\propto = 0.05$ for interpreting Pearson-Hartley Chart.

Table 7.7a

Control Group (TSI)—ANOVA for 'Before' and 'After' the Experiment
ANOVA-TSI-CB vs. CA

	Sum of sq.	Mean sq.	F	Sig.	Power*	ω^2
Between Groups	13.076	13.076	1.795	0.188	< 0.3	0.019
Within Groups	276.691	7.281				
Total	289.767					

Note: $*\propto = 0.05$ for interpreting Pearson-Hartley Chart.

Table 7.7b

Control Group (Mean DV)—ANOVA for 'Before' and 'After' the Experiment
ANOVA-mean DV-CB vs. CA

	Sum of sq.	Mean sq.	F	Sig.	Power*	ω^2
Between Groups	40.884	40.884	1.349	0.252	< 0.3	0.0086
Within Groups	1151.005	30.289				
Total	1191.889					

Note: $*\propto = 0.05$ for interpreting Pearson-Hartley Chart.

STUDY 3—DISCUSSION

There were some interesting and encouraging findings indeed. It seems contact with women managers in task situations does make a significant difference. For the experimental group we find that there is a significant effect at $p < 0.10$ (the significance values are quite close to 0.05 actually) on both the inaccuracy measures of TSI and mean DV. The effect size for both the measures is also more than 0.10 (which ultimately means that more than 10 per cent of the variance is explained by the treatment effects). An effect size of 0.06 has been classified as 'medium'(Cohen 1977) while an effect size of 0.15 or more has been classified as 'large'. Thus, we see that at 0.10, our effect size, though not equal or greater than the estimated 0.15 (when planning the sample size), denotes a significant amount of effect due to treatment effects. Calculating the power for both the experimental analyses (0.67 and 0.72), we find that the power values are quite high as well. We can therefore conclude that a high-power, high-effect experiment has successfully demonstrated that there is a significant reduction in inaccuracies in managerial gender stereotypes after contact with women in task situations.

Calculating the power analysis for the control group, however, provides a different picture. Not only are the F values low and the significance values greater than 0.15 (implying no significant effect of the experiment), but also the effect sizes are less than 0.01 (which has been denoted as 'small' [Cohen 1977]). The power values for these tests have also turned out to be low (<0.3). Had the effect size been large and the power values been low, then there could have been a possibility that despite a significant difference in the experimental variables, it was the low power of the test that was responsible for not detecting any significant difference. Thus we can again safely say that for the control groups (subjects who did not work with women), no significant effect was detected in inaccuracies of managerial gender stereotypes.

As we can see, both the variables, mean DV and TSI have shown a significant decrease after the experiment for the experimental group but not for the control group. The power of the experiment being high, we can say that a definite difference in inaccuracies of gender stereotypes can be brought about by facilitating contact with women managers while carrying out tasks.

While the findings of the experiment are encouraging, there are certain aspects that need discussion. The flip side to this encouraging finding is the use of MBA student samples for the experiment and extrapolating the results to managers, which might be flawed. It was, however, the best possible way, given the constraints of situation and time. Moreover, the use of an MBA sample for experimenting has been done before and it has been found that while results obtained from non-MBA student samples might give significantly erroneous conclusions if extrapolated to managers, the same cannot be said for MBA student samples, the assumption being that they are the future managers and therefore should have a mindset more or less similar to junior managers.

Findings of gender research have all along warned managers and organizations of the disruptive effects of gender-tokenism. It has been found that in industries and organizations where women managers are represented in token numbers, negative effects of gender stereotyping increase rather than decrease. This experiment found that a 50 per cent representation of women in task situations actually decreases inaccuracies of gender stereotyping. What this experiment has not investigated is the percentage of representation of women at which the improvement in accuracies actually starts. Nor has this experiment investigated if token representation actually results in more inaccurate stereotypes. These investigations could have provided more clarity in terms of the implications of the findings for organizations.

The single factor that was controlled in the experiment was the presence or absence of women in tasks that were designed to take into account the five quality conditions. We could think of designing a multi-factorial design experiment, taking into account all the seven 'contact' conditions. It is only then that we can conclusively say anything about 'quality of contact' surely helping in reducing inaccuracies in gender stereotypes. At present, we will have to make do with implying that the presence of women (50 per cent representation) in task situations significantly reduces inaccurate gender stereotypes.

Another factor which limits the understanding of the findings is that we have not gone into the depths of how the process of reduction of inaccuracy occurs. There are overlapping stages of decategorization, salient categorization and recategorization, through which such revision of stereotypes occurs (Pettigrew 1998). We have not explored such details. This lack of explanatory stages in the process of reduction of stereotypic inaccuracies could hamper the understanding of the process and thus limit its applicability in terms of planning a more elaborate experiment in future.

Also, in Study 3, we have measured a change in inaccuracies in gender stereotypes in terms of change in perception only. The other dimension of behavioural change has not been addressed; that dimension needs to be studied over time and with observational procedures. Thus, generalizing or concluding that contact with women managers would definitely result in behavioural change also (which is the prime concern in organizations) cannot be done emphatically. Whether the change in inaccuracies of gender stereotypes is retained or not is also something future research can address through longitudinal studies.

Moreover, in this study we have measured descriptive stereotypes of women managers (what women managers 'are observed' to be) and not prescriptive gender stereotypes (what women managers 'ought' to be). This is somewhat similar to implicit and explicit gender differences. It has been observed in research that while descriptive gender stereotypes have undergone (and are prone to undergo) change, prescriptive gender stereotypes have not changed much with time. However, though it might seem prudent to work with prescriptive gender stereotypes as well in future instead of concentrating only on the measurable and manipulable descriptive gender stereotypes, we also need to keep in mind that measurable criteria determine the choice of variable to represent a certain concept to a great extent.

IMPLICATIONS OF FINDINGS

In spite of the limitations mentioned above, the findings of Study 3 have important implications for India, especially for managerial gender stereotypes and the projection of social stereotypes into the managerial context. The very fact that contact with women has helped significantly reduce inaccuracies of managerial gender stereotypes shows how important gender diversity is in the Indian corporates of today; more so, when looking at the unwanted outcomes of inaccurate gender stereotypes in the organizational context.

With more and more women entering the Indian corporate world, it is time the authorities took cognizance of the writing on the wall and started looking at legislative interventions to ensure that debilitating gender stereotypes do not affect the growth and development of women managers in the country. The developed world has already embraced the concept of 'equal opportunities'. Maybe it is time to do so in this country as well, if we are to match pace with the world. Sceptics might point to industries which have already done a lot about such inclusion, but when we look at the hierarchical concentration of women in such industries, they are mostly to be found at the lower and middle echelons of the organizations. The ICICI Banks and the Biocons are hard to come by. They are more of exceptions which prove the rule. The overall numbers speak for themselves ('only two per cent of Indian managers are women', Rediff News, 6 October 2006) and without doubt we need a better representation of women in all spheres of the Indian corporate world, not only the services and the IT sectors.

In India, a very common perception, especially among the middle class, is that boys and girls should not interact much till they are actually compelled to do so by the organizational context. Our education system to a great extent reflects the same mentality, where most middle class children are educated separately in gender-specific environments. Even in cases where they are educated together, we have instances like the university in Bangalore (refer to Chapter 1) where they are segregated in the classroom. Most of our managerial input, however, comes from the 'great Indian middle class'. It is time we realized that even as students, if we allow boys and girls to undertake joint responsibilities and complete tasks together, we can go a long way in supplying a better-educated and less-stereotyped workforce in our organizations.

The implication for organizations and their leaders remains...just as in group processes, the responsibility lies with the leader to ensure participation from even the quietest group member, the responsibility lies on the policy makers in organizations to ensure better stereotypes in the workplace by getting more and more women managers to work with men (managers), even on tasks they 'perceive' to be out of bounds of women. Not by recruiting women because legislation demands it and keeping them more as showpieces to skirt the long arm of the law, but recruiting them and ensuring their participation in all spheres of organizational work. That is how the concept of equal opportunity can be embraced in its truest sense.

The representation of 50 per cent women in the task situations in the experiment also has strong implications for proportionate representation of women managers not only on boards, but also in organizations in general. There are strong arguments in favour of reservation for women in the Parliament of India. There are equally strong arguments against such a radical move. We can project similar arguments in favour of reservation for women in Indian organizations, keeping in mind that Scandinavian countries have already successfully shown the way in ensuring a fair representation of women in corporate management. How feasible or useful a move it will be is a matter of serious debate, but we already have a successful example to lead the way.

Even though the results of the experiment point to a reduction in inaccurate gender stereotyping, if we, as authorities, ensure equal representation of women in task situations through reservations or quotas, there are pitfalls which we have already discussed about the formation and maintenance of stereotypes in general. If we say we will reserve positions for women in the political and managerial context, there are other factors that we need to consider as well.

Even though my experiment has not explored what happens if we have the presence of women in task situations which are designed for quality contact and also have the presence of women in task situations where we do not control for quality contact, my hunch is that in the latter case, where we do not control for quality conditions, even if there is improvement in accuracies of stereotypes, the improvement will not be as significant as the one achieved in the experiment conducted. Without ensuring 'equal opportunity' in numbers only, we should ideally also take into account the quality factors in the interaction between men and women. This point has been amply demonstrated in the findings of Study 2.

So, even though we find that reservation for women on the boards of corporates in Scandinavian countries like Norway has resulted in a significant improvement in the number of women in the top echelons of Norwegian corporates, what we do not know is how such increased numbers have affected inaccurate stereotypes held of women managers. Yes, with time, these inaccuracies might reduce (as the presence of women has been found to have an alleviating effect on inaccurate gender stereotypes), but that is a debatable point which can be verified only with time and observation and study.

To conclude, while this experiment raises more questions than answers, the answers that it provides have far-reaching implications not only for organizational policies in India, but also have very strong social consequences. A detailed discussion on the implications of the findings of Study 3 is provided in context in the last chapter, which discusses the impact of the overall findings of the three studies constituting the backbone of this book.

ANNEXURE

Estimates' Survey

Please indicate below certain demographic details about yourself.

Name: .... **Academic Year:** 1st year/2nd year

Telephone number (residence or where you can be contacted):
....

Sex: M/F   **Age:** .... (Yrs)   **Work Experience:** .... (Yrs) .... (Months)

Level of management: Junior/Middle/Senior   **Education:** ....

1. Think about the students in your institution who are in the same management programme (PGDM) as you are. There would be male students and female management students. You will be asked to estimate what percentage of these male and female management students exhibits certain characteristics illustrated in the table below. Your estimates could be based on the interaction(s) that you have had with your peers/colleagues in the institution. Please think, estimate and then answer.

Please indicate in the space provided what **percentage of male and female management students**, in your institute, and according to **your own estimates**, exhibits the following characteristics:

Characteristic	Percentage of male students (%)	Percentage of female students (%)
1 Values Pleasant surroundings		
2 Adventurous		
3 Sympathetic		
4 Vigorous		
5 Timid		
6 Not uncomfortable about being aggressive		
7 Talkative		
8 Not conceited about appearance		
9 Submissive		
10 High need for power		
11 Interested in own appearance		
12 Strong need for achievement		
13 Shy		
14 Skilled in Business matters		
15 Humanitarian values		
16 Analytical Ability		
17 Sentimental		
18 Aggressive		
19 Kind		
20 Vulgar		

2. Please think about yourself in the context of situations where you need to interact with both male and female management students. To what extent are the following characteristics present *in you* in such situations of interaction(s). Please think, be honest, and indicate your response by circling/ticking on the numbers on the 6-point scale provided.

The numbers in the scale represent:

+3 Strongly Characteristic
+2 Characteristic
+1 Slightly Characteristic
−1 Slightly Uncharacteristic
−2 Uncharacteristic
−3 Strongly Uncharacteristic

	Characteristic						
1	Values Pleasant surroundings	+3	+2	+1	−1	−2	−3
2	Adventurous	+3	+2	+1	−1	−2	−3
3	Sympathetic	+3	+2	+1	−1	−2	−3
4	Vigorous	+3	+2	+1	−1	−2	−3
5	Timid	+3	+2	+1	−1	−2	−3
6	Not uncomfortable about being aggressive	+3	+2	+1	−1	−2	−3
7	Talkative	+3	+2	+1	−1	−2	−3
8	Not conceited about appearance	+3	+2	+1	−1	−2	−3
9	Submissive	+3	+2	+1	−1	−2	−3
10	High need for power	+3	+2	+1	−1	−2	−3
11	Interested in own appearance	+3	+2	+1	−1	−2	−3
12	Strong need for achievement	+3	+2	+1	−1	−2	−3
13	Shy	+3	+2	+1	−1	−2	−3
14	Skilled in Business matters	+3	+2	+1	−1	−2	−3
15	Humanitarian values	+3	+2	+1	−1	−2	−3
16	Analytical Ability	+3	+2	+1	−1	−2	−3
17	Sentimental	+3	+2	+1	−1	−2	−3
18	Aggressive	+3	+2	+1	−1	−2	−3
19	Kind	+3	+2	+1	−1	−2	−3
20	Vulgar	+3	+2	+1	−1	−2	−3

Thank you for your participation and your time.

REFERENCES

Aronson, E., N. Blaney, C. Stephan, J. Sikes and M. Snapp. (1978). *The Jigsaw Classroom*. Beverly Hills, CA: Sage Publications.

Cohen, J. (1977). *Statistical Power Analysis for the Behavioral Sciences*. New York: Academic Press.

Keppel, G. (1991). *Design and Analysis: A Researcher's Handbook*. NJ: Prentice-Hall Inc.

Pettigrew, T.F. (1998). 'Intergroup Contact Theory', *Annual Review of Psychology*, 49: 65–85.

DOES CONTACT HELP REDUCE INACCURATE GENDER STEREOTYPING?

8

The Implications: Where We Stand and What We Need To Do

After a detailed classroom discussion on the case of a bank in Canada where women had been given the short shrift in advancement and promotion for a long time because of stereotyped perceptions about their commitment and educational qualifications, we were discussing how perceptions influenced the way we interpreted reality and how inaccurate stereotypes coloured the way we looked at members of the group we were stereotyping, when one participant manager raised his hand and asked, 'But Ma'am, isn't it true that women managers themselves do not want to take up responsibility in higher positions as they fear that taking up so much responsibility will interfere with their family commitments?' …and this comment came just a day after Ms. Indra Nooyi was elected as Chairperson of the PepsiCo board.

It is this phenomenon that we need to fight against and that is why this book has been written…to reach out to a far wider audience than what my lectures can reach out to; to try and open our eyes to reality without the filters of inaccurate gender stereotypes.

This book has been about stereotypes; to be specific, gender stereotypes; to be even more specific, managerial gender stereotypes. Stereotypes per se are not dangerous or negative in nature. Stereotyping is supposed to be a very neutral phenomenon used by all human beings. The problem with stereotypes is that they mostly become inaccurate over time, especially when they are stereotypes held by men of women in workplaces, which traditionally have been male bastions.

There has been extensive research in the western world (mostly the US) about managerial gender stereotypes. In a review of global research on women in management the world over, the authors (Berthoin Anthal and Izraeli 1993) say, 'probably the single most important hurdle for women in management in all industrialized countries is the persistent stereotype that associates management with being male' (p. 63).

In the early 1970s, Schein (Schein 1973; 1975) demonstrated the 'think manager–think male' phenomenon clearly in her successive studies. What was striking then was that even women managers held perceptions that the managerial job was male in nature and therefore associated success at managerial jobs more with male managers than with female managers.

The 1970s was a different time in the US. The society underwent a lot of change after that period. This prompted Schein to replicate her study about a decade and a half later (Brenner et al. 1989), to check for attitudinal differences. The encouraging part of the findings was that women managers in the US no longer sex-stereotyped the managerial job and they made almost equal associations between success and men managers as they did between success and women managers. The discouraging and most alarming part of the findings was that the attitudes of men managers had hardly undergone any change. They stereotyped the managerial job as much, if not more, as they did 15 years ago.

The Schein studies were replicated again in the US using management students in 1989 (Schein et al. 1989) and 1995 (Dodge et al. 1995). The results were found to be very similar to the study using managers in 1989. Female students were found to hold a balanced view of managerial characteristics required for success and their association between men managers and women managers. They did not sex-type the managerial position, while male students did so significantly across studies.

The cross-cultural applicability of the 'think manager–think male' perception was undertaken by various researchers and the similarity of findings across countries (UK, Germany, China and Japan) revealed that it was an all-pervasive perceptual phenomenon. Male respondents across countries associated success at managerial jobs significantly more with men than with women managers.

Strikingly, with female respondents across countries the same phenomenon was observed. The perceptions of women in the US might have changed with changing time, but not in the countries surveyed. Women across the four countries made strong associations between men and managers, while at the same time making significantly lower associations between women and managers. Thus, quite unlike the US, the 'think manager–think male' perception extended to women as well. Managerial gender stereotypes across many countries of the world have therefore been found to be pervasively skewed in favour of men and against women. Would the Indian context be any different?

Apart from the problem of 'think manager–think male', the other greater problem associated with stereotyping is the probability of inaccuracies creeping into the process of stereo-type formation. Once inaccurate stereotypes set in, they have a tendency to self-feed their inaccuracy resulting in a host of negative consequences for women managers who want to make it to the top echelons of organizations. Holding inaccurate stereotypes in the workplace results in known negative con-sequences for women managers—the glass ceiling, lesser developmental opportunity, lesser career opportunities and unfair performance appraisals, to name a few. It becomes all the more important to deal with inaccurate stereotypes of women managers because of the 'Pygmalion' effect. If, because of inaccurate gender stereotypes, men managers (as bosses) expect women managers (as subordinates) to under-perform, there is a very high probability that they (women managers) would ultimately under-perform, thus validating the self-fulfilling prophecy of under-performance, which in turn would lead to further and stronger inaccurate stereotypes. That is a dangerous situation to deal with in organizations in growing economies like India.

Western society has taken cognizance of their extensive research findings and has accordingly made provisions to counter the negative effects of stereotypes and other related phenomena. Unfortunately, in India, which is rapidly growing and consequently employing more and more women in its workforce, not much research has been conducted in the sphere of gender stereotypes and how they can affect working relationships between managers. The number of women managers in India as compared to the developed countries is miniscule. Research is needed to understand how women are accepted and perceived in Indian organizations. This is all the more applicable in a country like India, which scores relatively high on the cultural dimension of masculinity and has been known to be a very conservative and traditional country.

According to Hofstede (1993), 'One of the conclusions of my own multilevel research has been that culture at the national level and culture at the organizational level, that is, corporate culture, are two very different phenomena and that the use of a common term for both is confusing' (p. 92). Even though the US and India are two very different nations whose national cultures vary to a great extent, the assumption behind this study was that since organizational cultures and national cultures are normally referred to as being different phenomena, the managerial context in India would prevail over the social context of gender stereotypes. Management philosophy in India has drawn deeply from the US, from the setting up of the first few premier management institutes in India to the curriculum that is followed even now in most management institutes.

Indian management principles have been quite a derived set. For example, the Indian Institutes of Management (IIMs), the premiere management institutes in the country which were set up to help develop managers who would manage the country's organizations, were established in collaboration with reputed management schools in the western world. Even now, most of the management education in India draws its feed from the US. Therefore, the assumption was that in Indian corporates, management philosophy would more or less follow that in the west. A similarity-assumption therefore seemed fair enough, though our societies are quite different.

However, we also cannot deny that we come from very different ethos. If the social context overshadowed the managerial context despite the managerial philosophical roots, then the gender stereotypes held in Indian organizations might follow the trend found in other countries in the world outside the US. So, while our managers might have been trained in the western management philosophy, where do we stand in respect of applicability of western assumptions regarding stereotypes in India? It is this curiosity and this identified gap in research that prompted this book and the three studies that were conducted.

The basis of this book was to explore managerial gender stereotypes in Indian organizations and try and trace them back to some antecedents. It was also to explore whether a positive difference could be made in inaccurate stereotypes held by men managers. In the following sections we will try and summarize the overall findings and their implications for Indian corporates.

STUDY 1

While it is intuitively understandable that Indian society is different from western society, a distinction was made between social stereotypes and managerial stereotypes. In the west, these two have been found to be reasonably different—the explanation being that the managerial setting overshadowed the social setting and therefore gender stereotypes in general would be inherently different from 'managerial' gender stereotypes. Based on the assumption that managerial characteristics would not be too different for Indian managers (as compared to the US), a comprehensive set of managerial stereotypic characteristics (SDI) were tested on an Indian managerial sample to explore what managerial gender stereotypes existed in the Indian organizations as compared to the US.

What was interesting about the first study was the result from the women managers in the sample. Traditionally in India, women have been known to be 'their own worst enemies'. Proverbs and popular sayings to that effect exist even now in Indian society. Soaps and serials on television propagate these social stereotypes even today. I was curious; does that mean that women managers would hold more negative stereotypes about themselves as compared to men, as was socially predicted? Or would they be even more prejudiced? Or could these sayings and proverbs have lost their significance in the managerial context? Exploring the stereotypes held by women managers could either dispel or validate the traditional social mindset and their thinking, when extended to the managerial context. One set of assumptions pointed to the rising managerial thinking, derived from the west, which would dispel such doubts, while another set pointed to strong cultural roots prevailing over the western philosophy in the workplace to confirm negative stereotypes held by women managers about women.

So, two very different analyses were conducted, one with women managers and the other with men managers. While the exploration of women managers' gender stereotypes was purely out of curiosity, the latter explorations gave us what managerial gender stereotypes were held by male managers. Since the number of women managers in Indian corporates is abysmally low, it was unlikely that the gender stereotypes held by women managers, even if found to be negative, would actually influence and affect the growth and development of women managers. Even today, most decision making positions in the top management of Indian organizations are dominated by men managers. It therefore made sense to move ahead with exploring the antecedents of the gender stereotypes held by male managers.

The findings were interesting. Men managers significantly associated success with themselves, but failed to associate success with female managers. Indian male managers closely associated successful managers with men managers, but they made no such associations between women managers and successful managers. Thus Indian male managers see men managers as more likely to possess characteristics necessary for success in the workplace than women managers.

When compared to similar studies in the US, Germany, UK, China and Japan, the association made between women managers and success was much lower than in the US or the UK. Indian male managers followed the international trend of 'think manager–think male' very strongly indeed. Moreover, traditionally success-related traits as found in the international studies, like 'analytical ability' and 'skilled in business matters', etc., were strongly attributed to men managers.

However, the results of the neutral characteristics (on which no significant difference was found in ratings between men and women managers) validated the assumption that the managerial or organizational context would overshadow the social context, especially social stereotypes.

A case in point is the social stereotype of 'quarrelsome', which is a social stereotype pervasively held by both men and women in India. The extent to which social stereotypes still exist can be gauged from a recent incident in one of the country's progressive state assembly. On 21 February 2007, the Speaker of the Karnataka State Assembly was heard admonishing a group of male MLAs in Kannada, the translation of which in English meant 'Stop quarrelling like women'. What came as a huge embarrassment to the Speaker was that he was accosted on the floor of the house by women MLAs, cutting across party affiliations. Even though the Speaker apologized later for his 'inappropriate remarks', what the incident brought to light was the still-strong stereotypes that male politicians held of women in India. What was ironic about this incident was that these social stereotypes still prevailed in the highest decision-making legislative body of a progressive state like Karnataka whose capital, Bengaluru, formerly Bangalore, is known as the Silicon Valley of India.

The encouraging point to be noted from the findings of Study 1 was that some traditionally social stereotypes like 'quarrelsome' have moved into the 'neutral' camp, where no distinction was made between men managers and women managers.

Similarly, some strongly held traditional 'international' managerial stereotypes like 'leadership ability' had also moved into the neutral camp. This phenomenon can be explained by the strong women leaders that the Indian subcontinent have produced in the political arena over the years. This explanation, however, contradicts the assumption that the social context would not contaminate the managerial context to a great extent.

Clearly, men managers in India were strongly prejudiced and stereotyped. Why these stereotypes were alarming was because the Indian male manager perceived men managers as more likely than women managers to possess characteristics necessary for managerial success. In other words, men managers would actually not expect women managers to hold the traits necessary for success in the Indian workplace and given the effect of self-fulfilling prophecies, this spells doom for the expectations that hardworking and competent women managers may have for equal treatment in selection, placement and promotion decisions in Indian organizations.

When it came to women managers and the perceptions they held of themselves, things were much brighter. Women managers associated success with men managers as much as they did with women managers. They saw men and women as equally likely to possess characteristics necessary for managerial success. Women managers thought of women managers as more intelligent, competent and persistent. Internationally, the stereotype of 'competent' has been found to be associated more with men managers than with women managers.

Another interesting revelation is the nature of stereotypes held by women managers about men managers, many of which had strong negative shades to them. One of the positive perceptions they held about men managers was that they (men managers) were as logical as required for success. The other stereotypes they held of men managers had some shades of negative in them (like devious, less grateful, less reserved, etc.). Unfortunately, these same characteristics were also rated as necessary for success in the Indian workplace. This finding does not paint a nice picture of the Indian workplace as it appears to the Indian woman manager. In her eyes, the Indian corporate might just be a strongly political place in which being manipulative and devious helps a manager succeed and rise in the corporate ladder and most men managers possess those characteristics which help them rise and succeed.

What are the implications of these findings in the Indian managerial context? Whatever our educational context is and however much we draw from the western world, India has its own quirks and fancies. Overall, Indian male managers turned out to be as we would have expected them to be—prejudiced and stereotyped. They followed the international trend almost with a vengeance. So, the next step was naturally to try and explore the presence of inaccuracies in these identified stereotypes and then trace the roots of such inaccuracies.

The interesting findings of Study 1 were of course the stereotypes held by women managers of themselves. Contrary to popular social belief, women managers did prove that the managerial lot of women were indeed a different set altogether. Not only did they not distinguish between associations of success between men and women managers, but they also thought better of themselves in terms of the qualities they possessed in relation to success in the workplace. The only other country where women managers are not influenced by stereotypical thinking today is the US. Even in the US, it took about two decades of affirmative action to bring about a change in the attitudes of women managers towards themselves. In the early 1970s, when women managers were a miniscule percentage of the managerial population in the US, women managers stereotyped women as much as men managers did. In India, where the percentage of women managers in the managerial population is abysmal compared to even the 1970s in the US, we still have such positive reflections from women managers about themselves. Moreover, given that socially women still tend to hold very negative perceptions about themselves, this finding is all the more interesting. Together, the two contradictory findings are extremely riveting.

One possible explanation for this interesting finding stems from the extremely oppressive society that India has traditionally been. It could have started with the foreign invasions of India, when women started being relegated to the background, both socially and politically. India was known to be one of the progressive societies in the world which boasted of female scholars like the great Gargi, who brought new insights into academics before foreign invasions destroyed the social and political fibre of the independent Indian states. Unfortunately the role of the woman in India later was a far cry from what it used to be centuries ago.

Indian women have therefore been known to be academically brilliant and competent, apart from the brilliant political leadership qualities some of them have demonstrated over years. Given that women in India could be assumed to carry a basic level of latent competence and intelligence, it was not surprising that when they were given a chance to prove themselves in a competitive and prejudiced environment like the Indian workplace, this very prejudice worked towards cementing bonds at the workplace, which were somehow not so socially relevant. It was these bonds, which, even in the absence of affirmative action (as in the US and the Scandinavian countries), might explain the positive perceptions that they held of themselves.

This has implications for industries that are trying to increase women's participation in their organizations. More women in management positions would mean that the real abilities and qualities of women managers would be tapped without prejudice or bias. Since Indian women managers are not influenced by stereotypical thinking, Indian organizations can expect their women managers to treat men and women more or less equally in selection and appraisals. Men managers, in contrast, would need training and counselling before women managers could report harmonious and satisfying working conditions under them. Recruiting and promoting women managers could lessen such burden on the organizations.

STUDY 2

Now that we knew what managerial gender stereotypes men managers held in Indian organizations, we arrived at a measure for assessing whether these stereotypes held were accurate or inaccurate. If inaccurate, were there significant inaccuracies? The basic premises on which Study 2 was based were drawn from social psychology.

Over the years it has been proposed that increasing the number of women in organizations would help reduce the inaccurate stereotypes held about them. Studies in the past have provided mixed results when trying to look at the beneficial effects of increasing the number of women in organizations.

In India, not too many studies have been conducted in the past on gender stereotypes and how to reduce their inaccuracies. The only studies that were conducted tried linking interaction with women managers in the banking industry to attitudes held towards women managers and found no significant correlation between the two.

Thus, the basic objective of Study 2 was to explore the entire range of 'interaction' with women managers and test whether quality interaction in the past made a difference. Thus, apart from quantity of contact with women managers in the past, it was also assumed that quality contact in the past would shape the inaccurate stereotypes held by men managers. Therefore, not only would the number of women managers and the frequency of interaction with them determine inaccuracies in gender stereotypes, but so would quality of contact conditions like equal status while interacting, having a common goal, having inter-dependent cooperation, perceived authority support and having friendship potential in the interaction situation. The assumption again was that managerial stereotypes were a different set from what social stereotypes were.

The findings of Study 2 revealed two things: (i) There existed significant inaccuracies in managerial gender stereotypes held by Indian men managers and (ii) Quite a substantial proportion of these inaccuracies could be traced back to lack of 'quality contact' with women managers in the past. The inaccuracies could also be traced significantly to the lack of number of women managers interacted with in the past. The word 'sub-stantial', instead of 'significant' conveys something. While the prediction was that a significant variance in the stereotypic in-accuracies would be predicted by a composite of quantity and quality contact with women managers in the past, the results, though encouraging, seemed to suggest that there was much more to the entire managerial stereotypic inaccuracy than just interaction with women managers in the past.

Therefore, the findings of Study 2 also revealed a strong possibility of the presence of societal and other individual-level antecedents which could explain inaccuracies in gender stereotypes to a greater extent than what only prior managerial contact did. For example, the upbringing of the manager, the ways of the society that one was born in, social cues from one's immediate and remote surroundings, extreme experiences with members of the other gender, etc. In other words, the validity of assumptions that social stereotypes and managerial stereotypes were somewhat exclusive and different was questioned by the findings. There existed the possibility of a strong overlap between social factors and experiences and managerial contact during organizational socialization.

Findings of Study 2 revealed interesting insights as well. First, when we think of increasing gender diversity in organizations, we usually think of it only in terms of increasing the number of women. What the findings of this study say is that inaccurate gender stereotypes can be bettered by not only increasing the quantity of women but also ensuring that men managers and women managers are given the opportunity to interact in situations where there is a common goal and where interdependent cooperation is ensured. More often than not, women are recruited and included in teams and committees and task forces because of the political correctness associated with including them, rather than the real complementary skills that they can bring to the table. If, instead of saving face, organizations can ensure interdependent cooperation and a common goal for both genders in a task situation, then stereotypic inaccuracies might reduce in future.

The findings also revealed that there should be equal status of both men managers and women managers in the task at hand. This might sound a bit confusing to most readers. This condition does not mean that if we have a woman (manager) holding the position of Assistant Manager in an organization, she has to be put in teams or committees comprising only of Assistant Managers. What it means has relevance for the working processes in any team. Within a team setting, norms and roles are allocated, as is the establishment of status systems. Let us consider a team without a woman in it. Even without the woman, status would be allocated based on the task at hand and the expertise that members bring to the table. An effective team would ensure that members do not bring their outside-team status to the team working scenario, so that smooth working and member satisfaction is ensured. A leader might take on the responsibility to ensure such smoothness in the functioning of the team. Now, when the woman manager joins the team, it should be similarly ensured that outside-team status (in-group vs. out-group status) should not encroach on the task at hand. That in itself would ensure that women being to the table equal status as they deserve and as is relevant to the task at hand. Thus, as is evident, this condition of ensuring equal status cannot happen if there is no perceived authority support for the same. In any situation perceived authority support might come from the organizational policies, the team leader, or any other intervention which ensures free and fair participation of women managers in task situations.

The other interesting aspect of the finding of Study 2 is the need to provide 'friendship potential' in such interaction situations in organizations. The finding regarding 'friendship potential' has a lot of implications for Indian society in general and by extension, to its managerial settings. India is a country where most women are traditionally brought up separate from men. This deep divide in upbringing, ostensibly to keep at bay unwanted consequences of liberal interaction, actually fuels inaccurate gender stereotyping. While the situation on the ground is changing for women of today, we are looking at a generation of men and women in this study who might have not been brought up with the neo-liberalism that is slowly pervading Indian society.

Let us take the case of an Indian boy, who we assume to have primarily come in contact with his mother and other socially related women in social situations over his formation and growing years. It could also be that he is sent to a boys' school, specifically keeping in mind that he should not get 'too friendly' with girls in a co-educational institution. We have a classic case of the principal of a co-educational college stipulating that women and men should sit separately in classrooms in one of southern India's most preferred cosmopolitan cities. We also have college principals stipulating dress codes for women attending graduate college in the eastern metropolis city of India.

Therefore, in all probability, before joining an organization, he would hardly have had the opportunity to interact with women in task situations (study groups, task groups, quiz teams, student committees, etc.). By this time, stereotypes about women would have formed in his mind, based on his limited interaction with women in social situations. India as we all know is socially not too conducive for women to display their managerial skills. Socially, the perceptions held of men and women are quite different. Men are perceived primarily as 'providers', while women are perceived primarily as 'nurturers'.

Therefore in most situations where there is social contact, men and women bring unequal socially-ascribed status to such situations of contact.

With this basis for stereotype formation, it is of little surprise that our Indian male manager will display prejudice and bias when it comes to stereotyping women and associating their characteristics with success in the workplace.

An example of traditional Indian male stereotyping about women is provided in an excerpt from a news item as follows:

'Why there are so few women managers in India'

'Women outperform in care-taking qualities and men outperform in taking-charge qualities,' says the CEO of another large family-managed Indian firm where women are non-existent in senior management.

While the CEO's son is heading an important division in the company, his daughter—an MBA graduate from a reputed foreign university—hasn't joined the business. 'It's not in our family culture for women to be in business. She is happily married,' the CEO says.

These stereotypes are the main reasons why surveys have shown that only four out of 10 CEOs in India considered the advancement of women to be critical for their organisations. The increasing feeling is that a majority of Indian companies still have a kind of institutional sexism that assumes women are less able than men.

Excerpt from Rediff News, 6 October 2006.

The Indra Nooyis and the Kiran Mazumdar Shaws are the exceptions in India which actually hide the trend. The trend remains that Indian women managers start from somewhat of an early disadvantage. Socially a majority of our men and women are not supposed to get to know each other, leave alone interacting in tasks and situations which may bring out managerial qualities of women. Even in graduate college, instances of separation of education for men and women abound. It is only at the post-graduate level that any such interaction is actually encouraged, but by the time the post-graduation level is reached, women students have already dwindled in number to an extent where even if interaction is encouraged, there just aren't enough women to ensure quality and quantity of interaction with a majority of the men. If such interaction is absent, it is little wonder that men and women managers enter organizations with very little scope for forming accurate perceptions about each other.

Moreover, given that men and women have traditionally not interacted in social situations, most men, and women as well, find occupational interaction beyond office hours a little awkward. The sense of discomfort is apparent in such occupational socialization scenes. This in turn creates the problem of the exclusion of women from the informal information network, which becomes very important for advancement in the upper echelons of organizations. Given that women too find such occupational socialization unnatural, they are then blamed for being uninterested in entering the men's club.

The list is endless. So, what do we suggest as remedial measures? While the findings of this study have implications for Indian corporates, I think the findings have more implications for our society and societal legislators and very much so for our educational institutions as well.

While in the west, legislation has been enacted to stop discrimination and to ensure that there is equal opportunity for men and women, we have no such a thing in India. We still feel that time will make things happen on their own. If that were the case, would we not have had substantial numbers of women managers in Indian organizations today which we could have been proud of? Without intervention, we might not even move one step forward in most spheres of organizational life. Just having enough women in the IT and ITES industries (even there the common perception is that women generally occupy the lower and middle levels) is not an indicator of a society that has progressed in all senses.

Else, we could go the Norwegian way. Norway, in January 2006, enacted a legislation which compels the top 500 publicly traded organizations to have 40 per cent women on their boards by the year 2008 (please refer to the news clip on page 192). There are proponents and opponents of this affirmative action in Norway as well. While this is a most controversial move, we need to realize that a measure like this, in isolation, might not work for a country like India.

Norway and, for that matter, the Scandinavian countries, are known to be very balanced in the cultural dimension of masculinity and femininity. Imposing boardroom quotas in such a country will work because they have already built a base for women and their advancement in organizations in their country. There would be enough women in the top rungs of the firms to make the next move to the boardroom. In a country like India, we cannot even dream of such a quota. We simply do not have the requisite number of women managers at the top management levels, ready to move into the boardrooms, in case a similar legislation is enacted in India.

'Why there are so few women managers in India'

Effective January 1 this year, Norway's government has imposed quotas under which the top 500 publicly traded firms have until 2008 to fill 40 per cent of their boardroom seats with women, or be delisted. France is imposing a 20 per cent quota, while Spain has decided to give preferential treatment to companies who appoint more women on their boards.

There may be huge problems in enforcing such a quota in India as it interferes with corporate freedom and overlooks merit. Besides, when the Department of Company Affairs proposed that 20 per cent of board seats should be reserved for women, lots of women managers themselves thought this was insulting and natural evolution is better than force. Every female director will now feel that she has been appointed just to fill the quota.

The consultant, however, says it may sound outlandish, but experience shows quotas may be the only means of achieving change. A survey done after Norway's move, by Egon Zhender International, showed precisely this.

While women's presence on boards in Scandinavia, where quotas have been introduced or mooted, has grown rapidly, in the rest of western Europe, the numbers have hardly changed and in Germany and the Netherlands they have even dropped back.

Women now account for nearly 29 per cent of directors in the biggest Norwegian companies, up from 22 per cent in 2004. In Sweden, Finland and Denmark, where Norway's move has attracted attention and increased pressure for action, the numbers have risen to 23 per cent, 20 per cent and 18 per cent, respectively.

Excerpt from Rediff News, 6 October 2006.

As of today, we have approximately 8 per cent women in the Parliament of India. Only 45 among the 543 seats in the Lower House of Parliament, or the Lok Sabha, are occupied by women. The numbers are worse in the State Legislative Assemblies, where less than 5 per cent on an average are women legislators. A simple legislation like reserving 33 per cent seats for women in the Parliament of India has always been scuttled by all parties alike. What is hailed as a landmark policy change is when in 1993, 33 per cent of seats in Panchayats (the local governing system) were reserved for women. How much has changed since women started representing a large chunk of the villages of India is a point under study in many sociological avenues. While there are innumerable instances of elected women being puppets of their menfolk, there are equally strong instances of positive action towards betterment taken by these elected women. My hunch is that while we cannot deny the positives of such a move, it will require intervention at a much deeper level to really eliminate the demons of discrimination.

While some may propose that reserving seats for women in Parliament is the only way to bring women into mainstream politics and therefore by consequence, bring about equally effective organizational legislature, there are equally vehement opponents of this view. Judging from the way the legislation for 33 per cent reservation for women in the Indian Parliament has been scuttled all along by all parties across the board, I guess the opponents are more in number than the proponents in the male-dominated Indian Parliament. Whether I support the move to provide reservation or not is not the point of debate;. the point of debate here is that changes in legislation alone would, in all probability, be ineffective, especially in a society like India, where there isn't enough support from educational and training programmes to promote gender consciousness.

The reason lies in what we have discussed till now; if we don't work at the upstream source of the problems, it will not be possible to achieve much by simply providing reservations downstream. On the contrary, it might just strengthen prejudice and bias against women, who will be looked upon as the new upstarts and being there by virtue of being women and not because they deserve it.

While in Scandinavian countries the quota system has worked pretty fine, the reason for such legislation succeeding in Norway has already been explained. Theirs is a society which does not hold itself back in terms of recognizing women and their abilities from a very young age. Scandinavian women are known to be effective and strong citizens of the state, with equality in their minds and in their actions. More importantly, Scandinavian societies are known across the world not only for their high standards of living, but more so because of the low gender discrimination that they practise. Unfortunately, India as a society is so different that such a quota will most probably not work in this setting.

We need to change the way we look at the concept of inter-action between men and women in our society. It has to start from the roots. Else, there is precious little that corporates alone can do in changing the inaccuracies that their men bring with them to the workplace. While they of course can ensure that the quality of interaction in their own workplace adheres to the desired conditions of contact as suggested by this study and consciously give more opportunities to women to bring out their managerial qualities, it isn't enough to address this malady so deep downstream.

Educational institutions need to realize that their narrow perspective and interpretation of interaction between men and women are sowing the seeds for future inaccuracies in stereotypes, which in turn is resulting in strong negative outcomes for women in the workplace. Legislators also need to take heed of the fact that their laid back attitude is fomenting trouble downstream.

If the west has woken up to this fact and if we are claiming to be a truly global India ready to march ahead keeping pace with the world, we need to understand that a truly global India, while not sacrificing its cultural heritage, has to wake up to the existence of an under-utilized and discriminated-against workforce which has enough potential in all fields to take this country forward. It has been proven in research that transformational leadership qualities are displayed more by women managers than by men managers (Bass 1999). Given that it is transformational leadership which is turning wheels in today's fast-paced complex organizations, shouldn't there be an automatic pull to bring in talented women and help them advance the hierarchy to positions where we can utilize their leadership skills? In almost all important board examinations, girls outperform boys academically. What happens to this bright lot of girls when it comes to entering professional courses and further, in moving up in the echelons of organizations? We need to sit back and think hard about where we need to start changing the rules. This study points a finger at a possible area of concern.

Just because the concern for intervention has shifted to the roots does not mean that the downstream be neglected. It has to be through a concerted joint effort not only at the educational level but also at the workplace level, that we introduce joint legislation to ensure equal representation of women, to ensure that women are given the right to participate equally, the opportunity to display their managerial abilities and later on continue the same in organizations.

The need for Equal Opportunity Laws in the workplace is just one of the various measures that can bring about a change in these inaccurate perceptions that our men managers hold of their women colleagues.

STUDY 3

While the findings of Study 2 explained where to look when tracing back inaccurate managerial gender stereotypes, it also became necessary to know if a futuristic intervention can help reduce existing inaccurate gender stereotypes.

The experiment conducted with business management students established without doubt that working on interactional tasks with women does help in reducing inaccuracies of gender stereotypes. A significant reduction in inaccuracies of managerial gender stereotypes was found after male students interacted with an equal number of women students for a prolonged interactional task. Thus, we can safely say that 50 per cent representation of women in task situations can make positive stereotypic differences.

If that is true, then it should hold true for situations in educational institutions and training institutions as well. If we have to introduce quotas at all to help women advance, we should introduce laws at the primary and secondary educational levels and at the training levels so as to make interaction with women under professional task situations mandatory. For example, it can be made mandatory that 33 per cent of all co-educational school and college student committees should comprise of girls. It can also be made mandatory that resident welfare boards should comprise 33 per cent women. In educational institutions, boys and girls should be encouraged to interact in situations which bring out task-related professional abilities of both genders. Educational institutions can counsel parents on why such interaction is necessary. Training programmes can offer discounts to organizations which nominate more women from their managerial cadre for development. Training programmes can then be designed so that quality interaction is ensured between men and women managers while they learn. Course curriculum can be designed in educational institutions so that girls and boys have to participate in as many joint tasks as possible.

It is only when we introduce such forward-looking legislation upstream, can India move ahead with all oars rowing in tandem. Introducing legislation in isolation at a stage when it is already too late will be equivalent to trying to uproot a poisonous tree by trimming its visible branches and leaves. The roots need to taken care of, if the tree is to be truly uprooted. Else, we will remain in this dichotomous situation for a long time to come—one India trying to move forward, while the other India pulls right back.

FUTURE IMPLICATIONS AND SUGGESTIONS

Gender stereotypes and their inaccuracies in the Indian context have not been measured before. As mentioned before, Indian studies like Bhatnagar and Swamy (1995) have tried to link 'interaction' with 'attitudes towards women managers', but specifically stereotype related studies have not been done so far. In my opinion, the most important implication of this study lies in its wide range of applicability to contexts other than gender. This study can be extended to the multi-cultural context of India to study inter-caste stereotypes. Caste stereotypes might uncover important lessons for the country as well, especially in the volatile situation that exists today. Ethnic stereotypes, in a diverse country like India, can also be studied and appropriate affirmative action suggested.

Business schools in India have already taken steps to incorporate conditions of teamwork in their course curriculum to prepare their would-be managers for working better in teams in the organizations they join. On similar lines, they should also make an effort to reduce inaccuracies in gender stereotypes of their students, especially when the majority of the students have no work experience and could, therefore, rightly be assumed to hold inaccurate managerial gender stereotypes. Thus, ensuring conditions of quality contact between male and female students prior to joining organizations could allow us to build a better 'educated' workforce who do not hold inaccurate managerial gender stereotypes. Perhaps we need to ask ourselves the question, why is it that women are so under-represented in the managerial educational institutions? If something can be done to increase the number of female students, fine; if not, then we can work on other ways to draw out better the professional abilities of female students already absorbed in the courses.

The lesson for managers in organizations lies in a combination of the findings of the three studies. Knowing what stereotypes are held by Indian managers can help in important situations like selection, performance appraisals and career planning and development. Also, it is possible for an aware manager to ensure quality of contact conditions for subordinates in team tasks in organizations. It is also possible for team members to be aware of how, unconsciously, their stereotypes affect perceptions of success of women managers in their teams. Training modules can make the inclusion of women compulsory when pre-deciding the training group composition. Educational institutes, especially B-schools in India, can do their bit in forming workgroups keeping the inclusion of women students in mind. They can also design workgroup interaction, keeping in mind the quality of contact conditions. Instead of boardroom quotas, professional educational institutes can think of compulsorily recruiting more women in their student bodies. Apart from recruiting more women, they can also facilitate situations in which women can hold leadership positions in educational institutes. As women are observed more in positions where their managerial and leadership qualities become more pronounced, there is a finite chance that stereotypic inaccuracies would reduce, thus paving the way to healthier organizations and policies.

A reconsideration on these lines, at the pre-organization as well as at all the organizational levels of managers, could well result in a decrease in the negative outcomes that women managers face in organizations, resulting in not only a better and satisfied overall workforce, but also ensuring a better-utilized talent pool (including competent women who are also 'perceived to be' competent) in all organizations.

On that hopeful note, I will conclude, referring to another Calvin and Hobbes masterpiece, just as I started with him.

Calvin bars girls from climbing up to his tree house. This time though, it seems that Susie has found her feet. Susie is more in her element when she waves aside Calvin's diktat, re-fusing to even consider it an attractive option.

Unfortunately, it will take ages for Indian women managers to really take the fun out of sex discrimination on their own. It will take awareness, legislation and a general change in societal mindset to get to a level where the Susies of Indian organizations can hold their own against discrimination and inaccurate stereotypes. Till then I intend to continue with my writing in an attempt to spread awareness to as many unsuspecting souls as possible.

REFERENCES

Bass, B.M. (1999). 'Two decades of research and development in transformational leadership', *European Journal of Work & Organizational Psychology*, 8(1): 9–32.

Berthoin Anthal, A. and D.N. Izraeli. (1993). 'A global comparison of women in management: Women managers in their homelands and as expatriates', in E. Fagenson (ed.), *Women in Management: Trends, Issues and Challenges in Managing Diversity*, pp. 52–96. Newbury Park, CA: Sage.

Bhatnagar, D. and R. Swamy. (1995). 'Attitudes toward women as managers: Does Interaction make a difference?', *Human Relations*, 48(11): 1285–307.

Brenner, O.C., V.E. Schein and J. Tomkiewicz. (1989). 'The relationship between sex role stereotypes and requisite management characteristics revisited', *Academy of Management Journal*, 32(3): 662–69.

Dodge, K.A., F.D. Gilroy and L.M. Fenzel. (1995). 'Requisite management characteristics revisited: Two decades later', *Journal of Social Behavior and Personality*, 10: 253–64.

Hofstede, G. (1993). 'Cultural Constraints in Management Theories', *Academy of Management Executive*, 7(1): 81–94.

Schein, V.E. (1973). 'The relationship between sex role stereotypes and requisite management characteristics', *Journal of Applied Psychology*, 57: 95–100.

———. (1975). 'Relations between sex role stereotypes and requisite management characteristics among female managers', *Journal of Applied Psychology*, 60: 340–44.

Schein, V.E., R. Mueller and C. Jacobson. (1989). 'The relationship between sex role stereotypes and requisite management characteristics among college students', *Sex Roles*, 20: 103–10.

Bibliography

Abate, M. and F.K. Berrien. (1967). 'Validation of stereotypes—Japanese versus American students', *Journal of Personality and Social Psychology*, 7: 435–38.

Adams, J. and J.D. Yoder. (1985). 'When sex roles and work roles conflict: A critical look at standards of evaluation'. Paper presented at Academy of Management, San Diego.

Adler, M.A. (1994). 'Male-female power differences at work: A comparison of supervisors and policymakers', *Social Inquiry*, 37: 45–9.

Adler, N.J. and D.N. Izraeli (eds). (1988). *Women in Management Worldwide*. Armonk, NY: Sharpe.

Agars M.D. (2004). 'Reconsidering the impact of gender stereotypes on the advancement of women in organizations', *Psychology of Women Quarterly*, 28: 103–11.

Allport, G.W. (1954). *The Nature of Prejudice*. Reading, MA: Addison-Wesley.

———. (1979). *The Nature of Prejudice*. Reading, MA: Addison-Wesley. (Originally published in 1954).

Anderson, L.S. (1995). 'Outdoor adventure recreation and social integration: a social-psychological perspective'. PhD thesis, University of Minnesota, Minneapolis, MN.

Araragi, C. (1983). 'The effect of the jigsaw learning method on children's academic performance and learning attitude', *Japanese Journal of Educational Psychology*, 31: 102–12.

Aronson, E. and S. Patnoe. (1997). *The Jigsaw Classroom*. New York: Longman. 150 pp. 2nd ed.

Aronson, E. and A. Gonzalez. (1988). 'Desegregation, jigsaw, and the Mexican-American experience', in P. Katz and D. Taylor (eds), *Eliminating Racism: Profiles in Controversy*, pp. 301–14. New York: Plenum.

Ashmore, R.D. and F.K. Del Boca. (1979). 'Sex stereotypes and implicit personality theory: Toward a cognitive-social psychological conceptualization', *Sex Roles*, 5: 219–48.

Aven, F.F., B. Parker and G.M. McEvoy. (1993). 'Gender and attitudinal commitment to organizations: A meta analysis', *Journal of Business Research*, 26: 63–73.

Bartol, K. (1978). 'The sex structuring of organizations: A search for possible causes', *Academy of Management Review*, 3: 805–15.

Basow, S.A. (1992). *Gender: Stereotypes and Roles*. Pacific Grove, CA: Brooks/Cole.

Bass, B.M. (1999). 'Two decades of research and development in transformational leadership', *European Journal of Work & Organizational Psychology*, 8(1): 9–32.

Ben-Ari, R. and Y. Amir. (1986). 'Contact between Arab and Jewish youth in Israel: Reality and potential', in M. Hewstone and R. Brown (eds), *Contact and Conflict in Intergroup Encounters*, pp. 45–58. Oxford: Blackwell.

Berger, J., B.P. Cohen and M. Zelditch. (1972). 'Status characteristics and social interaction', *American Sociological Review*, 37: 241–55.

———. (1973). 'Status characteristics and social interaction', in R. Ofshe (ed.), *Interpersonal Behavior in Small Groups*, pp. 194–216. Englewood Cliffs, NJ: Prentice Hall.

Berthoin Anthal, A. and D.N. Izraeli. (1993). 'A global comparison of women in management: Women managers in their homelands and as expatriates', in E. Fagenson (ed.), *Women in Management: Trends, Issues and Challenges in Managing Diversity*, pp. 52–96. Newbury Park, CA: Sage.

Bettencourt, B.A., M.B. Brewer, M.R. Rogers-Croak and N. Miller. (1992). 'Cooperation and the reduction of intergroup bias: The role of reward structure and social orientation', *Journal of Experimental & Social Psychology*, 28: 301–19.

Betz, N.E. and L.F. Fitzergald. (1987). *The Career Psychology of Women*. Orlando, FL: Academic Press.

Beutel, N.J. and O.C. Brenner. (1986). 'Sex differences in work variability', *Journal of Vocational Behavior*, 28: 29–41.

Bhatnagar, D. and R. Swamy. (1995). 'Attitudes toward women as managers: Does interaction make a difference?', *Human Relations*, 48(11): 1285–1307.

Blalock, H.M. (1967). *Toward a Theory of Minority Group Relationships*. New York: John Wiley & Sons.

Bornman, E. and J.C. Mynhardt. (1991). 'Social identification and intergroup contact in South Africa with specific reference to the work situation', *Genet. Sociology and General Psychological Monographs*, 117: 437–62.

Bradburn, N., S. Sudman and G.L. Gockel. (1971). *Side by Side: Integrated Neighborhoods in America*. Chicago: Quadrangle Books.

Brenner, O.C. (1982). 'Relationship of education to sex, managerial status, and the managerial stereotype', *Journal of Applied Psychology*, 67: 380–83.

Brenner, O.C. and J.H. Greenhaus. (1979). 'Managerial status, sex and selected personality characteristics', *Journal of Applied Psychology*, 5: 107–13.

Brenner, O.C., V.E. Schein and J. Tomkiewicz. (1989). 'The relationship between sex role stereotypes and requisite management characteristics revisited', *Academy of Management Journal*, 32(3). 662–69.

Brewer, M.B. (1991). 'The social self: On being the same and different at the same time', *Personality and Social Psychology Bulletin*, 84: 888–914.

Brewer, M.B. and N. Miller. (1984). 'Beyond the contact hypothesis: Theoretical perspectives on desegregation', in M. Hewstone and R.J. Brown (eds), *Contact and Conflict in Intergroup Encounters*, pp. 281–302. Oxford: Blackwell.

———. (1988). 'Contact and co-operation: When do they work?', in P. Katz and D. Taylor (eds), *Eliminating Racism: Profiles in Controversy*, pp. 315–26. New York: Plenum.

Brewer, M.B. and R.M. Kramer. (1985). 'The psychology of intergroup attitudes and behavior', *Annual Review of Psychology*, 36: 219–43.

Brief, A.P. and R.L. Oliver. (1976). Male-female differences in work attitudes among retail sales managers', *Journal of Applied Psychology*, 61: 526–28.

Brigham, J.C. (1971a). 'Ethnic Stereotypes'. *Psychological Bulletin*, 76: 15–38.

———. (1971b). 'Racial stereotypes, attitudes and evaluations of and behavioral intentions towards negroes and whites', *Sociometry*, 34: 360–80.

———. (1973). 'Ethnic stereotypes and attitudes: A different mode of analysis', *Journal of Personality*, 41: 206–23.

———. (1974). 'Views of black and white children concerning the distribution of personality characteristics', *Journal of Personality*, 42: 144–58.

Brooks, D. (1975). *Race and Labour in London Transport*. London: Oxford University Press.

Broverman, I.K., S.R. Vogel, D.M. Broverman, F.E. Clarkson and P.S. Rosenkratz. (1972). 'Sex roles stereotypes: A current appraisal', *Journal of Social Issues*, 28: 59–79.

Cantor, N. and W. Mischel. (1979). 'Prototypes in person perception', in L. Berkowitz (ed.), *Advances in Experimental Social Psychology*, 12, 4–52. New York: Academic Press.

Carr Rufino, N. (1985). *The Promotable Woman: Becoming a Successful Manager*. Wadsworth, Belmont: California.

Caspi, A. (1984). 'Contact hypothesis and interage attitudes: A field study of cross-age contact', *Social Psychology Quarterly*, 47: 74–80.

Catalyst. (2003) 'Women and men in U.S. corporate leadership: Same workplace, different realities?'. (http://www.catalystwomen.org/bookstore/files/exe/wmicl4executivesummary.pdf)

Chang, H. (1973). 'Attitudes of Chinese students in the United States', *Sociol. Soc. Res.,* 58: 66–77.

Chapman, L.J. (1967). 'Illusory correlation in observational report', *Journal of Verbal Learning and Verbal Behavior*, 6: 151–55.

Christensen, D. and R. Rosenthal. (1982). 'Gender and nonverbal encoding skill as determinants of interpersonal expectancy effects', *Journal of Personality and Social Psychology*, 42: 75–87.

Chu, D. and D. Griffey. (1985). 'The contact theory of racial integration: The case of sport', *Sociology in Sport Journal*, 2: 323–33.

Chusmir, L.H. (1985). 'Motivation of managers: Is gender a factor?', *Psychology of Women Quarterly*, 9: 153–59.

Cohen, E.G. and R.A. Lotan. (1995). 'Producing equal-status interaction in the heterogeneous classroom', *American Educational Research Journal*, 32: 99–120.

Cohen, E.G. (1982). 'Expectation states and interracial interaction in school settings', *Annual Review of Sociology*, 8: 209–35.

Cohen, J. (1977). *Statistical Power Analysis for the Behavioral Sciences*. New York: Academic Press.

Cook, E.P. (1993). 'The gendered context of life: Implications for women's and men's career-life plans', *The Career Development Quarterly*, 41: 227–37.

Cook, S.W. (1962). 'The systematic analysis of socially significant events: a strategy for social research', *Journal of Social Issues*, 18: 66–84.

Cook, S.W. (1978). 'Interpersonal and attitudinal outcomes in cooperating interracial groups', *Journal of Research & Developmental Education*, 12: 97–113.

———. (1984). 'Cooperative interaction in multiethnic contexts', in M. Brewer (ed.), *Groups in Contact: The Psychology of Desegregation*, pp. 155–85. Orlando, FL: Academic.

———. (1985). 'Experimenting on social issues: The case of school desegregation', *American Psychologist*, 40: 452–60.

Daily, C. and C. Trevis. (1999). 'A decade of corporate women: Some progress in the boardroom, none in the executive suit', *Strategic Management Journal*, 20(1): 93–9.

Day, D.R. and R.M. Stogdill. (1972). 'Leader behavior of male and female supervisors: A comparative study', *Personnel Psychology*, 25: 353–60.

Deaux, K. (1976). 'Sex: A perspective on the attribution process', in J. Harvey, W.J. Ickes and R.F. Kidd (eds), *New Directions in Attribution Research, Vol. 1*, pp. 335–52. Hillsdale NJ: Erlbaum.

Deaux, K. (1984). 'From individual differences to social categories: Analysis of a decade's research on gender', *American Psychologist*, 39: 105–16.

Deaux, K. and L.L. Lewis. (1984). 'Structure of gender stereotypes: Inter-relationships among components and gender label', *Journal of Personality and Social Psychology*, 46: 991–1004.

Desforges, D.M., C.G. Lord, S.L. Ramsey, J.A. Mason and M.D. Van Leeuwen, S.C. West and M.R. Lepper. (1991). 'Effects of structured cooperative contact on changing negative attitudes toward stigmatized social groups', *Journal of Personality and Social Psychology*, 60: 531–44.

Devine, P.G.S.R. Evett and K.A. Vasquez-Suson. (1996). 'Exploring the interpersonal dynamics of intergroup contact', in R.M. Sorrentino, E.T. Higgins (eds), *Handbook of Motivation and Cognition: The Interpersonal Context, Vol. 3*, pp. 423–64. New York: Guilford.

Dobbins, G.H. and S.J. Platz. (1986). 'Sex differences in leadership: How real are they?', *Academy of Management Review*, 11: 118–27.

Dobbins, G.H. and W. Trahan. (1985). 'Sex Bias in Performance Appraisal: A Meta-Analysis and Critical Review'. Paper presented at the Academy of Management, Chicago.

Dodge, K.A., F.D. Gilroy and L.M. Fenzel. (1995). 'Requisite management characteristics revisited: Two decades later', *Journal of Social Behavior and Personality*, 10: 253–64.

Donnell, S.M. and J. Hall. (1980). 'Men and women as managers: A significant case of no significant difference', *Organizational Dynamics*, 11: 60–77.

Dovidio, J.F., J.C. Brigham, B.T. Johnson and S.L. Gaertner. (1996). 'Stereo-typing, prejudice, and discrimination: Another look', in N. Macrae, C. Stangor and M. Hewstone (eds), *Foundations of Stereotypes and Stereotyping*, pp. 276–322. New York: Guilford.

Drew, B. (1988). 'Intergenerational Contact in the Workplace: An Anthro-pological Study of Relationships in the Secondary Labor Market'. PhD thesis. New Brunswick, NJ: Rutgers University.

Dubno, P. (1985). 'Attitudes towards women executives: A longitudinal ap-proach', *Academy of Management Journal*, 28: 235–39.

Durkheim, E. (1960). *The Division of Labor*, 439 pp. Glencoe, IL: Free Press.

Eagly, A.H. (1983). 'Gender and Social influence: A social psychological analysis', *American Psychologist*, 21(September): 971–81.

Eagly, A. and B.T. Jonhson. (1990). 'Gender and leadership style: A meta-analysis', *Psychological Bullettin*, 108: 233–56.

Eagly, A.H. and V.J. Steffen. (1984). 'Gender stereotypes stem from the distribution of women and men into social roles', *Journal of Personality and Social Psychology*, 46: 735–54.

Eppler, R. and G.L. Huber. (1990). 'Wissenserwerb im Team: Empirische Untersuchung von Effekten des Gruppen-Puzzles', *Psychol Erzieh. Unterr*, 37: 172–78.

Eskilson, A. (1995). 'Trends in Homophobia and Gender Attitudes: 1987–1993'. Presented at Annual Meeting of the American Sociological Association. 90th, Washington, DC.

Fagenson, E.A. (1986). 'Women's work orientation: Something old, something new', *Group and Organization Studies*, 11: 75–100.

———. (1990). 'Perceived masculine and feminine attributes examined as a function of individuals' sex and level in the organizational power hierarchy: A test of four theoretical perspectives', *Journal of Applied Psychology*, 75: 204–21.

Fairhurst, G.T. and B.K. Snavaley. (1983). 'A test of the social isolation of male tokens', *Academy of Management Journal*, 26: 353–61.

Falkenberg, L. and C. Rychel. (1985). 'Gender stereotypes in the workplace'. Concordia University Faculty of Commerce and Administration Working Paper Series, Montreal, Quebec, pp. 85–123.

Feather, N.T. (1984). 'Masculinity, Femininity, psychological androgyny and the structure of values', *Journal of Personality and Social Psychology*, 47: 604–21.

Feldman, R. and E. Glenn. (1979). 'Male & Female: Job vs. Gender models in the sociology of work', *Social Problems*, 26: 525–35.

Fine, G.A. (1979). 'The Pinkston settlement: An historical and social psychological investigation of the contact hypothesis', *Phylon*, 40: 229–42.

Ford, W.S. (1986). 'Favorable intergroup contact may not reduce prejudice: Inconclusive journal evidence 1960–1984', *Sociological & Social Research*, 70: 256–58.

Foster, L.W. and T. Kolinko. (1979). 'Changes to be a managerial woman: An examination of individual variables and career choice', *Sex Roles*, 5: 627–34.

Freedman, S.M. and J.S. Phillips. (1988). 'The changing nature of research on women at work', *Journal of Management*, 14: 231–51.

Gaertner, S., J. Mann, A. Murrell and J. Dovidio. (1989). 'Reducing intergroup bias: The benefits of recategorization', *Journal of Personality and Social Psychology*, 57: 239–49.

Gaertner, S.L., J.F. Dovidio, P.A. Anastasio, B.A. Bachman and M.C. Rust. (1993). 'The common ingroup identity model: Recategorization and the reduction of intergroup bias', *European Review of Social Psychology*, 4: 1–26.

Gaertner, S.L., M.C. Rust, J.F. Dovidio, B.A. Bachman and P.A. Anastasio. (1994). 'The contact hypothesis: The role of a common ingroup identity on reducing intergroup bias', *Small Group Research*, 25: 224–49.

Golin, C. and C. Rouse. (1997). 'Orchestrating Impartiality: The Impact of "Blind" Auditions on Female Musicians'. Working Paper No. 376, Industrial Relations Section, Princeton University.

Gomez-Mejia, L. (1983). 'Sex differences during occupational socialization', *Academy of Management Journal*, 26: 492–99.

Greenhaus, J.H. and Parasuraman. (1993). 'Job performance attributions and career advancement prospects: An examination of gender and race effects', *Organizational Behavior and Human Decision Processes*, 55: 273–97.

Gregory, A. (1990). 'Are women different and why women are thought to be different: Theoretical and methodological perspectives', *Journal of Business Ethics*, 9: 257–66.

Gutek, B.A., S. Searle and L. Klepa. (1991). 'Rational vs. Gender-role explanations for work-family conflict', *Journal of Applied Psychology*, 76: 560–68.

Hamilton, D.L. (1979). 'A cognitive-attributional analysis of stereotyping', in L. Berkowitz (ed.), *Advances in Experimental Social Psychology*, pp. 3–84. New York: Academic Press.

———. (1981). 'Illusory correlation as a basis for stereotyping', in D.L. Hamilton (ed.), *Cognitive Processes in Stereotyping and Intergroup Behavior*, pp. 115–44. Hillsdale, NJ: Erlbaum.

Hamilton, D.L. and T. Rose. (1980). 'Illusory correlation and the maintenance of stereotypic beliefs', *Journal of Personality and Social Psychology*, 39: 832–45.

Harlan, A. and C.L. Weiss. (1982). 'Sex differences in factors affecting managerial career advances', in Phylis A. Wallace (ed.), *Women in the Workplace*, pp. 59–100. Boston: Auburn House.

Harragan, B.L. (1977). *Games Mother Never Taught You: Corporate Gamesmanship for Women*. New York: Warner Books.

Heilbrun, A.B. (1976). 'Measurement of masculine and feminine sex role identities as independent dimensions', *Journal of Consulting and Clinical Psychology*, 44: 183–90.

Heilman, M.E. (1983). 'Sex bias in work settings: The lack of fit model', in B.M. Staw and L.I. Cumings (eds), *Research in Organizational Behaviour*, *Vol. 5*, pp. 269–98. Greenwich, CT: JAI Press.

———. (1995). 'Sex stereotypes and their effects in the workplace: What we know and what we don't know', *Journal of Social Behaviour and Personality*, 10: 3–26.

Heilman, M.E., R.F. Martell and M.C. Simon. (1989). 'Has anything changed? Current characterisations of men, women and managers', *Journal of Applied Psychology*, 74: 935–42.

Heilman M.E. and M.C. Simon. (1995). 'Sex stereotypes: Do they influence perceptions of managers', *Journal of Social Behaviour & Personality*, 10: 237–47.

Hennig, M. and A. Jardim. (1976). *The Managerial Woman*. New York: Anchor Press.

Herek, G.M. and J.P. Capitanio. (1996). '"Some of my best friends": Intergroup contact, concealable stigma, and heterosexuals' attitudes toward gay men and lesbians', *Personnel & Social Psychological Bulletin*, 22: 412–24.

Hewstone, M. and R. Brown (eds). (1986). *Contact and Conflict in Intergroup Encounters*. Oxford: Blackwell.

Hewstone, M. (1996). 'Contact and categorization: Social-psychological interventions to change intergroup relations', in C.N. Macrae, C. Stagnor and M. Hewstone (eds), *Foundations of Stereotypes and Stereotyping*, pp. 323–68. New York: Guilford.

Hofstede, G. (1993). 'Cultural Constraints in Management Theories', *Academy of Management Executive*, 7(1): 81–94.

Horner, M.S. (1968). 'Sex differences in achievement motivation and performance in competitive and non-competitive situations'. Doctoral Dissertation, University of Michigan. University Microfilms, Ann Arbor.

———. (1972). 'Towards an understanding of achievement related conflicts in women', *Journal of Social Issues*, 28: 157–76.

Huffman, M.L. and S.C. Valasco. (1997). 'When more is less: Sex composition, organizations, and earnings in U.S. firms', *Work & Occupations*, 39: 214–38.

Jackman, M.R. and M. Crane. (1986). '"Some of my best friends are black...": Interracial friendship and whites' racial attitudes', *Public Opinion Quarterly*, 50: 459–86.

Jensen, L.C., R. Christensen and D.J. Wilson. (1985). 'Predicting young women's role preference for parenting and work', *Sex Roles*, 13: 507–14.

Johnson, D.W., R.T. Johnson and G. Maruyama. (1984). 'Goal interdependence and interpersonal-personal attraction in heterogeneous classrooms: A meta-analysis', in N. Miller and M.B. Brewer, *Groups in Contact: The Psychology of Desegregation*, pp. 187–212. New York: Academic Press.

Johnston, L. and M. Hewstone. (1992). 'Cognitive models of stereotype change: III. Subtyping and the perceived typicality of disconfirming group members', *Journal of Experimental & Social Psychology*, 28: 360–86.

Kanter, R.M. (1977a). *Men and Women of the Corporation*. New York: Basic Books.

———. (1977b). 'Some effects of proportions on group life: Skewed sex ratios and responses to token women', *American Journal of Sociology*, 82: 965–90.

Kaolin, R. and D.C. Hodgins. (1984). 'Sex bias and occupational suitability', *Canadian Journal of Behavioral Science*, 16: 311–25.

Katz, D. and K.W. Braly. (1933). 'Racial stereotypes of one hundred college students', *Journal of Abnormal and Social Psychology*, 28: 280–90.

Kelly, H.H. (1972). 'Attribution in social interaction', in E.E. Jones, D.E. Kanouse, H.H. Kelly, R.E. Nisbett, S. Valens and B. Weiner (eds), *Attribution: Perceiving the Causes of Behavior*, pp. 1–26. Morristown, NJ: General Learning Press.

Keppel, G. (1991). *Design and Analysis: A Researcher's Handbook*. NJ: Prentice-Hall Inc.

Kidder, L.H. (1981). *Selltiz, Wirghtman and Cooks: Research Method in Social Relations*. New York: Holt, Rinehart and Winston.

Kinloch, G.C. (1981). 'Comparative race and ethnic relations', *International Journal of Comparative Sociology*, 22: 257–71.

———. (1991). 'Inequality, repression, discrimination and violence: A comparative study', *International Journal of Comparative Sociology*, 28: 85–98.

Konrad, A.M and B.A. Gutek. (1987). 'Theory and research on group composition: Applications to the status of women and minorities', in S. Oskamp and S. Spacapan (eds), *Interpersonal Processes: The Claremont Symposium on Applied Social Psychology*, pp. 85–121. Newbury Park, CA: Sage.

Kulkarni, S.S. (2002). 'Women and professional competency—a survey report', *Indian Journal of Training and Development*, XXXII(2): 72–83.

Landis, D., R.O. Hope and H.R. Day. (1984). 'Training for desegregation in the military', in N. Miller and M.B. Brewer (eds), *Groups in Contact: The Psychology of Desegregation*, pp. 257–78. Orlando, FL: Academic Press.

Larouche, J. and R. Ryan. (1984). *Janice Larouche's Strategies for Women at Work*. New York: Avon.

Larwood, L., E. Szajkowski and S. Rose. (1988). 'When discrimination makes "sense": The rational bias theory', in B.A. Gutek and L. Larwood (eds), *Women and Work: An Annual Review*, Vol. 3, pp. 265–88. Newbury Park, CA: Sage.

Larwood, L. and U.E. Gattiker. (1987). 'A comparison of career paths used by successful women and men', in B.A. Gutek and L. Larwood (eds), *Women's Career Development*, pp. 129–56. Newbury Park, CA: Sage.

Lippmann, W. (1922). *Public Opinion*. New York: Harcourt, Brace.

Lips, H.M. (1999). 'Women, Education and Economic Participation'. Keynote address at the Northern Regional Seminar. National Council of women of New Zealand. Available at http://www.runet.edu

Locksley, A., E. Bongida, N. Brekke and C. Hepburn. (1980). 'Sex Stereotypes and Social Judgment', *Journal of Personality & Social Psychology*, 39: 821–30.

Loden, M. (1985). *Feminine Leadership or How to Succeed in Business without being One of the Boys*. New York: Times Books.

Lott, B. (1985). 'The devaluation of women's competence', *Journal of Social Issues*, 41: 43–60.

Lyness, K. and D. Thompson. (1997). 'Above the glass ceiling? A comparison of matched samples of female and male executives', *Journal of Applied Psychology*, 82(3): 359–75.

Mainiero, L. (1986). 'Coping with powerlessness: The relationship of gender and job dependency to empowerment strategy usage', *Administrative Science Quarterly*, 31: 633–53.

Manley, J.E. (1995). 'Sex-segregated work in the system of professions: The development and stratification of nursing', *Social Quarterly*, 36: 297–308.

Marshall, J. (1984). *Women Managers: Travellers in a Male World*. Chichester, UK: John Wiley & Sons..

Martin, C.L. (1987). 'A ratio measure of sex stereotyping', *Journal of Personality and Social Psychology*, 52: 489–99.

Martin, C.L. and C.F. Halverson. (1981). 'A schematic processing model of sex-typing and stereotyping in children', *Child Development*, 52: 1119–1134.

Martin, Y.M., D. Harrison and D. Dinitto. (1983). 'Advancement for women in hierarchical organizations: A multi-level analysis for advancements and prospects', *Journal of Applied Behavioral Science*, 19: 19–33.

McCarty, P.A. (1986). 'Effects of feedback on the self confidence of men and women', *Academy of Management Journal*, 29: 840–47.

McCauley, C. and C.L. Stitt. (1978). 'An individual and quantitative measure of stereotypes', *Journal of Personality and Social Psychology*, 36: 929–40.

McCauley, C., C.L. Stitt and M. Segal. (1980). 'Stereotyping: From prejudice to prediction', *Psychological Bulletin*, 87: 195–208.

McCauley, C.D., M.N. Ruderman, P.J. Ohlott and J.E. Morrow. (1994). 'Assessing the developmental components of managerial jobs', *Journal of Applied Psychology*, 79: 544–60.

McGarty, C. and A.M. de la Haye. (1997). 'Stereotype formation: Beyond illusory correlation', in R. Spears, P.J. Oakes, N. Ellemers and S.A. Haslam (eds), *The Social Psychology of Stereotyping and Group Life*, pp. 144–70. Oxford: Blackwell.

McGinnis, S.P. (1990). 'Descriptive and evaluative components of stereotypes of computer programmers and their determinants'. PhD thesis. New York: City Univ. NY.

McGrath, J.E. (1964). 'Toward a "Theory of Method" for research in organizations', in W.W. Cooper, H.J. Leavitt and M.W. Shelley (eds), *New Perspectives in Organization Research*, pp. 533–56. New York: John Wiley & Sons.

McKay, S. and Pitman, J. (1993). 'Determinants of Anglo-Australian stereotypes of the Vietnamese in Australia', *Australian Journal of Psychology*, 45: 17–23.

Meeker, B.F. and P.A. Weitzel-O-Neill. (1977). 'Sex roles and interpersonal behavior in task-oriented groups', *American Sociological Review*, 42: 91–105.

Meer, B. and E. Freedman. (1966). 'The impact of Negro neighbors on white house owners', *Social Forces*, 45: 11–19.

Miller, J.B. (1976). *Toward a new Psychology of Women*. Boston: Beacon Press.

Miller, N. and M.B. Brewer (eds). (1984). *Groups in Contact: The Psychology of Desegregation*. Orlando, FL: Academic.

Miracle, A.W. (1981). 'Factors affecting interracial cooperation: A case study of a high school football team', *Human Organization*, 40: 150–54.

Morrison, A.M. (1992). *The New Leaders Guidelines on Leadership Diversity*. San Francisco: Jossey Bass.

Morrison, E.W. and J.M. Herlihy. (1992). 'Becoming the best place to work: Managing diversity at American Express Travel related services', in S.E. Jackson (ed.), *Diversity in the Workplace,* pp. 203–26. New York: Guilford.

Neft, N. and A.D. Levine. (1997). *Where Women Stand: An International Report on the Status of Women in 140 Countries*. New York: Random House.

Nieva, V.F. and B.A. Gutek. (1980). 'Sex Effects on Evaluation', *Academy of Management Review*, 5: 267–76.

Ohm, R.M. (1988). *Constructing and reconstructing social distance attitudes*. PhD thesis. 316 pp. Arizona State University. Tempe.

O'Leary, V.E. (1974). 'Some attitudinal barriers to occupational aspirations in women', *Psychological Bulletin*, 81: 809–26.

Olson, J.E., D.C. Good and I.H. Frieze. (1985). 'Income differentials of male and female MBAs: The effects of job type and industry'. Paper presented at Academy of Management, San Diego.

Parker, J.H. (1968). 'The interaction of Negroes and whites in an integrated church setting', *Social Forces*, 46: 359–66.

Patchen, M. (1982). *Black-White Contact in Schools: Its Social and Academic Effects*. West Lafayette, IN: Purdue Univ. Press.

Paul, A.M. (1998). 'Where bias begins: The truth about stereotypes'. *Psychology Today*. http://www.runet.edu/~junnever/articles/bias_article.htm. (Accessed in May/June 1998)

Pazy, A. (1986). 'Persistence of pro-male bias despite identical information regarding causes of success', *Organizational Behavior & Human Decision Processes*, 38: 366–73.

Perdue, C.W., J.F. Dovidio, M.B. Gurtman and R.B. Tyler. (1990). 'Us and them: Social categorization and the process of intergroup bias', *Journal of Personality and Social Psychology*, 59: 475–86.

Pettigrew, T.F. (1971). *Racially Separate or Together?* New York: McGraw-Hill.

———. (1975). 'The racial integration of the schools', in T.F. Pettigrew (ed.), *Racial Discrimination in the United States*, pp. 224–39, 429. New York: Harper & Row.

———. (1986). 'The contact hypothesis revisited', in M. Hewstone and R. Brown (eds), *Contact and Conflict in Intergroup Encounters*, pp. 169–95. Oxford, UK: Blackwell.

———. (1991a). 'The importance of cumulative effects: a neglected emphasis of Sheriffs work', in D. Granberg, G. Sarup (eds), *Social Judgment and Inter-group Relations: Essays in Honor of Muzafer Sherif*, pp. 89–103. New York: Springer-Verlag.

———. (1991b). 'Toward unity and bold theory: Popperian suggestions for two persistent problems of social psychology', in C.W. Stephan, W. Stephan and T.F. Pettigrew (eds), *The Future of Social Psychology*, pp. 13–27. New York: Springer-Verlag.

———. (1996). *How to Think Like a Social Scientist*. New York: Harper-Collins.

Pettigrew, T.F. (1997a). 'Generalized intergroup contact effects on prejudice', *Personality & Social Psychologicy Bulletin*, 23: 173–85.

———. (1997b). 'The affective component of prejudice: Empirical support for the new view', in S.A. Tuch and J.K. Martin (eds), *Racial Attitudes in the 1990s: Continuity and Change,* pp. 76–90. Westport, CT: Praeger.

———. (1997c). 'Ingroup reappraisal: Another intergroup contact process that reduces prejudice'. Unpublished manuscript. University of California, Santa Cruz.

———. (1998). 'Intergroup Contact Theory', *Annual Review of Psychology*, 49: 65–85.

Pettigrew, T.F. and R.W. Meertens. (1995). 'Subtle and blatant prejudice in western Europe', *European Journal of Social Psychology*, 25: 57–75.

Pettigrew T.F., S. Wright and L. Tropp. (1998). 'Intergroup contact and prejudice: A meta-analytic test of Allport's hypothesis'. Unpublished manuscript. Department of Psychology, University of California, Santa Cruz.

Powell, G.N. (1987). 'The effects of sex and gender on recruitment', *Academy of Management Review*, 12: 731–43.

———. (1988). *Women and Men in Management.* Beverly Hills, CA: Sage.

———. (1993). *Women and Men in Management.* 2nd. Edition. Newbury Park, CA: Sage.

———. (1994). *Gender & Diversity in the Workplace: Learning Activities and Exercises.* New York: Sage.

Powell, G.N. and A. Butterfield. (1979). 'The "good manager": Masculine or androgynous?, *Academy of Management Journal*, 22: 345–403.

Powell, G.N., B.Z. Posner and W.H. Schmidt. (1984). 'Sex effects in managerial value systems', *Human Relations*, 37: 909–21.

Powell, G.N. and L.A. Mainiero. (1992). 'Cross currents in the river of time: Conceptualizing the complexities of women's careers', *Journal of Management*, 18: 215–37.

Powers, D.A. and C.G. Ellison. (1995). 'Interracial contact and black racial attitudes: The contact hypothesis and selectivity bias', *Social Forces*, 74: 205–26.

Pulakos, E.D. and K.N. Wexley. (1983). 'The Relationship Among Perceptual Similarity, Sex, and Performance Ratings in Manager-Subordinate Dyads', *Academy of Management Journal*, 26(1): 129–39.

Putnam, L. and S.J. Heinen. (1976). 'Women in management: The fallacy of the trait approach', *MSU Business Topics*, Summer, 47–53.

Ragins, B.R. and J. Cotton. (1996, April). 'The influence of gender ratios on organizational attitudes and outcomes'. Poster session presented at the 11th Annual Conference for the Society for Industrial and Organizational Psychology. San Diego, CA.

Rely, G. (1994) 'The Effects of Demographics and social Identity on Relationships Among Professional Women', *Administrative Science Quarterly*, 39: 203–38.

Remus, W.L. and L. Kelley. (1983). 'Evidence of sex discrimination: In similar populations man are paid better than women', *American Journal of Economics and Sociology*, 42: 149–52.

Riger, S. and P. Galligan. (1980). 'Women in management: An exploration of competing paradigms', *American Psychologist*, 35: 902–10.

Riordan, C. (1978). 'Equal-status interracial contact: A review and revision of the concept', *International Journal of Intercultural Relations*, 2: 161–85.

———. (1987). 'Intergroup contact in small cities', *International Journal of Intercultural Relations*, 11: 143–54.

Riordan, C. and J. Ruggiero. (1980). 'Producing equal-status interracial interaction: A replication', *Social Psychology Quarterly*, 43: 131–36.

Robinson, J.L. Jr. (1980). 'Physical distance and racial attitudes: A further examination of the contact hypothesis', *Phylon*, 41: 325–32.

Robinson, J.W. Jr. and J.D. Preston. (1976). 'Equal-status contact and modification of racial prejudice', *Social Forces*, 54: 911–24.

Rose, T.L. (1981). 'Cognitive and dyadic processes in intergroup contact', in D.L. Hamilton (ed.), *Cognitive Processes in Stereotyping and Intergroup Behavior*, pp. 145–81. Hillsdale, NJ: Erlbaum.

Rosen, B. and M.F. Mericle. (1979). 'Influence of strong vs. weak fair employment policies and applicants' sex on selection decisions and salary recommendations in a management simulation', *Journal of Applied Psychology*, 64: 435–39.

Rosenkratz, P., S. Vogel, H. Bee, I. Broverman and D.M. Broverman. (1968). 'Sex role stereotypes and self-concepts in college students', *Journal of Consulting and Clinical Psychology*, 32: 343–55.

Ruble, T.L. (1983). 'Sex stereotypes: Issues of change in the 1970s', *Sex Roles*, 9: 397–402.

Ruble, T.L., R. Cohen and D.M. Ruble. (1984). 'Sex stereotypes: Occupational barriers for women', *American Behavioral Scientist*, 27: 339–56.

Ruderman, M.N. and P.J. Ohlott. (1992, August). 'Managerial promotions as a diversity practice'. Paper presented at the 52nd annual meeting of the Academy of Management, Las Vegas.

Sackett, P.R. C.L.Z. Dubois and A.W. Noe. (1991). 'Tokenism in performance evaluation: The effects of work group representation on male-female and white-black differences in performance ratings'. *Journal of Applied Psychology*, 76: 263.

Sagiv, L. and S.H. Schwartz. (1995). 'Value priorities and readiness for out-group social contact', *Journal of Personality and Social Psychology*, 69: 437–48.

Schein, V.E. (1972). 'Fair employment of women through personnel research', *Personnel Research*, 51: 330–35.

———. (1973). 'The relationship between sex role stereotypes and requisite management characteristics', *Journal of Applied Psychology*, 57: 95–100.

———. (1975). 'Relations between sex role stereotypes and requisite management characteristics among female managers', *Journal of Applied Psychology*, 60: 340–44.

———. (1978). 'Sex role stereotyping, ability and performance: Prior research and new directions', *Personnel Psychology*, 31: 259–68.

———. (2001), 'A global look at psychological barriers to women's progress in management', *Journal of Social Issues*, 57(4): 675–88.

Schein, V.E., R. Mueller and C. Jacobson. (1989). 'The relationship between sex role stereotypes and requisite management characteristics among college students', *Sex Roles*, 20: 103–10.

Schneer, J.A. (1985). 'Gender context: An alternative perspective on sex differences in organization'. Paper presented at the Academy of Management, San Diego.

Schofield, J.W. (1989). *Black and White in School: Trust, Tension, or Tolerance?* New York: Teachers College Press.

Schuman, H. (1966). 'Social change and the validity of regional stereotypes in East Pakistan', *Sociometry*, 29: 428–40.

Sherif, M. (1966). *In Common Predicament*. Boston: Houghton Mifflin.

Sigelman, L. and S. Welch. (1993). 'The contact hypothesis revisited: Black-white interaction and positive racial attitudes', *Social Forces*, 71: 781–95.

Singh, K. (2003). 'Women managers: Perception vs. performance analysis', *Journal of Management Research*, 3(1): 31–42.

Sitterley, C. and B.W. Duke. (1988). *A Woman's Place: Management*. Englewood Cliffs, NY: Prentice Hall.

Slavin, R.E. (1983). *Cooperative Learning.* New York: Longman.

Slavin, R.E. and N.A. Madden. (1979). 'Social practices that improve race relations', *American Educational Research Journal*, 16: 169–80.

Smircich, L. (1985). 'Toward a woman-centred organization theory'. Paper presented at the Annual Meeting of the Acedemy of Management, August, San Diego, CA.

Smith, C.B. (1994). 'Back and to the future: The intergroup contact hypothesis revisited', *Social Inquiry*, 64: 438–55.

Spears, R., P.J. Oakes, N. Ellemers and S.A. Haslam (eds). (1997). *The Social Psychology of Stereotyping and Group Life*. Oxford, UK: Blackwell.

Spence, J.T. and R.L. Helmreich. (1978). *Masculinity and Femininity: Their Psychologican Dimensions, Correlates and Antecedents*. Austin: University of Texas Press.

Spence, J.T., R. Helmreich and J. Stapp. (1974). 'The personal attributes questionnaire: A measure of sex role stereotypes and masculinity-femininity', *Journal of Supplemental Abstract Service Catalog of Selected Documents in Psychology*, 4: 43–45.

———. (1975). 'Ratings of self and peers on sex role attributes and their relation to self-esteem and conceptions of masculinity and femininity', *Journal of Personality and Social Psychology*, 32: 29–39.

Staw, B.M. (1980). 'The experimental organization: Strategies and issues in improving causal inference within administrative settings', in E.E. Lawler, D.A. Nadler and C. Cammann (eds), *Organizational Assessment: Perspectives on the Measurement of Organizational Behavior and Quality of Worklife*. New York: John Wiley and Sons.

Steffy, B.D. and J.W. Jones. (1988). 'The impact of family and career variables on the organizational career and community commitment of professional women', *Journal of Vocational Behaviour*, 32: 196–212.

Steinberg, R. and S. Shapiro. (1982). 'Sex differences in personality traits of female and male MBA students', *Journal of Applied Psychology*, 67: 306–10.

Stephan, W.G. and C.W. Stephan. (1984). 'The role of ignorance in intergroup relations', in N. Miller and M. Brewer (eds), *Groups in Contact*, pp. 229–55. New York: Academic Press.

———. (1985). 'Intergroup anxiety', *Journal of Social Issues*, 41: 157–75.

———. (1989). 'Antecedents of intergroup anxiety in Asian-Americans and Hispanic-Americans', *International Journal of Intercultural Relations*, 13: 203–19.

Stewart, L.P. and W.B. Gudykunst. (1982). 'Differential factors influencing the hierarchical level and numbers of promotions of males and females within the organization', *Academy of Management Journal*, 25: 587–97.

Strober, M.H. (1982). 'The MBA: Same passport to success for men and women?', in A. Wallace Phylis (ed.), *Women in the Workplace*, pp. 25–58. Auburn House: Boston.

Stroh, L.K., J.M. Brett and A.H. Reilly. (1992). 'All the right stuff: A comparison of female and male managers' career progression', *Journal of Applied Psychology*, 77: 251–57.

Susman, G.I. (1983). 'Action Research: A socio-technical systems' perspective'. *Beyond Method: Strategies for Social Research*, pp. 95–113. Beverly Hills, CA: Sage.

Swim, J.K. and L.J. Sanna. (1996). 'He's skilled, she's lucky: A meta-analysis of observed attributions for women's and men's successes and failures', *Personality and Social Psychology Bulletin,* 22: 507–19.

Taylor, D.M., L. Dube and J. Bellerose. (1986). 'Intergroup contact in Quebec: Myth or Reality?', in M. Hewstone and R. Brown (eds), *Contact and Conflict in Intergroup Encounters*, pp. 107–18. Oxford: Basil Blackwell.

Taylor, M.S. and D.R. Ilgen. (1981). 'Sex discrimination against women in initial placement decisions: A laboratory investigation', *Academy of Management Journal*, 24: 859–65.

Terborg, J.R. (1981). 'Interactional psychology and research in human behavior in organizations', *Academy of Management Review*, 6: 569–76.

———. (1977). 'Women in management: A research review', *Journal of Applied Psychology*, 62: 647–64.

Terborg, J.R. and D.R. Ilgen. (1975). 'A theoretical approach to sex discrimination in traditionally masculine occupations', *Organization Behavior & Human Performance*, 13: 352–76.

Thompson, J.D. (1967). *Organizations in Action*. New York: McGraw Hill.

Tsui, A.S. and B.A. Gutek. (1984). 'A role analysis of gender difference in performance affective relationships and career success of industrial middle managers', *Academy of Management Journal*, 27: 619–35.

Van Fleet, D.D. and J.G. Saurage. (1984). 'Recent Research on women in management', *Akron Business and Economic Review*, 15(2): 15–24.

Vernon-Gerstenfeld, S. and E. Burke. (1985). '*Affirmative Action in Nine Large Companies: A Field Study'*, *Personnel Journal*, 54: 55–59.

Wagner, U., M. Hewstone and U. Machleit. (1989). 'Contact and prejudice between Germans and Turks', *Human Relations*, 42: 561–74.

Walker, I. and M. Crogan. (1997). 'Academic performance, prejudice, and the jigsaw classroom: New pieces to the puzzle'. Presented at Annual Meeting of Social Psychology, 3rd, Wollongong.

Weber, R. and J. Crocker. (1983). 'Cognitive processes in the revision of stereotypic beliefs', *Journal of Personality and Social Psychology*, 45: 961–77.

Webster, M. and J.B. Kervin. (1971). 'Artificiality in Experimental Psychology', *Canadian Revenue of Sociology and Anthropology*, 8: 263–72.

Weldon, D.E., D.E. Carlston, A.K. Rissman, L. Slobodin and H.C. Triandis. (1975). 'A laboratory test of effects of culture assimilator training', *Journal of Personality and Social Psychology*, 32: 300–310.

Werth, J.L. and C.G. Lord. (1992). 'Previous conceptions of the typical group member and the contact hypothesis', *Basic and Applied Social Psychology*, 13: 351–69.

Wilder, D.A. and P.N. Shapiro. (1989). 'Role of competition-induced anxiety in limiting beneficial impact of positive behavior by an outgroup member', *Journal of Personality and Social Psychology*, 56: 60–69.

Wilder, D.A. and J.E. Thompson. (1980). 'Intergroup contact with independent manipulations of in-group and out-group interaction', *Journal of Personality and Social Psychology*, 38: 589–603.

Wilder, D.A. (1984). 'Intergroup contact: the typical member and the exception to the rule', *Journal of Experimental and Social Psychology*, 20: 177–94.

Wilder, D.A. (1993a). 'The role of anxiety in facilitating stereotypic judgments of outgroup behavior', in D.M. Mackie and D.L. Hamilton (eds), *Affect, Cognition, and Stereotyping: Interactive Processes in Group Perception*, pp. 87–109. San Diego: Academic.

———. (1993b). 'Freezing intergroup evaluations: Anxiety fosters resistance to counterstereotypic information', in M.A. Hogg and D. Abrams (ed.), *Group Motivation: Social Psychological Perspectives*, pp. 68–86. London: Harvester Wheatsheaf.

Williams, J.E. and S.M. Bennett. (1975). 'The definition of sex stereotypes via the Adjective Checklist', *Sex Roles*, 1: 327–37.

Wilson, F. (1997). *Organization Behavior and Gender*. New York: McGraw-Hill.

Wolf, W.C. and N.D. Fligstein. (1979). 'Sex and authority in the workplace: The causes of sexual inequality', *American Sociological Review*, 44: 235–52.

Yoder, J.D. (1991). 'Rethinking tokenism: Looking beyond numbers', *Gender and Society*, 5(2): 178–92.

Zajonc, R.B. (1968). 'Attitudinal effects of mere exposure', *Journal of Personality and Social Psychology*, 9: 1–27.

Zuel, C.R. and C.R. Humphrey. (1971). 'The integration of black residents in suburban neighborhoods', *Social Problems*, 18: 462–74.

About the Author

Sujoya Basu is an Assistant Professor in the Behavioural Sciences Area at the Indian Institute of Management Calcutta (IIMC). She graduated as an engineer from Jadavpur University, Kolkata, in 1995. After working in Kolkata for three years, she completed her PhD in management, specializing in Organization Behaviour from the Indian Institute of Management Ahmedabad (IIMA) in 2003. She worked as an organization redesign consultant for CSIR (IGIB) for about a year and joined IIMC in 2004. Her research interests include gender stereotypes, virtual trust and cross-cultural management issues. She has several papers published in the proceedings of national and international conferences to her credit.

Insight Phrase Book
Italian
Original text: Elisabeth Graf-Riemann
Editor: Sabine von Loeffelholz
English edition translated by: Paul Fletcher
Edited by: Renée Holler and Cathy Muscat

Managing Editor: Tony Halliday
Editorial Director: Brian Bell

CONTACTING THE EDITORS: As every effort is made to provide accurate information in this publication, we would appreciate it if readers would call our attention to any errors and omissions by contacting:
Apa Publications, PO Box 7910, London SE1 1WE, England.
Fax: (44 20) 7403 0290
e-mail: insight@apaguide.demon.co.uk

Information has been obtained from sources believed to be reliable,
but its accuracy and completeness, and the opinions based thereon,
are not guaranteed.

© 2000 APA Publications GmbH & Co. Verlag KG Singapore Branch, Singapore.

1st edition 2000

Printed in Singapore by Insight Print Services (Pte) Ltd

Original edition © Polyglott-Verlag Dr Bolte KG, Munich

Distributed in the UK & Ireland by:
GeoCenter International Ltd
The Viables Centre, Harrow Way, Basingstoke,
Hampshire RG22 4BJ
Tel: (44 1256) 817987, Fax: (44 1256) 817-988

Distributed in the United States by:
Langenscheidt Publishers, Inc.
46–35 54th Road, Maspeth, NY 11378
Tel: (1 718) 784-0055, Fax: (1 718) 784-0640

Worldwide distribution enquiries:
APA Publications GmbH & Co. Verlag KG (Singapore Branch)
38 Joo Koon Road, Singapore 628990
Tel: (65) 865-1600, Fax: (65) 861-6438

INSIGHT PHRASE BOOK

Italian

Apa Publications

Contents

Introduction

About this book

Insight Phrase Books are the perfect companion when touring abroad as they cover all the everyday situations faced by travellers who are not familiar with the language of their holiday hosts.

The sentences and expressions translated here have been chosen carefully so that you can make yourself understood quickly and easily. You will not find any complicated sentence constructions or long word lists. Nearly all the sentences have been compiled from basic phrases so that by substituting words and other expressions, you will be able to cope with a variety of conversational situations.

The word lists at the end of each section are themed and this will make it easy for you to vary what you want to say. You will be able to make yourself understood quickly in Italian with the minimum vocabulary. You won't need to spend a long time searching for the word you want.

So that you can understand what others are saying to you in everyday situations, for example at the doctors, at the border, we have marked with an asterisk (*) those phrases and questions that you are likely to hear frequently.

The simplified pronunciation guide geared towards English speakers will help you to say correctly the words you need. You will also find a summary of basic pronunciation information, together with a brief introduction to Italian grammar.

This introduction is followed by nine chapters containing examples of sentences from general and tourist-related situations. You will find general tips and guidance not just in the chapter entitled *Practical Information*, but also elsewhere in the book. The various feature boxes contain useful information on such matters as meal times, using public transport and telephones, the different categories of hotels and restaurants and lots more.

At the end of the book you will find an English-Italian dictionary, which can be used for reference and as an index, the page number referring to an entry in one of the nine chapters. The Italian-English dictionary contains a selection of important words and abbreviations, which you are likely to encounter on signs, notices and information boards.

Hoping you have lots of fun on your travels, Buon viaggio! [bwon **vyaj**jo] *(Have a good trip!).*

Pronunciation

All the Italian words included in this guide are given a phonetic rendering. This always appears in square brackets after the translation and there are no special symbols to remember.

You will see that where a word has more than one syllable, the stressed syllable is shown in bold, e.g. momento [mo**men**to] *(moment)*, tavolo [**ta**volo] *(table)*.

Italian is an easy and logical language to read and you will probably find yourself reading straight from the translation before long.

Although the phonetic rendering can be read as though it were English, the following points about pronunciation should be noted:

– **c** and **cc** when they precede the vowels a, o and u are pronounced as a k, e.g. camera [**ka**maira] *(room)*; coda [**ko**da] *(traffic jam)*. Before e and i as ch, e.g. cinque [**cheen**kway] *(five)*; centro [**chen**tro] *(centre)*.

- **ch** and **cch** are pronounced as k, e.g. che [kay] *(what)*; chiesa [k**ay**za] *(church)*.

- **ci** and **cci** when they precede the vowels a, o and u are pronounced as ch, e.g. ciao [chow] *(hi!)*; cioccolata [choko**la**ta] *(chocolate)*.

- **g** before an a, o and u is a hard g like the English goal, e.g. ragazza [ra**gat**za] *(girl)*; when followed by an e or an i, then it becomes a soft g like gentle, e.g. gente [**jen**tay] *(people)*; oggi [**oj**jee] *(today)*.

- **gh** is always pronounced like a g, e.g. funghi [**foon**gee] *(mushrooms)*.

- **gi** or **ggi** are pronounced as a soft g, e.g. mangiare [man**ja**ray] *(to eat)*; oggi [**oj**jee] *(today)*.

- **gl** makes an ly sound as in stallion, e.g. figlia [**feel**ya] *(daughter)*; moglie [**mol**yay] *(wife)*.

- **gn** sounds like ny as in onion, e.g. signora [seen**yo**ra] *(woman)*; montagna [mon**tan**ya] *(mountain)*.

- the **h** is always silent, e.g. hai [a-ee] *([you] have)*; hotel [o**tel**] *(hotel)*.

- **qu** is a kw sound, e.g. acqua [**ak**wa] *(water)*; quando [**kwan**do] *(when)*.

- the **r** is rolled, e.g. rosso [**ros**so] *(red)*.

- **sc** before a, o and u sounds like sk, e.g. scusa [**skoo**za] *(sorry)*; but before e and i as a sh sound, e.g. uscita [oo**shee**ta] *(exit)*.

- **sch** is always sk, e.g. pesche [**pes**kay] *(peaches)*; Ischia [**eesk**ya] *(Ischia)*.

- **sci** makes a sh sound when before a, o and u, e.g. lasciare [la**sha**ray] *(to leave)*.

When two or more vowels occur next to each other, then each vowel is heard, e.g. paese [pa-**ay**zay] *(country)*; europeo [ayooro**pay**o] *(European)*; cucchiaino [kookya-**ee**no] *(spoon)*; when an i occurs before a stressed vowel or between two vowels, then it is pronounced as a y, e.g. escursione [eskoorsy**o**nay] *(excursion)*; lieve [l**yay**vay] *(light)*.

Stress and accent

Generally speaking, it is the last but one syllable which is stressed when the word ends in a vowel, e.g. buon giorno [bwon⌣**jor**no] *(hello, good-day)*; turismo [too**ree**zmo] *(tourism)*; escursione [eskoorsy**o**nay] *(excursion)*.

If the stress occurs on a different syllable, then an accent shows the stressed syllable, e.g. perché [per**kay**] *(why)*; lui può [**loo**ee pwo] *(he can)*; nazionalità [natsyonalee**ta**] *(nationality)*; libertà [leebair**ta**] *(freedom)*.

The Italian alphabet

A a	[a]
B b	[bee]
C c	[chee]
D d	[dee]
E e	[eh]
F f	[**ef**fay]
G g	[jee]
H h	[**ak**ka]
I i	[ee]
J j	[ee **loon**go]
K k	[**kap**pa]
L l	[**el**lay]
M m	[**em**may]
N n	[**en**nay]
O o	[o]
P p	[pee]
Q q	[koo]
R r	[**er**ray]
S s	[**es**say]
T t	[tee]
U u	[oo]
V v	[vu]
W w	[vu **dop**pyo]
X x	[eex]
Y y	[**eep**seelon]
Z z	[**tzay**ta]

7

Italian Grammar In Brief

The article

In Italian all nouns are either masculine *[m]* or feminine *[f]*.

The definite article

Masculine singular: **il** and **lo**. Lo is shortened to l' before nouns that begin with a vowel:
il cane [eel **ka**nay] *(the dog);* lo sportello [lo spor**tel**lo] *(the booking office);* l'occhio [**lok**yo] *(the eye).*

Masculine plural: **i** and **gli**
i cani [ee **ka**nee] *(the dogs);* gli occhi; [lyee **ok**kee] *(the eyes).*

Feminine singular: **la**
la casa [la **ka**za] *(the house);* la scuola [la **skwo**la] *(the school).*

Feminine plural: **le**
le case [lay **ka**zay] *(the houses);* le scuole [lay **skwo**lay] *(the schools).*

Indefinite article

Masculine singular **un** and **uno**
un libro [oon **lee**bro] *(a book);* uno stivale [**oo**no stee**va**lay] *(a boot).*

The *plural* of the indefinite article is formed by the partitive article di and the plural form of the definite article **dei (di+i), degli (di+gli):**
dei libri [**day**ee **lee**bree] *(books);* degli stivali [**day**lyee stee**va**lee] *(boots).*

Feminine singular: **una**
una casa [**oo**na **ka**za] *(a house);* una barca [**oo**na **bar**ka] *(a boat).*

Feminine plural: **delle (di+le)**
delle case [**del**lay **ka**zay] *(houses);* delle barche [**del**lay **bar**kay] *(boats).*

Nouns

The gender of the noun in Italian can usually be established by the ending in

its singular form. Masculine nouns usually end in -**o**, e.g. il libro [eel **lee**bro] *(the book);* feminine nouns in -**a**: la casa [la **ka**za] *(the house).*

There are a few exceptions to this rule, e.g. il telegramma [eel tele**gram**ma] *(the telegram);* il problema [eel pro**blay**ma] *(the problem).*

Nouns ending in -**e** can be either masculine or feminine, e.g. la madre [la **ma**dray] *(the mother);* il padre [eel **pa**dray] *(the father).*

Forming plurals

Nouns ending in -**a** form the plural in -**e:** la mela [la **may**la] *(the apple)* – le mele [lay **may**lay] *(the apples).*

Nouns ending in -**o** form the plural in-**i:** il libro [il **lee**bro] *(the book)* – i libri [ee **lee**bree] *(the books).*

Adjectives

Most adjectives are like nouns and end in -**o**. They form the feminine plural with -**a**, plural with -**e**, e.g. buono/buona [**bwo**no/**bwo**na] *(good);* caro/cara [**ka**ro/**ka**ra] *(dear, expensive).*

Il vino buono [eel **vee**no **bwo**no] *(the good wine),* i vini buoni [ee **vee**nee **bwo**nee] *(the good wines);* la casa bella [la **ka**za **bel**la] *(the beautiful house),* le case belle [lay **ka**zay **bel**lay] *(the beautiful houses).*

The adjective always matches the gender and number of the noun, even when it is not next to the noun in the sentence, e.g. un libro bello [oon **lee**bro **bel**lo] *(a beautiful book);* Il libro è bello. [eel **lee**bro ay **bel**lo] *(The book is beautiful.)*

Adjectives ending in -**e** usually do not have their own feminine form, e.g. grande [**gran**day] *(large);* verde [**vair**day] *(green).*

osition of the adjective

he describing word usually goes next
) the noun, e.g. la casa grande [la ka**za**
granday] *(the large house)*; la città bella
a chee**tta bel**la] *(the beautiful town).*

some common adjectives such as molto
molto] *(many),* poco [po**ko**] *(few)* or
buono [**bwo**no] *(good)* can go before the
noun, e.g. Buon viaggio [bwon⌣v**yaj**jo]
(Have a good trip!)

omparison of adjectives

To create the comparative form of an
adjective, Italian uses più [pyoo] *(more),*
e.g. caro [**ka**ro] *(expensive),* più caro
pyoo **ka**ro] *(more expensive).* For the
superlative form, the definite article is
required, e.g. il più caro [eel pyoo **ka**ro]
(the most expensive). Direct comparisons
are formed with **di,** e.g. più caro di ...
pyoo **ka**ro dee] *(more expensive than ...).*

Some adjectives do not follow this
pattern, e.g. buono – migliore – ottimo
[bwono – meel**yo**ray – o**ttee**mo] *(good –
better – best);* cattivo – peggiore – pessi-
mo [ka**ttee**vo – pe**jo**ray – **pess**eemo] *(bad –
worse – worst).*

Another form of the superlative, the
absolute superlative, can be created
with the ending -**issimo**: bellissimo
[bel**lees**seemo] *(very beautiful);* carissimo
karee**ssee**mo] *(very expensive).*

Adverbs

The adverb is usually derived from the
feminine form of the adjective by the
addition of the suffix -**mente**: chiaro/
chiara [**kya**ro/**kya**ra] – chiaramente
[kyara**men**tay] *(clearly, obviously);* Chiara-
mente vengo domani da te. [kyara**men**tay
vengo do**ma**nee da tay] *(I will obviously
come to see you tomorrow.)*

Irregular adverbs are: bene [**bay**nay]
(well), male [**ma**lay] *(badly):* Tutto bene.
[too**tto bay**nay] *(Everything is fine.);*
Dove fa male? [**do**vay fa **ma**lay] *(Where
does it hurt?)*

Pronouns

Subject pronouns

io [ee-o] *(I)*
tu [too] *(you [singular/familiar])*
lui [**loo**-ee] *(he);* lei [**lay**] *(she);* lei [**lay**]
(you [singular/formal])
noi [noy] *(we)*
voi [voy] *(you [plural/familiar])*
loro [**lo**ro] *(they);* Loro [**lo**ro] *(you
[plural/formal]).*

Object pronouns

mi [mee] *(me/to me)*
ti [tee] *(you/to you [singular/familiar])*
gli [lyee] *(to him);* le [**lay**] *(to her);*
Le [**lay**] *(to you [singular/formal])*
lo [lo] *(him);* la [la] *(her);* La [la] *] (you
[singular/formal])*
ci [chee] *(us)*
vi [vee] *(you [plural/familiar])*
gli [lyee] *(to them);* Loro [**lo**ro] *(to you
[plural/formal])*
li [lee] *(them [m]);* le [**lay**] *(them [f]);*
Li [lee] *(you [m]);* Le [**lay**] *(you [f]
[plural/formal])*

Possessive pronouns

mio/mia [**mee**-o/**mee**-a] *(my)*
tuo/tua [**too**-o/**too**-a] *(your
[singular/familiar])*
suo/sua [**soo**-o/**soo**-a] *(his; her; your
[singular/formal])*
nostro/nostra [**nos**tro/**nos**tra] *(our)*
vostro/vostra [**vos**tro/**vos**tra]
(your [plural/familiar])
loro [**lo**ro] *(their);*
Loro [**lo**ro] *(your [plural/formal]).*

The possessive pronouns are used with
both the definite and indefinite articles,
e.g. la mia casa [la **mee**-a ka**za**] *(my
house);* una mia amica [**oo**na **mee**-a
a**mee**ka] *(one of my friends).*

Other uses include a casa mia [a ka**za**
mee-a] *(at my house; to my house);* a
casa nostra [a **ka**za **nos**tra] *(at our house;
to our house).*

Demonstrative pronouns

questo [**kwes**to] *(this [m. sing])* –
questi [**kwes**tee] *(these [m.plural])*;
questa [**kwes**ta] *(this [f.sing])* – queste
[**kwes**tay] *(these [f.plural])* - quello
[**kwel**lo] *(that [m.sing])* – quelli
[**kwel**lee] *(those [m.plural])* - quella
[**kwel**la] *(that [f.sing])* – quelle
[**kwel**lay] *(those [f.plural])*

Questo and quello can be used without
a noun, e.g. Cosa è questo? [**ko**za ay
kwesto] *(What is this?)*.

Prepositions

di [dee] *(from, of)*
a [a] *(to, at)*
da [da] *(from, of, to)*
in [een] *(in, to)*
con [kon] *(with, through)*
su [soo] *(on, above)*

The prepositions **di**, **a**, **da**, **in** and **su**
merge with the definite article:
di+il = del [del]
di+lo = dello [**del**lo]
di+la = della [**del**la]
di+i = dei [**day**ee]
di+gli = degli [**day**lyee]
di+le = delle [**del**lay]

There are also the forms al (a+il) [al], allo
(a+lo) [**al**lo], ai (a+i) [**a**-ee], dal (da+il)
[dal], nel (in+il) [nel] and sul (su+il) [sool],
e.g. Penso alle ferie. [**pen**so al**lay fair**yay]
(I am thinking of the holidays.); sul
tavolo [sool **ta**volo] *(on the table)*.

Verbs

There are three groups of regular verbs.
Their endings are -**are**, -**ere** and -**ire**.
Pronouns are usually left out, as the verb
subject is usually indicated by the ending.

Present tense of regular verbs

-**are**: mandare [man**dar**ay] *(to send)*
io mando [**ee**-o **man**do] *(I send)*
tu mandi [too **man**dee] *(you
[singular/familiar] send)*
lui/lei/Lei manda[**loo**-ee/**lay man**da]
(he/she sends; you [sing./formal] send)

noi mandiamo [noy man**dya**mo] *(we send*
voi mandate [voy man**da**tay] *(you
[plural/familiar] send)*
loro/Loro mandano [**loro man**dano]
(they send; you [plural/formal] send)

-**ere**: vendere [**ven**deray] *(to sell)*
io vendo [**ee**-o **ven**do] *(I sell)*
tu vendi [too **ven**dee] *(you
[singular/familiar] send)*
lui/lei/Lei venda[**loo**-ee/**lay ven**da]
(he/she sells; you [sing./formal] sell)
noi vendiamo [noy ven**dya**mo] *(we send*
voi vendete [voy ven**det**tay] *(you
[plural/familiar] sell)*
loro/Loro vendono [**loro ven**dono] *(the
sell; you [plural/formal] sell)*

-**ire**: partire [par**tir**ay] *(to leave)*
io parto [**ee**-o **par**to] *(I leave)*
tu parti [too **par**tee] *(you
[singular/familiar] leave)*
lui/lei/Lei parte [**loo**-ee/**lay par**tay] *(he/
she leaves; you [singular/formal] leave*
noi partiamo [noy par**tya**mo] *(we leave*
voi partite [voy par**tee**tay] *(you
[plural/familiar] leave)*
loro/Loro partono [**loro par**tono] *(they
leave; you [plural/formal] leave)*

Present tense of some irregular verbs

avere [a**vair**ay] *(to have)*
io ho [**ee**-oo] *(I have)*
tu hai [too **a**-ee] *(you [singular/
familiar] have)*
lui/lei/Lei ha [**loo**-ee/**lay** a] *(he/she
has); you [singular/formal] have)*
noi abbiamo [noy ab**bya**mo] *(we have)*
voi avete [voy a**vay**tay] *(you
[plural/familiar] have)*
loro/Loro hanno [**loro an**no] *(they
have; you [plural/formal] have)*

essere [**ess**airay] *(to be)*
io sono [**ee**-o **so**no] *(I am)*
tu sei [too **say**] *(you [singular/
familiar] are)*
lui/lei/Lei è [**loo**-ee/**lay** ay] *(he/she is;
you [singular/formal] are)*
noi siamo [**noy sya**mo] *(we are)*
voi siete [voy s**yay**tay] *(you [plural/
familiar] are)*
loro/Loro sono [**loro so**no] *(they are;
you [plural/ formal] are)*

andare [andaray] *(to go)*
io vado [ee-o vado] *(I go)*
tu vai [too **va**-ee] *(you [singular/ familiar] go)*
lui/lei/Lei va [loo-ee//**lay** va] *(he/she goes; you [singular/formal] go)*
noi andiamo [noy and**ya**mo] *(we go)*
voi andate [voy an**da**tay] *(you [plural/ familiar] go)*
loro/Loro vanno [loro **van**no] *(they go; you [plural/ formal] go)*

fare [**fa**ray] *(to make, to do)*
io faccio [ee-o **fa**cho] *(I do)*
tu fai [too **fa**-ee] *(you [singular/ familiar] do)*
lui/lei/Lei fa [loo-ee/**lay** fa] *(he/she does; you [singular/formal] do)*
noi facciamo [noy fa**cha**mo] *(we do)*
voi fate [voy **fa**tay] *(you [plural/ familiar] do)*
loro/Loro fanno [loro **fan**no] *(they do; you [plural/formal] do)*

potere [po**tai**ray] *(to be able to)*
io posso [ee-o **pos**so] *(I can)*
tu puoi [too pwoy] *(you [singular/ familiar] can)*
lui/lei/Lei può [loo-ee/**lay** pwo] *(he/she can; you [singular/ formal] can)*
noi possiamo [noy pos**sya**mo] *(we can)*
voi potete [voy po**tay**tay] *(you [plural/ familiar] can)*
loro/Loro possono [loro **pos**sono] *(they can; you [plural/formal] can)*

venire [ve**nee**ray] *(to come)*
io vengo [ee-o **ven**go] *(I come)*
tu vieni [too v**ya**nee] *(you [singular/ familiar] come)*
lui/lei/Lei viene [loo-ee/**lay** v**yay**nay] *(he/she comes; you [singular/ formal] come)*
noi veniamo [noy ven**ya**mo] *(we come)*
voi venite [voy ve**nee**tay] *(you [plural/familiar] come)*
loro/Loro vengono [loro **ven**gono] *(they come; you [plural/formal] come)*

volere [vo**lai**ray] *(to wish/to want)*
io voglio [ee-o **vol**yo] *(I wish/want)*
tu vuoi [too vwoy] *(you [singular/ familiar] wish/want)*
lui/lei/Lei vuole [loo-ee/**lay** vwo**lay**] *(he/she wishes/wants; you [singular/ formal] wish/want)*
noi vogliamo [noy vol**ya**mo] *(we wish/want)*
voi volete [voy vo**lay**tay] *(you [plural/ familiar] wish/want)*
loro/Loro vogliono [loro **vol**yono] *(they wish/want; you [plural/formal] wish)*

Perfect

The perfect tense in Italian is formed with the auxiliary verb **avere** *(to have)* or **essere** *(to be)* and the past participle:

io ho avuto [eeo-o a**voo**to] *(I have had)*
tu hai avuto [too a-ee a**voo**to] *(you have had)*
lui/lei ha avuto [loo-ee/**lay** a a**voo**to] *(he/she has had)*
noi abbiamo avuto [noy ab**bya**mo a**voo**to] *(we have had)*
voi avete avuto [voy a**vay**tay a**voo**to] *(you [plural/familiar] have had)*
loro hanno avuto [loro **an**no a**voo**to] *(they have had)*

io sono stato *(m)*/stata *(f)* [ee-o **so**no **sta**to/**sta**ta] *(I have been)*
tu sei stato *(m)*/stata *(f)* [too say **sta**to/ **sta**ta] *(you [singular/familiar] have been)*
lui/lei è stato*(m)*/stata *(f)* [loo-ee/**lay** ay **sta**to/**sta**ta] *(he/she has been)*
noi siamo stati *(m)*/state *(f)* [noy s**ya**mo **sta**tee/**sta**tay] *(we have been)*
voi siete stati *(m)*/state *(f)* [voy s**yay**tay **sta**tee/**sta**tay] *(you [plural/familiar] have been)*
loro sono stati *(m)*/state *(f)* [loro **so**no **sta**tee/**sta**tay] *(they have been)*

Negatives

The negative **non** always precedes the verb, e.g. Non parlo italiano. [non **par**lo eetal**ya**no] *(I don't speak Italian.)*
Niente *(nothing)* and **mai** *(never)* require a double negative, e.g. Non ho niente. [non o n**yen**tay] *(I have nothing)*

Two people-watchers on the piazza

General

Hello and goodbye

Good morning/afternoon.	Buon giorno. [bwon **jor**no]
Good evening.	Buona sera. [bwona **sair**a]
Good night.	Buona notte. [bwona **not**tay]
Hello!	Ciao! [chow]
How are you doing?	Come va? [**ko**may va]
How are you?	Come stai?/Come sta? [**ko**may sta-ee/**ko**may sta]
* Bene, grazie. [**bay**nay **grat**syay]	Fine, thank you.
And you?	E tu?/E Lei? [ay too/ay lay/]
Goodbye.	Arrivederci. [arreevay**dair**chee]
Bye.	Ciao! [chow]
See you soon.	A fra poco. [a fra **pok**ko]
See you tomorrow.	A domani. [a do**man**ee]
Regards to the family.	Saluti alla famiglia. [sa**loo**tee **al**la fa**meel**ya]
Thank you for everything.	Grazie di tutto. [**grat**syay dee **too**to]
We really enjoyed it.	Ci è piaciuto molto. [chee ay pee-a**choo**to **mol**to]
* Buon viaggio! [bwon **vyaj**jo]	Have a good journey!

Introducing yourself

Mr/Mrs/Miss ...	Signore/Signora/Signorina ... [seen**yor**ay/seen**yor**a/seenyo**ree**na]
What's your name?	Come ti chiami?/Come si chiama? [**ko**may tee **kyam**ee/**ko**may see **kyam**a]
My name is ...	Mi chiamo ... [mee **kya**mo]

12

This is/These are	Questo è/Questa è/Questi sono
	[kwesto ay/kwesta ay/kwestee sono]
my husband/my boyfriend	mio marito/il mio amico
	[mee-o mareeto/eel mee-o ameeko]
my wife/my girlfriend	mia moglie/la mia amica
	[mee-a molyay/la mee-a ameeka]
my son/my daughter/	mio figlio/mia figlia/i miei figli. [mee-o
my children.	feelyo/mee-a feelya/ee myayee feelyee]
Pleased to meet you.	Piacere./Molto lieto. [peeachairay/molto lyayto]
And you.	Altrettanto. [altraytanto]
Where are you from?	Di dove sei?/Di dov'è? [dee dovay say/dee dovay]
I'm	Io sono [ee-o sono]
English	inglese [eenglayzay]
American	americano/-a [amereekano/-a]
Australian	australiano/-a. [owstralyano/-a]
We live in .../	Noi abitiamo a .../in hotel ...
stay at the ... Hotel	[no-ee abeetyamo a/een otel]

Communication

Do you speak English?	Tu parli/Lei parla/ inglese?
	[too parlee/lay parla eenglayzay]
What's that called?	Come si chiama questo? [komay see kyama kwesto]
Pardon?/Sorry??	Come prego? [komay praygo]
What does that mean?	Cosa significa questo? [koza seenyeefeeka kwesto]
Did you understand that?	Hai/Ha capito? [a-ee/a kapeeto]
I don't understand.	Io non capisco. [ee-o non kapeesko]
Could you speak more slowly, please?	Prego lentamente! [praygo lentamentay]
Could you repeat that, please?	Prego un'altra volta! [praygo oonaltra volta]
Could you ... for me?	Può/Puoi [pwo/pwoy]
write that down	scrivermelo [skreevairmaylo]
explain/translate that	chiarire/tradurre? [keeareeray/tradooray]

Civilities

Please.	Prego. [praygo]
Thank you (very much).	(Molte) grazie. [(moltay) gratsyay]
Thank you, the same to you.	Grazie, altrettanto. [gratsyay altretanto]
Thank you for your help.	Grazie per l'aiuto. [gratsyay pair layooto]
* Prego./Non c'è di che. [praygo/non chay dee kay]	You're welcome./Don't mention it.
Sorry/Excuse me.	Scusa/Scusi. [skooza/skoozee]
* Non fa niente. [non fa nyentay]	It doesn't matter.

Do you have a moment, please!	Un momento, prego! [oon mo**men**to **pray**go]
That's very nice of you.	É molto gentile da parte tua/sua. [ay **mol**to jen**tee**lay da **par**tay **too**-a/**soo**-a]
I'm sorry about that.	Mi dispiace. [mee deespy**a**chay]
That's a pity.	Peccato. [pe**ka**to]
Welcome!	Un cordiale benvenuto! [oon kord**ya**lay benve**noo**to]
Congratulations!	Cordiali auguri! [kord**ya**lee ow**goo**ree]
Happy birthday!	Auguri (per il compleanno)! [ow**goo**ree (pair eel kompla**yan**no)]
Have fun!	Buon divertimento! [bwon deevairtee**men**to]
Get well soon!	Buona guarigione! [**bwo**na gwaree**jo**nay]
Good luck!	Molto successo! [**mol**to soo**chay**sso]
Have a nice day!	Una bella giornata! [**oo**na **bel**la jor**na**ta]
Have a good journey!	Buon viaggio! [bwon **vyaj**jo]
Have a good holiday!	Buone vacanze! [**bwo**nay va**kant**say]
Merry Christmas!	Buon Natale! [bwon na**ta**lay]
Happy New Year!	Felice Anno nuovo! [fe**lee**chay **an**no **nwo**vo]

Meeting people

Do you mind if I sit here?	Posso sedermi con te/con Lei? [**pos**so se**dair**mee kon tay/kon lay]
Do you mind?	Permetti? [pair**met**tee]
Are you	**Sei/È** [say/ay]
on you own	solo (-a) in giro [**so**lo (-a) een **jee**ro]
travelling with somebody	con qualcuno in giro [kon kwal**koo**no een **jee**ro]
married?	sposato (-a)? [spo**za**to (-a)]
Do you have a boyfriend/girlfriend?	Hai un amico/un'amica? [a-ee oon a**mee**ko/oon a**mee**ka]
How old are you?	Quanti anni hai? [**kwan**tee **an**nee a-ee]
I am 25 years old.	Io ho venticinque anni. [**ee**-o o ventee**cheen**kway **an**nee]
What do you do for a living?	Che lavoro fai/fa? [kay la**vo**ro **fa**-ee/fa]
I'm	**Sono** [**so**no]
still at school	scolaro (scolara) [sko**la**ro (sko**la**ra)]
a student	studente (studentessa) [stoo**dayn**tay (stoodayn**tes**sa)]
employed.	impiegata (impiegato). [eempeeay**ga**ta/(-o)]
Can I buy you a drink?	Vuoi/Vuole bere qualcosa? [vwoy/ **vwo**lay **bai**ray kwal**ko**za]
Thank you, that's a nice idea.	Si, volentieri, buona idea. [see volenty**air**ee **bwo**na ee**da**ya]
Why not?	Perché no? [pair**kay** no]
No, thank you.	No grazie. [no **grats**yay]
Perhaps another time.	Forse un'altra volta. [**for**say oo**nal**tra **vol**ta]
Maybe later.	Forse più tardi. [**for**say pyoo **tar**dee]
Do you like it here?	Ti/Le piace qui. [tee/lay **pya**chay kwee]

Greetings

Buon giorno means "good morning" and also "hello" or "good-day". In the early evening, the normal greeting is *buona sera*. *Buona notte* is used later in the evening to bid someone goodnight. A more easy-going greeting, however, is *ciao (hello/goodbye)*. The formal way to say goodbye is *arrivederci/ arrivederla! (until the next time!). Come stai/sta? (how are you?)* is often added to the initial greeting, but nobody expects an honest answer to the question. It is best to respond with a simple *bene (OK)* or *molto bene (very well)*.

I like it very much here.	Mi piace molto. [mee pyachay **mol**to]
Is this your first time here?	Sei/È qui per la prima volta? [say/ay kwee pair la **pree**ma **vol**ta]
No, I've been to ... before.	No, sono già stato (-a) una volta a ... [no **so**no ja **sta**to (-a) **oo**na **vol**ta a]
Have you ever been to England?	Conosci/Conosce la Inghilterra? [ko**no**shee/ko**no**shay la eengeel**tai**ra]
You must visit me.	Vienimi a trovare./Mi venga a trovare. [v**yen**eemee a tro**var**ay/mee **ven**ga a tro**var**ay]
Here's my address.	Questo è il mio indirizzo. [**kwes**to ay eel **mee**-o eendee**ree**tzo]
How long have you been staying here?	Da quanto tempo sei/è già qui? [da **kwan**to **tem**po say/ay ja kwee]
For a week./For two days.	Da una settimana/due giorni. [da **oo**na setee**ma**na/**doo**ay **jor**nee]
How much longer are you staying?	Quanto tempo rimani/rimane ancora qui? [**kwan**to **tem**po ree**ma**nee/ree**ma**nay an**ko**ra kwee]
Another week/two days.	Ancora una settimana/due giorni. [an**ko**ra **oo**na setee**ma**na/**doo**ay **jor**nee]

Shall we ... together today/tomorrow?	**Vogliamo oggi/domani ... insieme?** [vol**ya**mo **oj**jee/do**ma**nee ... eensy**ay**may]
have a meal	mangiare [man**jar**ay]
go out	uscire [oo**sheer**ay]
go to the cinema/go dancing	andare al cinema/a ballare [an**dar**ay al **chee**nayma/a bal**lar**ay]
do something sporty	fare dello sport [**far**ay **del**lo sport]
play	giocare [jo**kar**ay]
O.K., let's do that!	D'accordo, va bene! [da**kor**do va **bay**nay]
No, thank you.	No, grazie. [no **grats**yay]
I can't, sorry.	Mi dispiace non posso. [mee deespy**a**chay non **pos**so]
What time/Where shall we meet?	Quando/Dove ci incontriamo? [**kwan**do/**do**vay chee eenkontry**a**mo]
At 7 o'clock in front of the cinema.	Alle sette davanti al cinema. [**al**-lay **set**tay da**van**tee al **chee**nayma]

Shall I
  pick you up
  take you home

  take you to the bus stop?

Posso venire a [po**s**so ve**nee**ray a]
  prenderti/prenderla [**pren**dairtee/**pren**dairla]
  accompagnarti/accompagnarla a casa
  [akompan**yar**tee/akompan**yar**la a **ka**za]
  accompagnarti/accompagnarla all'autobus?
  [akompan**yar**tee/akompan**yar**la al-**ow**toboos]

No, that's not necessary.

No, grazie non è necessario.
[no **grats**yay non ay neche**ssar**yo]

It's been very nice.

È stato molto bello. [ay **sta**to **mol**to **bel**lo]

When can we see each other
again?
I don't like that.

Quando ci incontriamo di nuovo?
[**kwan**do chee eenkont**rya**mo dee **nwo**vo]
Questo non mi piace.
[**kwes**to non mee **pya**chay]

I don't feel like it.

Non ne ho voglia. [non nay o **vol**ya]

Leave me alone!

Lasciami/Mi lasci/ in pace!
[**la**shamee/mee **la**shee een **pa**chay]

Please go away!

Per favore, vattene/se ne vada/.
[**pair** fa**vo**ray **va**tenay/say nay **va**da]

Questions

What's that?
How much is that?
Where is ...?/can I get ...?
Where does ... go?
How do you say it?
What's that called?
How long does it last?
When does the concert start?

Cosa è questo? [**ko**za ay **kwes**to]
Quanto costa questo? [**kwan**to **kos**ta **kwes**to]
Dov'è ...?/C'è ...? [do**vay**/chay]
Dove va ...? [**do**vay va]
Come si dice? [**ko**may see **dee**chay]
Come si chiama [**ko**may see **kya**ma]
Quanto dura? [**kwan**to **doo**ra]
Quando comincia il concerto?
[**kwan**do ko**meen**cha eel kon**chair**to]

How many kilometres/minutes
is it?

Quanti chilometri/minuti sono?
[**kwan**tee kee**lo**metree/mee**noo**tee **so**no]

Could you
  help me
  show me, please?

Puoi/Può [pwoi/pwo]
  aiutarmi [ayoo**tar**mee]
  mostrarmi questo? [most**rar**mee **kwes**to]

Can I help you?

Posso aiutarti/aiutarla? [**pos**so ayoo**tar**tee/la]

Interrogatives

What?
Who?
Which?
Where?/Where to?
How?
How much
How many?
When?
How long?
Why?
What ... for?

Cosa? [**ko**za]
Chi? [kee]
Quale? *(Sing)* [**kwa**lay]; Quali? *(Pl)* [**kwa**lee]
Dove? [**do**vay]
Come? [**ko**may]
Quanto [**kwan**to]
Quanti *(m/Pl)* [**kwan**tee]/Quante *(f/Pl)* [**kwan**tay]
Quando? [**kwan**do]
Per quanto tempo? [pair **kwan**to **tem**po]
Perché? [pair**kay**]
Per cosa? [pair **ko**za]

Days of the week

Monday lunedì [loonaydee]
Tuesday martedì [martaydee]
Wednesday mercoledì [mairkolaydee]
Thursday giovedì [jovaydee]
Friday venerdì [venairdee]
Saturday sabato [sabato]
Sunday domenica [domeneeka]

Months

January gennaio [jennayo]
February febbraio [febbrayo]
March marzo [martso]
April aprile [apreelay]
May maggio [majjo]

June giugno [joonyo]
July luglio [loolyo]
August agosto [agosto]
September settembre [settembray]
October ottobre [ottobray]
November novembre [novembray]
December dicembre [deechembray]

Seasons

spring primavera [preemavaira]
summer estate [estatay]
autumn autunno [owtoonno]
winter inverno [eenvairno]
peak/off peak season alta/fuori stagione [alta/fworee stajonay]

Time

What's the (exact) time, please?
Che ore sono (di preciso), prego?
[kay oray sono (dee precheezo) praygo]

It's
1 o'clock/2 o'clock
quarter past three
quarter to five

twenty past three
half past three
five to six
noon/midnight.

È/Sono [ay/sono]
l'una/le due [loona/lay dooay]
le tre e un quarto [lay tray ay oon kwarto]
le cinque meno un quarto
[lay cheenkway mayno oon kwarto]
le quindici e venti [lay kweendeechee ay ventee]
le tre e mezza [lay tray ay metza]
le sei meno cinque [lay say mayno cheenkway]
mezzogiorno/mezzanotte.
[metzojorno/metzanottay]

What time do we have to be there?
A che ora dobbiamo essere lì?
[a kay ora dobbyamo essairay lee]
Around twelve/At twelve o'clock sharp.
Più o meno alle dodici/Alle dodici in punto.
[pyoo o mayno allay dodeechee/... een poonto]
When is breakfast/lunch/dinner?
Quando c'è colazione/pranzo/cena?
[kwando chay kolatsyonay/prandzo/chayna]

* Dalle otto alle nove.
[dallay otto allay novay]
From eight to nine.

Date

What's the date today?
Che giorno è oggi?
[kay jorno ay ojjee]

Today's the 1st/2nd/15th of August.
Oggi è il primo/due/quindici agosto.
[ojjee ay eel preemo/dooay/kweendeechee agosto]

We'll arrive on the 20th of May.
Noi arriviamo il venti maggio.
[noy areevyamo eel ventee majjo]

We're staying until August 31st.
Noi rimaniamo fino al trentuno agosto. [noy reemanyamo **feeno** al trentoono a**gos**to]

I was born on January 12th (1960).
Sono nato il dodici gennaio (millenovecentosessanta). [**so**no **na**to eel **do**deechee jennayo (meelaynovaychentosessanta)]

Indication of time

in the evening	la sera [la **sai**ra]
at the weekend	a fine settimana [a **fee**nay settee**ma**na]
until tomorrow	fino a domani [**fee**no a do**ma**nee]
yesterday	ieri [ee**ai**ree]
today	oggi [**oj**jee]
tonight	stasera [sta**sai**ra]
in a fortnight	fra quindici giorni [fra **kween**deechee **jor**nee]
(this/next/every) year	(quest'/il prossimo/passato/ogni) anno [(**kwest**/eel **pros**seemo/**on**yee) **an**no]
last year	l'anno scorso [**lan**no **skor**so]
now	adesso [a**des**so]
sometimes	qualche volta [**kwal**kay **vol**ta]
minute	minuto [mee**noo**to]
at midday	a mezzogiorno [a metzo**jor**no]
tomorrow	domani [do**ma**nee]
in the morning	la mattina [la mat**tee**na]
in the afternoon	il pomeriggio [eel pomai**ree**jo]
at night	la notte [la **not**tay]
in time	per tempo [pair **tem**po]
second	secondo [se**kon**do]
late/too late	tardi/troppo tardi [**tar**dee/**trop**po **tar**dee]
later	più tardi [pyoo **tar**dee]
hour	l'ora [**lo**ra]
daily	giornalmente [jornal**men**tay]
day	giorno [**jor**no]
day after tomorrow	dopodomani [doppodo**ma**nee]
(two days) ago	(due giorni) fa [(**doo**ay **jor**nee) fa]
day before yesterday	l'altro ieri [**lal**tro ee**ai**ree]
before	prima [**pree**ma]
week	settimana [settee**ma**na]
at the moment	al momento [al mo**men**to]

Measurements

centimetre/metre/kilometre	centimetro/metro/chilometro [chen**tee**metro/**me**tro/kee**lo**metro]
square metre/square kilometre/hectare	metro quadrato/chilometro quadrato/ettaro [**me**tro kwa**dra**to/kee**lo**metro kwa**dra**to/**et**taro]
cubic metre	metro cubo [**me**tro **koo**bo]
kilometres per hour	chilometri orari [kee**lo**metree o**ra**ree]
quarter of a litre	un quarto di litro [oon **kwar**to dee **lee**tro]
half a litre	mezzo litro [**me**tzo **lee**tro]
gram/half a kilo/ kilogramme/ton	grammo/mezzo chilo/chilo/tonnellata [**gram**mo/**me**tzo **kee**lo/**kee**lo/tonnay**la**ta]
second/minute/hour	secondo/minuto/ora [se**kon**do/mee**noo**to/**o**ra]

day/week/month/year — giorno/settimana/mese/anno [**jor**no/sette**ema**na/**may**zay/**an**no]

a dozen/a couple/a portion — una dozzina/un paio/una porzione [**oo**na dot**zee**na/oon **pa**-yo/**oo**na port**syo**nay]

Weather

Is it going to stay nice/bad — Rimane così bello/brutto? [ree**ma**nay ko**zee** **bel**lo/**broo**tto]

What does the weather forecast say? — Cosa dice la previsione del tempo? [**ko**za **dee**chay la preveez**yo**nay del **tem**po]

It's going to get colder/warmer. — Farà freddo/caldo. [fa**ra** **frayd**do/**kal**do]

It is hot/close/stormy/foggy. — È caldo/afoso/tempestoso/nebbioso. [ay **kal**do/a**fo**zo/tempe**sto**zo/neb**yo**zo]

It is windy. — C'è vento. [chay **ven**to]

It is going to rain/snow today/tomorrow. — Oggi/Domani dovrebbe piovere/nevicare. [**oj**jee/**do**manee dov**reb**bay pyo**va**ray/nevee**ka**ray]

For how long has it been raining? — Da quanto tempo piove già? [da **kwan**to **tem**po **pyo**vay ja]

When is it going to stop raining? — Quando smette di piovere? [**kwan**do **zmet**tay dee **pyo**vairay]

What's the temperature? — Quanti gradi abbiamo? [**kwan**tee **gra**dee ab**bya**mo]

25 degrees (in the shade). — Venticinque gradi. [ventee**cheen**kway **gra**dee]

Colours

I'm looking for a pair of blue/black trousers. — Io cerco pantaloni blu/neri. [**ee**-o **chair**ko panta**lo**nee bloo/**nai**ree]

Do you have this shirt — **Ha questa camicia** [a **kwes**ta ka**mee**cha]

in white, too — anche in bianco [**an**kay een **byan**ko]

in another colour? — in un altro colore? [een oon **al**tro ko**lo**ray]

I don't like this colour. — Questo colore non mi piace. [**kwes**to ko**lo**ray non mee **pya**chay]

This colour is too light/dark — Questo colore è troppo chiaro/troppo scuro. [**kwes**to ko**lo**ray ay **trop**po **kya**ro/**trop**po **skoo**ro]

Colours and patterns

beige beige [bayj]	patterned stampato/-a [stampato/-a]
black nero/-a [**nai**ro/-a]	pink rosa [**ro**za]
blue blu [bloo]	plain-coloured tinta unita [**teen**ta oo**nee**ta]
brown marrone [mar**ro**nay]	purple viola [**vyo**la]
checked a quadri [a **kwa**dree]	red rosso/-a [**ros**so/-a]
colourful colorato/-a [ko**lo**rato/-a]	striped rigato/-a [ree**ga**to/-a]
dark scuro/-a [**skoo**ro/-a]	turquoise turchese [toor**kay**zay]
green verde [**vair**day]	white bianco/-a [**byan**ko/-a]
grey grigio/-a [**gree**jo/-a]	yellow giallo/-a [**jal**lo/-a]
light chiaro/-a [**kya**ro/-a]	

It's often a tight squeeze for traffic in the medieval town centres

Getting Around

Customs formalities

* Il Suo passaporto, prego!
[eel **soo**-o passa**por**to **pray**go]

Your passport, please!

* La Sua patente, prego!
[la **soo**-a pa**ten**tay **pray**go]

Your driving licence, please!

* I documenti della macchina, prego! [ee doko**omen**tee **del**la **mak**kena **pray**go]

Your vehicle registration papers, please!

* Lei dove è diretto?
[lay **do**vay ay dee**ray**tto]

Where are you going to?

I'm/We're going to ...

Io vado/Noi andiamo a ...
[**ee**-o **va**do/noy and**ya**mo a]

I'm
  a tourist.
  on a business trip.

Io sono [**ee**o **so**no]
  turista [too**rees**ta]
  in viaggio di affari. [een **vyaj**jo dee af**fa**ree]

How many ... are duty free?

Quanti *(m)*/Quante *(f)* ... sono liberi da dogana?
[**kwan**tee/**kwan**tay ... sono **lee**bairee da do**ga**na]

  cigarettes
  litres of wine/spirit

  sigarette [seega**ray**ttay]
  litri di vino/liquore [**lee**tree dee **vee**no/leek**wo**ray]

*Prego apra il cofano!
[**pray**go apra eel **ko**fano]

Open the suitcase, please!

Can I call
  my embassy
  my consulate

Posso parlare con [**pos**so par**la**ray kon]
  la mia ambasciata [la **mee**-a amba**sha**ta]
  il mio consolato? [eel **mee**-o konso**la**to]

21

Asking Directions

How do I get	Come arrivo [komay arreevo]
to ...	a ... [a]
on to the motorway	all'autostrada [alla-ootostrada]
to the city centre	al centro [al chentro]
to ... Square	in piazza ... [een pyatza]
to ... Street	in via ... [een veea]
to the station/bus station	alla stazione/alla stazione dei pullman
	[alla statssyonay/alla stasyonay dayee poolman]
to the airport/harbour?	all'aeroporto/al porto? [al-airoporto/al porto]

* All'incrocio [alleenkrocho]	At the crossroads
* Dopo il semaforo	After the traffic lights
[dopo eel semaforo]	

* Dopo cinquecento metri	After 500 metres
[dopo cheenkwaychento maytree]	
* girare a destra/sinistra	turn right/left
[jeeraray a destra/seeneestra]	
* andare dritto	go straight ahead
[andaray dreetto]	
* tornare indietro.	turn around.
[tornaray eendyaytro]	

Is this the road to ...?	È questa la strada per ...?
	[ay kwesta la strada pair]
How far is it to...?	Quanto è lontano fino a ...?
	[kwanto ay lontano feeno a]
Can you show me that on the map?	Può indicarmelo sulla carta?
	[pwo eendeekarmaylo soolla karta]

Car, motorbike and bicycle hire

I'd like to hire	Io vorrei affittare [eeo vorrayee affeettaray]
a car	una macchina [oona makkeena]
a four-wheel drive	un fuoristrada [oon fworeestrada]
a minibus	un pullmino [oon poolmeeno]
a camper van	un camper [oon kampair]
a motorbike	una motocicletta [oona motocheekletta]
a moped	un motorino [oon motoreeno]
a scooter	una vespa [oona vespa]
a bicycle	una bicicletta [oona beecheekletta]
a mountain bike	una mountainbike [oona maoontenbaeek]
for two days/one week	per due giorni/una settimana
	[pair dooay jornee/oona setteemana]
from today/tomorrow	da oggi/domani. [da ojjee/domanee]

What do you charge	Quanto costa questo veicolo
	[kwanto kosta kwesto vayeekolo]
per day/per week	al giorno/alla settimana
	[al jorno/alla setteemana]
per kilometre?	secondo i chilometri percorsi?
	[sekondo ee keelometree pairkorsee]

Is there a mileage limit?	C'è un limite di chilometraggio? [chay un **lee**meetay dee keelome**traj**jo]
Is there a free allowance?	È senza limite di chilometraggio? [ay **sen**tsa **lee**meetay dee keelome**traj**jo]
How many kilometres are included in the price?	Quanti kilometri sono liberi? [**kwan**tee keelometree sono **lee**bairee]
What petrol does it take?	Quale benzina devo mettere? [**kwa**lay bend**zee**na **day**vo **met**tairay]
How much is the deposit?	Quant'è la cauzione? [kwan**tay** la ka-oots**yo**nay]
Does the vehicle have comprehensive insurance?	Questo veicolo ha una polizza di assicurazione kasko? [**kwes**to vay**ee**kolo a **oo**na po**leet**za dee asseekoorats**yo**nay **kas**ko]
Can I take the car back in … hours/days?	Posso portare questo veicolo in … ore/giorni indietro? [**pos**so por**ta**ray **kwes**to vay**ee**kolo een … oray/**jor**nee eend**yay**tro]
When do I have to be back by?	Fino a quando devo portare questo veicolo indietro? [**fee**no a **kwan**do **day**vo por**ta**ray **kwes**to vay**ee**kolo eend**yay**tro]
Could you explain how everything works, please!	Per favore mi spieghi precisamente tutte le funzioni. [pair fa**vo**ray mee sp**yay**gee precheeza**men**tay **toot**tay lay foonts**yo**nee]

Parking

Can I park here?	Posso parcheggiare qui? [**pos**so parkay**ja**ray kwee]
Is there a … near here?	C'è … qui vicino [chay … kwee vee**chee**no]
a (supervised) car park	un parcheggio (custodito) [oon par**kay**jo (koosto**dee**to)]
a (multi-storey) car park/ a garage	un autosilo/un garage? [oon owto**see**lo/oon gara**jay**]

Traffic signs

Accendere i fari Use your headlights!
Attenzione Caution!
Autostrada (con obbligo di pedaggio) motorway (subject to toll)
Camion lorries
Cantiere edile construction site
Cassa toll booth
Circonvallazione bypass
Coda traffic jam
Controllo radar radar control
Corsia slow lane
Corsia per ciclisti cycle track

Curva pericolosa dangerous bend
Dare la precedenza give way
Deviazione diversion
Disco orario parking disc
Divieto di parcheggio no parking
Divieto di sorpasso no overtaking
Autosilo car park
Guidare a destra keep right
Lasciare libera l'uscita keep clear
Lavori in corso road works
Pericolo danger
Rallentare reduce speed
Senso unico one-way-street
Vicolo cieco cul de sac

Travelling by car

The Italians are very attached to their cars and drive everywhere. In Italy about 75 percent of all journeys are made by car and so the Italian road network is very extensive. Motorways *(autostrade)* criss-cross the whole country. All of them levy a toll except the section from Salerno to Reggio Calabria.

The customer is still king at the petrol station *(distributore)*. Attended service is the norm rather than the exception. If requested, the pump attendant will clean your windscreen and check your oil and water. He will take your money and will expect a small tip. Only at night or on Sunday is a self-service system in operation and for this you will need a good supply of high-value notes.

You will find plenty of small garages *(officina)* in every town. To call the Italian Automobile Club *(ACI)*, if you have a breakdown, dial 116. The emergency number *(Numero di Emergenza)* is 113.

Is the car park open during the night?	È aperto di notte il parcheggio? [ay apairto dee nottay eel parkayjo]
* Occupato. [okkoopato]	Full.
* Libero. [leebairo]	Spaces.

How much is it

   per hour
   per day
   per night?

Quanto è la tariffa di parcheggio
[kwanto ay la tareeffa dee parkayjo]
   all'ora [allora]
   al giorno [al jorno]
   a notte? [a nottay]

Petrol

Where's the nearest petrol station, please?

Dov'è il prossimo distributore di benzina? [dovay eel prosseemo deestreebootoray dee bendzeena]

Fill up, please.

Prego il pieno. [praygo eel pyayno]

20 litres of . . . , please.
   regular
   super
   diesel
     unleaded/leaded.

   mixture for a two-stroke engine.

Prego venti litri di [praygo ventee leetree dee]
   benzina normale [bendzeena normalay]
   benzina super [bendzeena soopair]
   diesel [deezel]
     senza piombo/con piombo
     [sendsa pyombo/kon pyombo]
   miscela a due tempi.
   [meeshayla a dooay tempee]

I'd like half a litre of oil, please.

Io vorrei mezzo litro di olio [eeo vorrayee metzo leetro dee olyo]

Please check
   the oil
   the tyre pressure

   the water.

Prego controlli [praygo kontrollee]
   il livello dell'olio [eel leevello dellolyo]
   la pressione delle gomme
   [la pressyone dellay gommay]
   l'acqua. [lakwa]

Breakdown and accident

I have	Io ho [ee-o o]
a flat tyre	un guasto (alle gomme) [oon **gwas**to (**al**lay **gom**may)]
had an accident.	un incidente. [oon eenchee**den**tay]

Could you give me a lift — Per favore mi dia un passaggio fino [pair fa**vor**ay mee **dee**a oon pas**saj**jo **fee**no]

to the nearest petrol station — al prossimo distributore di benzina [al **pros**seemo deestreeboo**tor**ay dee bend**zee**na]

to a garage? — ad un'officina. [ad oonoffee**chee**na]

Could you — Per favore può [pair fa**vor**ay pwo]

tow my car away — rimorchiarmi [reemork**yar**may]

help me (push) — aiutarmi (spingere) [ayoo**tar**mee (**speen**jairay)]

help me jump-start my car — aiutarmi a partire con la sua batteria [ayoo**tar**mee a par**tee**ray kon la **soo**-a bat**tai**reea]

lend me some petrol — prestarmi benzina [pre**star**mee bend**zee**na]

lend me your jack — prestarmi il cricco [pre**star**mee eel **kree**ko]

call for a breakdown truck — informare il servizio di soccorso stradale [eenfor**mar**ay eel sair**veet**syo dee so**kor**so strada**la**lay]

call the police/fire brigade — chiamare la polizia/i pompieri [kya**mar**ay la poleet**see**a/ee pomp**yai**ree]

call an ambulance — chiamare una autoambulanza [kya**mar**ay **oo**na owtoamboo**lan**tsa]

call a doctor? — chiamare un medico? [kya**mar**ay oon **med**eeko]

Are you injured? — È ferito? [ay fai**ree**to]

Nobody is injured. — Non c'è nessuno ferito. [non chay nes**soo**no fai**ree**to]

Somebody is (seriously) injured. — C'è qualcuno ferito (grave). [chay kwal**koo**no fai**ree**to (**gra**vay)]

Car, motorbike, bicycle

air-conditioning	aria condizionata [aarya kondeetsyonata]
battery	batteria [battaireea]
bicycle tyre	copertone per bicicletta [kopairtonay pair beecheeklaytta]
brake	freno [frayno]
car key	chiave della macchina [kyavay della makkeena]
catalytic converter	catalizzatore [kataleetzatoray]
chain	catena [katayna]
child seat	sedile per bambini [sedeelay pair bambeenee]
engine	motore [motoray]
exhaust	tubo di scarico [toobo dee skareeko]
fan belt	cinghia [cheengya]
first-aid kit	materiale di pronto soccorso [matairyalay dee pronto sokorso]
fuse	valvola di sicurezza [valvola dee seekooretza]
gearshift	cambio [kambyo]
handbrake	freno a mano [frayno a mano]
headlights	faro [faro]/luce anteriore [loochay antairyoray]
horn	clacson [klakson]
light bulb	lampadina [lampadeena]
pump	pompa dell'aria [pompa dellarya]
puncture repair kit	arnesi da rappezzo [arnayzee da rapetzo]
radiator	radiatore [radyatoray]
rear light	luce posteriore [loochay postairyoray]
repair	riparazione [reeparatsyonay]
screw	vite [veetay]
screwdriver	cacciavite [kachaveetay]
seat belt	cintura di sicurezza [cheentoora dee seekooraytza]
spare part	pezzo di ricambio [petzo dee reekambyo]
spare tyre	ruota di scorta [roo-ota dee skorta]
spark plugs	candela di accensione [kandayla dee achensyonay]
steering	sterzo [stairtso]
tank	serbatoio [sairbatoyo]
tools	arnese da lavoro [arnayzay da lavoro]
tow rope	cavo da rimorchio [kavo da reemorkyo]
tube	gomma [gomma]
tyre	ruota [roo-ota]
valve	valvola [valvola]
warning triangle	triangolo di avvertimento [treeangolo dee avairteemanto]
windscreen wipers	tergicristallo [tairjeekreestallo]

Give me . . ., please.	Prego mi dia [**pray**go mee **dee**-a]
your name and address	il Suo nome e indirizzo
	[eel **soo**-o **no**may ay eendee**ree**tzo]
your insurance number	il Suo numero di assicurazione.
	[eel **soo**-o **noo**mairo dee asseekooratsyonay]

I was/You were/He was	**Io sono/Lei è/Lui è** [**ee**-o **so**no/lay ay /**loo**-ee ay]
driving too fast	andato troppo veloce
	[an**da**to **trop**po vay**lo**chay]
driving too close.	andato troppo vicino.
	[an**da**to **trop**po vee**chee**no]

I/You/He	**Io non ho/Lei non ha/Lui non ha**
	[**ee**-o non o/lay non a/**loo**-ee non a]
ignored the right of way	rispettato la precedenza
	[reespet**ta**to la preche**den**tsa]
went through a red light.	visto la luce rossa [**vees**to la **loo**chay **ros**sa]

Did you witness the accident?	Lei è testimone dell'incidente?
	[lay ay testee**mo**nay delleenchee**den**tay]
Thank you very much for your help.	Molte grazie per il Suo aiuto.
	[**mol**tay **grats**yay pair eel **soo**-o a**yoo**to]

Garage

Where's the nearest (Fiat) garage?	C'è qui un'officina (per la Fiat)?
	[chay kwee oonoffee**chee**na (pair la **fee**-at)]

The engine	**Il motore** [eel mo**tor**ay]
won't start	non parte [non **par**tay]
is losing oil	perde olio [**pair**day **o**lyo]
isn't working.	non funziona bene. [non foont**syo**na **bay**nay]

The brakes don't work.	I freni non sono in ordine.
	[ee **fray**nee non **so**no een **or**deenay]
The warning light is on.	La lampada di controllo è accesa.
	[la **lam**pada dee kon**trol**lo ay a**chay**za]
The exhaust/radiator is leaking/is faulty.	Il tubo di scarico/Il radiatore non è impermeabile/è difettoso.
	[eel **too**bo dee **ska**reeko/eel radya**tor**ay non ay eempairmayabeelay/ay deefet**to**zo]
How much will the repairs be?	Quanto costa la riparazione?
	[**kwan**to **ko**sta la reeparats**yo**nay]
When will the car be ready?	Quando è pronta la macchina?
	[**kwan**do ay **pron**ta la **mak**keena]

Hitchhiking

Are you going to …?	Lei va a …? [lay va a]
Could you give me a lift to …?	Può darmi un passaggio?
	[pwo **dar**mee oon pas**saj**jo]
I'd like to get out here, please!	Vorrei scendere qui! [vor**ray**ee **shen**dairay kwee]
Thanks for the lift!	Grazie per il passaggio! [**grats**yay pair eel pas**saj**jo]

27

Public transport

Bus, tram and underground

Is there a bus to ...?
C'è un autobus per ...? [chay oon **ow**toboos pair]

How long does it take?
Quanto dura il viaggio?
[**kwan**to **doo**ra eel **vyaj**jo]

Excuse me, where's the nearest
Scusi, dov'è la prossima
[**skoo**zee, dovay la **pross**ema]

bus stop
fermata dell'autobus [fair**ma**ta dell**ow**toboos]

tram stop
fermata del tram [fair**ma**ta del tram]

underground station?
stazione della metropolitana?
[stats**yo**nay **del**la metropoleetana]

... goes to ...?
... va a ...? [va a]

Which bus
Quale autobus [**kwa**lay **ow**toboos]

Which tram
Quale tram [**kwa**lay tram]

Which tube line
Quale metropolitana [**kwa**lay metropolee**ta**na]

When does the last bus leave?
Quando ritorna l'ultimo autobus?
[**kwan**do ree**tor**na **lool**teemo **ow**toboos]

Does this bus go to...?
È questo l'autobus per ...?
[ay **kwes**to **low**toboos pair]

Where do I have to
Dove devo [**do**vay **day**vo]

get off
scendere [**shen**dairay]

change for ...
cambiare per ... [kamb**ya**ray pair]

change
cambiare [kamb**ya**ray]

to get to the station
per la stazione [pair la stats**yo**nay]

to get to the airport
per l'aeroporto [pair la-ayro**por**to]

to get to the ... Hotel
per l'albergo ... [pair lal**bair**go]

to get to the city centre?
per il centro? [pair eel **chen**tro]

Could you tell me when I have to get off, please.
Per favore, mi dica quando devo scendere.
[pair fa**vo**ray mee **dee**ka **kwan**do **day**vo **shen**dairay]

A ticket to ..., please.
Un biglietto per ..., prego.
[oon beel**yet**to pair ... **pray**go]

How much is it?
Quanto costa il biglietto per ...?
[**kwan**to **kos**ta eel beel**yet**to pair]

Could you stop here, please!
Prego faccia una fermata qui!
[**pray**go **fa**cha **oo**na fair**ma**ta kwee]

Taxi

Where's the nearest taxi rank?
Dov'è la prossima stazione dei taxi?
[**do**vay la **pross**eema stats**yo**nay **day**ee **ta**xee]

Can you take me ...please?
Mi porti per favore [mee **por**tee pair fa**vo**ray]

to the station
alla stazione [**al**la stats**yo**nay]

to the hotel
all'albergo [allal**bair**go]

to the airport
all'aeroporto [alla-ayro**por**to]

to the centre of town
al centro [al **chen**tro]

to ...
a ... [a]

Signs

Acqua (non) potabile (not) drinking water!
Banchina platform
Binario platform
Freno d'allarme emergency brake
Gabinetti toilets
Informazioni information
Lavabo washroom
Libero free
Occupato occupied
Uscita exit
Vagone cuccette couchette
Vagone letto sleeper/sleeping car
Vagone ristorante dining car

How much is it to ...? — Quanto costa il viaggio per ...? [**kwan**to **kos**ta eel v**yaj**jo pair]

Could you switch on the meter, please? — Inserisca per favore il tassametro. [eensai**rees**ka pair fa**vor**ay eel tas**sa**metro]

Could you stop here, please. — Si fermi qui prego. [see **fair**mee kwee **pray**go]

That's for you! — Questo è per Lei! [**kwes**to ay pair lay]

Getting around by train and bus

Where's the (bus) station, please? — Scusi, dov'è la stazione (dei pullman)? [**skoo**zee do**vay** la stats**yo**nay (**day**ee **pool**man)]

When's the next train/bus to ...? — Quando parte un treno/pullman per ...? [**kwan**do **par**tay oon **tray**no/**pool**man pair]

Do I have to change? — Devo scendere? [**day**vo **shen**dairay]

Which platform does the train leave from? — Da quale binario parte il treno? [da **kwa**lay bee**na**reeo **par**tay eel **tray**no)]

When does the train/bus arrive in ...? — Quando arriva il treno/pullman a ...? [**kwan**do ar**ree**va eel **tray**no/**pool**man a]

Is there a connection to ... in ...? — C'è una coincidenza a ... per ...? [chay **oo**na koeenchee**den**tsa a ... pair]

How much is it? — Quanto costa il viaggio? [**kwan**to **ko**sta eel v**yaj**jo]

Are there special rates for children? — C'è uno sconto per bambini? [chay **oo**no **skon**to pair bam**bee**nee]

A ... ticket/tickets, please — **Prego un biglietto/dei biglietti** [**pray**go oon beel**yet**to/**day**ee beel**yet**tee]

- to ... — per ... [pair]
  - single/return — semplice/andata e ritorno [**sem**pleechay/an**da**ta ay ree**tor**no]
  - first-class/second-class — prima/seconda classe [**pree**ma/se**kon**da **klas**say]
  - for two adults and two children. — per due adulti e due bambini. [pair **doo**ay a**dool**tee ay **doo**ay bam**bee**nee]

I'd like to book ...	**Prego riservi per il treno/per l'autobus per ...**
on the train/bus to ...	[**pray**go ree**sair**vee pair eel **tray**no/pair **low**toboos pair]
a (window) seat	un posto vicino alla finestra
	[oon **pos**to vee**chee**no **alla** fee**nes**tra]
a non- smoker/smoker	non fumatori/fumatori
seat	[non fooma**tor**ee/fooma**tor**ee]
a couchette	un posto cuccetta [oon **pos**to koo**chet**ta]
a sleeper.	un posto vagone letto.
	[oon **pos**to va**gon**ay **let**to]
on the two o'clock train/bus	alle ore quattordici [**al**lay **or**ay kwat**tor**deechee]

I'd like	**Io vorrei** [ee-o vor**ray**ee]
to take my bycicle with me.	portare la mia bicicletta
	[por**tar**ay la **mee**-a beechee**klet**ta]
to check in my luggage.	consegnare questo pacco.
	[konsen**yar**ay **kwes**to **pak**ko]

Where can I find	**Scusi, dove trovo** [**skoo**zee, **do**vay **tro**vo]
the information desk	lo sportello per le informazioni
	[lo spor**tel**lo pair lay eenformats**yo**nee]
the left-luggage office	il deposito bagagli [eel de**po**seeto ba**gal**yee]
the lockers	la cassetta di custodia?
	[la kas**set**ta dee koos**to**deea]

Is this the train/bus to ...?	È questo il treno/l'autobus per ...?
	[ay **kwes**to eel **tray**no/**low**toboos pair]
Is this seat taken, please?	**Scusi**, è libero questo posto?
	[**skoo**zee ay **lee**bairo **kwes**to **pos**to]

Getting around by plane

I'd like to	**Io vorrei** [ee-o vor**ray**ee]
to book a flight to ...	riservare un volo per ...
	[reesair**var**ay oon **vo**lo pair]
for 1 person/2 people	per una persona/due persone
	[pair **oo**na pair**so**na/**doo**ay pair**so**nay]
on ...	il ... [eel]
one-way/return	semplice/andata e volo di ritorno
	[**sem**pleechay/an**da**ta ay **vo**lo dee ree**tor**no]
economy class/first class.	classe turistica/prima classe
	[**klas**say too**ree**steeka/**pree**ma **klas**say]
to confirm a flight	confermare un volo [konfair**mar**ay oon **vo**lo]
to cancel/change the flight.	stornare/prenotare per un altro volo.
	[stor**nar**ay/preno**tar**ay pair oon **al**tro **vo**lo]

Where is	**Dov'è** [do**vay**]
terminal 1/2/3	il terminale uno/due/tre
	[eel tairmee**na**lay **oo**no/**doo**ay/tray]
the information desk?	lo sportello per le informazioni?
	[lo spor**tel**lo pair lay eenformats**yo**nee]

When does the plane from ...	Quando atterra l'aereo da ...?
arrive?	[**kwan**do at**tair**ra la-**ay**rayo da]

Are there any seats ... left?	**Ci sono ancora posti liberi**
	[chee **so**no an**ko**ra **pos**tee **lee**bairee]
by the window/aisle	vicino alla finestra/al corridoio
	[vee**chee**no **a**lla fee**nes**tra/al korree**do**yo]
smoking/non-smoking	per fumatori/non fumatori?
	[pair fooma**to**ree/non fooma**to**ree]
How much is the ticket?	Quanto costa il volo? [**kwan**to **kos**ta eel **vo**lo]
Are there any special rates/	Ci sono tariffe speciali/posti stand by?
stand-by seats?	[chee **so**no ta**ree**ffay spe**cha**lee/**pos**tee stand by]
When do I have to be at the	Quando devo essere all'aeroporto?
airport?	[**kwan**do **day**vo **es**sairay alla-airo**por**to]
How much is the airport tax?	Quant'è la tariffa per l'aeroporto?
	[kwan**tay** la ta**ree**ffa pair la-airo**por**to]
My suitcase/My bag	**La mia valigia/La mia borsa**
	[la **mee**-a va**lee**ja/la **mee**-a **bor**sa]
has been damaged	è danneggiata [ay danna**ja**ta]
is missing.	è sparita. [ay spa**ree**ta]

Getting around by boat

When does the next boat/(car)	Quando parte una nave/un traghetto per ...?
ferry leave for ...?	[**kwan**do **par**tay **oo**na **na**vay/oon tra**get**to pair]
How long does the crossing	Quanto dura la traversata?
take?	[**kwan**to **doo**ra la travair**sa**ta]
I'd like	**Io vorrei** [**ee**-o vorra**yee**]
a ticket to ...	un biglietto per ... [oon beel**yet**to pair]
first class/tourist class	prima/seconda classe
	[**pree**ma/se**kon**da **klas**say]
reclining seats	sedile a sdraio [se**dee**lay a **zdra**yo]
a single cabin	una cabina singola [**oo**na ka**bee**na **seen**gola]
a double cabin	una cabina doppia [**oo**na ka**bee**na **dop**ya]
an outside/inside cabin.	una cabina esterna/interna.
	[**oo**na ka**bee**na es**tair**na/een**tair**na]
I'd like to take the car	Io vorrei portare la mia auto.
with me.	[**ee**-o vorra**yee** por**ta**ray la **mee**-a **ow**to]
When do I/we have to be	Quando devo/dobbiamo stare a bordo?
on board?	[**kwan**do **day**vo/dobb**ya**mo **sta**ray a **bor**do]
When do we arrive at ...?	Quando ancoriamo a ...?
	[**kwan**do ankoree**a**mo a]
How long are we stopping	Per quanto tempo ci fermiamo?
for?	[pair **kwan**to **tem**po chee fairm**ya**mo]
I'm looking for	**Io cerco** [**ee**-o **chair**ko]
cabin number...	la cabina numero ... [la ka**bee**na **noo**mairo]
the restaurant	il ristorante [eel reesto**ran**tay]
the shop	un negozio [oon ne**got**syo]
the toilets	i gabinetti [ee gabee**net**tee]
the parking deck	il ponte di parcheggio [eel **pon**tay dee par**kay**jo]
a steward.	un cameriere di bordo.
	[oon kamairee**yai**ray dee **bor**do]

31

Accommodation

Hotel and guesthouse

Where can I find
a good/cheap hotel

a guesthouse
close to the beach
in the centre of town
in a quiet location?

C'è ... qui vicino [chay kwee vee**chee**no]
un albergo buono/semplice
[oon al**bair**go bwono **sem**pleechay]
una pensione [oona pen**syo**nay]
vicino alla spiaggia [vee**chee**no alla spyajja]
nel centro [nel **chen**tro]
in un posto tranquillo
[een oon **pos**to trank**wee**llo]

Where is the ... hotel/
guesthouse?

Dov'è l'albergo/la pensione ...?
[do**vay** lal**bair**go/la pen**syo**nay]

At the reception desk

I have a reservation.

Io ho fatto riservare una camera.
[ee-o o **fat**to reesair**va**ray oona **ka**maira]

My name is ...

Il mio nome è ... [eel **mee**-o **no**may ay]

Have you got any vacancies
for 1 night
for 1 day
for 2/3 days
for 1 week?

Ha una camera libera [a **oo**na **ka**maira **lee**baira]
per una notte [pair **oo**na **not**tay]
per un giorno [pair oon **jor**no]
per due/tre giorni [pair **doo**ay/tray **jor**nee]
per una settimana? [pair **oo**na sette**ma**na]

* Noi siamo purtroppo al
completo. [noy **sya**mo
poor**trop**po al kom**play**to]

I'm afraid we're fully booked.

There's a vacancy from ...

Dal... ci sarà qualcosa libero.
[dal... chee sa**ra** kwal**ko**za **lee**bairo]

32

I'd like/We'd like

a room with a shower

a single room
a double room
a room with twin beds

  with a bath and toilet

  with a balcony
  facing the beach/at the
  front.

How much is the room

  per person
  per night
  per week
    with/without breakfast
    with half board
    with full board

  for children?

Does the room have a
television/telephone?

I'd like to see the room.

This room is nice/is O.K.

I don't like this room.

Do you have another room?

Can I pay by cheque/credit
card?

Do you have
  a car park
  a (supervised) garage

  a safe
  a swimming-pool?
  a sauna
  your own beach?

Where is
  the breakfast room

  the dining room?

Io vorrei/Noi vorremmo
[**ee**-o vor**ray**ee/noy vor**ray**mo]
una camera con doccia
[**oo**na ka**mai**ra kon **do**cha]
una camera singola [**oo**na ka**mai**ra **seen**gola]
una camera doppia [**oo**na ka**mai**ra **dop**ya]
una camera a due letti
[**oo**na ka**mai**ra a **doo**ay **let**tee]
con bagno e gabinetto
[**kon ban**yo ay gabee**net**to]
con balcone [kon bal**ko**nay]
sulla spiaggia/sulla strada.
[**sool**la **spyaj**ja/**sool**la **stra**da]

Quanto costa la camera
[**kwan**to **kos**ta la ka**mai**ra]
a persona [a pair**so**na]
per notte [pair **not**tay]
per settimana [pair sette**ma**na]
con/senza colazione [kon/**sen**dza kolats**yo**nay]
con mezza pensione [kon **met**za pens**yo**nay]
con pensione completa
[kon pens**yo**nay kom**play**ta]
per bambini? [pair bam**bee**nee]

La camera è con televisione/telefono?
[la **ka**maira ay kon telayveez**yo**nay/te**lay**fono]

Vorrei vedere la camera.
[vor**ray**ee ve**dair**ay la **ka**maira]

La camera è bella/in ordine.
[la **ka**maira ay **bel**la/een **or**deenay]

La camera non mi piace.
[la **ka**maira non mee **pya**chay]

Ha un'altra camera?
[a oon**al**tra **ka**maira]

Posso pagare con assegno/carta di credito?
[**pos**so pa**ga**ray kon as**sen**yo/**kar**ta dee **kray**deeto]

Avete [a**vay**tay]
un parcheggio [oon par**kay**jo]
un garage (sorvegliato)
[oon ga**raj** (sorvel**ya**to)]
una cassaforte [**oo**na kassa**for**tay]
una piscina [**oo**na pee**shee**na]
una sauna [**oo**na **sa**oona]
una spiaggia propria?
[**oo**na **spyaj**ja **pro**preea]

Dov'è [do**vay**]
il posto per la colazione
[eel **pos**to pair la kolats**yo**nay]
la sala da pranzo? [la **sa**la da **pran**dzo]

What time is
  breakfast
  lunch/dinner?

Quando è l'ora di [kwando ay lora dee]
  colazione [kolatsyonay]
  pranzo/cena? [**prandzo/chay**na]

▶ (Food and Drink, see page 40)

Would you wake me
tomorrow at 7, please!

Mi svegli domani alle sette per piacere!
[mee **svay**lyee do**ma**nee **a**llay **set**tay pair
pee**a**chairay]

My key, please!

La mia chiave, per favore!
[la **mee**-a **kya**vay pair fa**vo**ray]

Room number 10, please!

Camera numero dieci prego!
[**ka**maira **noo**mairo d**yay**chee **pray**go]

Where can I
  change money
  cash traveller's cheques

  buy stamps/postcards

  make a phone call?

È possibile [ay pos**see**beelay]
  cambiare soldi [kamb**yar**ay **sol**dee]
  riscuotere traveller's cheques [reesk**wot**airay
  travellers sheks]
  comprare francobolli/cartoline
  [kom**pra**ray franko**bol**lee/karto**lee**nay]
  telefonare? [telayfo**nar**ay]

Can I make a phone call to
England from my room?

Posso telefonare dalla mia camera in Inghilterra?
[**pos**so telayfo**nar**ay **da**lla **mee**-a **ka**maira een
eengeel**tai**ra]

Please put me through to
the following number ...!

Mi può collegare con il numero ... per favore?
[mee pwo kolle**gar**ay kon eel **noo**mairo ... pair
fa**vo**ray]

Are there any letters for me?

C'è posta per me? [chay **pos**ta pair may]

Complaints

The room is dirty/too loud.

La camera è sporca/rumorosa.
[la **ka**maira ay **spor**ka/roomo**ro**za]

There's no (hot) water.

Noi non abbiamo acqua (calda).
[noy non ab**by**amo **a**kwa (**kal**da)]

... does not work.
  The light
  The shower
  The toilet
  The heating

... non funziona. [non foont**syo**na]
  La luce [la **loo**chay]
  La doccia [la **do**cha]
  Il gabinetto [eel gabee**net**to]
  Il riscaldamento [eel reeskalda**men**to]

There are no
  towels
  hangers.
There is no toilet paper.

Mancano [**man**kano]
  asciugamani [ashooga**ma**nee]
  grucce [**groo**chay]
Manca carta igienica [**man**ka **kar**ta eej**ye**neeka]

Could we have (another)

  blanket
  pillow?

Noi abbiamo (ancora) bisogno di
[noy ab**by**amo (**an**kora) bee**zon**yo dee]
  una coperta [**oo**na ko**pair**ta]
  un cuscino. [oon koo**shee**no]

I've lost the key to my room.

Io ho perso la mia chiave della camera.
[**ee**-o o **pair**so la **mee**-a **kya**vay **del**la ka**ma**ira]

Hotel reservation by fax

Hotel Lungomare
Salerno
FAX ...

Hotel Lungomare
Salerno
FAX ...

Gentili Signore e Signori,

Dear sir,

io vorrei/noi vorremmo prenotare dal 1 al 15 agosto 2001 una camera per 1/2 persone, si e possibile con doccia e balcone. Prego mi/ci informi dei prezzi per camera singola/camera doppia con colazione/mezza pensione/ pensione completa e mi/ci informi subito sull'effettuato prenotamento.

I/We would like to reserve a room from 1 to 15 August 2001 for one/two persons, if possible with shower and balcony. Please let me/us know the price for a single/double room with breakfast/half-board/full board so that I/we can confirm my/our booking as soon as possible.

Distinti saluti.

Best wishes

Departure

I'm leaving/We're leaving tomorrow/today.

Io parto/Noi partiamo domani/oggi.
[**ee**-o **par**to/noy part**ya**mo do**ma**nee/**oj**jee]

I'd like my bill, please.

Il conto prego. [eel **kon**to **pray**go]

Would you call a taxi for me, please.

Chiami per favore un taxi.
[**kya**mee pair fa**vo**ray oon **ta**xee]

It's been very nice here.

A noi è piaciuto molto qui.
[a noy ay peea**choo**to **mol**to kwee]

Thank you very much!

Molte grazie! [**mol**tay **grats**yay]

Good-bye.

Arrivederci. [arreevay**dair**chee]

Holiday cottage and holiday flat

We're looking for

Noi cerchiamo [noy chair**kya**mo]

a holiday cottage

una casa per le vacanze
[**oo**na **ka**za pair le va**kant**say]

a holiday flat

un appartamento per le vacanze
[oon apparta**men**to pair lay va**kant**say]

a (quiet) holiday flat

un appartamento (tranquillo)
[oon apparta**men**to (trank**weel**lo)]

for 2/4 people

per 2/4 persone [pair **doo**ay/**kwat**tro pair**so**nay]

for 6 days/2 weeks.

per sei giorni/due settimane.
[pair **say**ee **jor**nee/**doo**ay settee**ma**nay]

How many rooms does the flat have?

Quante camere ha l'appartamento [**kwan**tay **ka**mairay a lapparta**men**to]

How much is the cottage?

Quanto costa la casa [**kwan**to **kos**ta la **ka**za]

Are there any additional costs?

Le spese accessorie sono da pagare a parte?
[lay **spay**zay aches**sor**yay **so**no da pa**ga**ray a **par**tay]

Are pets/dogs allowed?

Sono permessi animali domestici/cani?
[**so**no pair**mes**see anee**ma**lee do**mays**teechee/**ka**nee]

Do we have to clean it before we leave?

Dobbiamo fare noi le pulizie finali?
[dobbyamo faray noy lay pooleetsyay feenalee]

Where can I
go shopping
make a phone call
do the laundry?

Dove si può [dovay see pwo]
fare la spesa [**far**ay la **spay**za]
telefonare [telayfo**nar**ay]
lavare biancheria? [**la**varay beeankai**ree**a]

Camping

Have you got room for
a tent
a caravan
a camper van?

Avete posto per [a**vay**tay **pos**to pair]
una tenda [**oo**na **ten**da]
una roulotte [**oo**na roo**lott**]
un camper? [oon **kam**pair]

What's the charge

for one person
for a car
for a camper van
for a caravan
for a tent?

Quanto costa il posto
[**kwan**to **kos**ta eel **pos**to]
a persona [a pair**so**na]
per una macchina [pair **oo**na **mak**keena]
per un camper [pair oon **kam**pair]
per una roulotte [pair **oo**na roo**lott**]
per una tenda? [pair **oo**na **ten**da]

Do you also rent out
caravans
tents
bungalows/cabins?

Affitta anche [af**feet**ta an**kay**]
roulotte [roo**lott**]
tende [**ten**day]
villini/capanne? [veel**lee**nee/ka**pan**nay]

Where are the showers/ toilets?

Dove sono le docce/i gabinetti?
[**do**vay sono lay **do**chay/ee gabee**net**tee]

We need

a power point

a tap for water

a sewerage connection.

Noi abbiamo bisogno di un
[**no**-ee ab**by**amo bee**zon**yo dee oon]
collegamento per la corrente
[kollega**men**to pair la kor**ren**tay]
collegamento per l'acqua
[kollega**men**to pair **lak**wa]
collegamento alla canalizzazione.
[kollega**men**to alla kanaleetzatsyo**nay**]

When is the gate locked at night?
Is the camp-site guarded at night?

Quando viene chiuso il portone di notte?
[**kwan**do vyay**nay kyoo**zo eel **por**tonay dee **not**tay]
Il posto è sorvegliato di notte?
[eel **pos**to ay sorvel**ya**to dee **not**tay]

Does the camp-site have

a supermarket
washing machines

cool boxes

a playground?

C'è al campeggio
[chay al kam**pay**jo]
un supermercato [oon soopairmair**ka**to]
una lavatrice a gettoni
[**oo**na lava**tree**chay a jet**to**nee]
un frigorifero da affittare
[oon freego**ree**fairo da affet**tar**ay]
un parco giochi? [oon **par**ko **jo**kee]

Youth Hostel

Is there a youth hostel around here?	C'è un ostello della gioventù qui vicino? [chay oon ostello della joventoo kwee veecheeno]
How much is it per night per person (with breakfast)?	Quanto costa un pernottamento a persona (con colazione)? [kwanto kosta oon pairnottamento a pairsona (kon kolatsyonay)]
I/We will stay for two days/ weeks.	Io rimango/Noi rimaniamo due giorni/ settimane. [ee-o reemango/noy reemanyamo dooay jornee/setteemanay]

Accommodation

adapter	spina di riduzione [speena dee reedootsyonay]
air-conditioning	aria condizionata [arya kondeetsyonata]
apartment	appartamento [appartamento]
ashtray	portacenere [portachaynairay]
balcony	balcone [balkonay]
bathtub	vasca da bagno [vaska da banyo]
bed	letto [letto]
bedlinen	lenzuola e coperte [lenzwola e kopairtay]
bill	conto [konto]
blanket	coperta da letto [kopairta da letto]
bottled gas	bombola di gas [bombola dee gaz]
camper van	camper [kampair]
caravan	roulotte [roolott]
car park	parcheggio [parkayjo]
chambermaid	cameriera [kamaireeyaira]
change	spiccioli *(m/Pl)* [speecholee]
clean	pulire [pooleeray]
coat hanger	gruccia [groocha]
coffee machine	caffettiera [kaffetyaira]
coin	moneta [monayta]
cooker	cucina [koocheena]
cot	letto per bambini [letto pair bambeenee]
crockery	piatti [peeattee]
dining room	sala da pranzo [sala da prandzo]
drinking water	acqua potabile [akwa potabeelay]
electricity	corrente elettrica [korrentay elayttreeka]
extra costs	spese accessorie [spayzay achessoryay]
family room	camera per famiglia [kamaira pair fameelya]
fan	ventilatore [vaynteelatoray]
final cleaning	pulizie finali [pooleetsyay feenalee]
garage	garage [garaj]
guesthouse	pensione [pensyonay]
heating	riscaldamento [reeskaldamento]

I need/I don't need bedlinen.

Io (non) ho bisogno di lenzuola e coperte.
[**ee**-o (non) o beez**on**yo dee lenz**wo**la ay ko**pair**tay]

When is the front door
locked?

Quando viene chiusa la porta di entrata?
[**kwan**do **vyay**nay **kyoo**za la **por**ta dee en**tra**ta]

How far is it to

Quanto è lontano fino
[**kwan**to ay lon**tan**o **fee**no]

the beach
the town centre
the station?

alla spiaggia [**alla** sp**yaj**ja]
in città [een **cheet**ta]
alla stazione? [**alla** stats**yo**nay]

hire	noleggiare [nolay**jar**ay]
hire charge	tassa di noleggio [**tas**sa dee no**lay**jo]
kitchen	cucina [koo**chee**na]
key	chiave [**kya**vay]
lift	ascensore [ashen**sor**ay]
light	luce [**loo**chay]
luggage	bagaglio [ba**gal**yo]
pillow	cuscino [ku**shee**no]
pots	pentole [**pen**tolay]
power point	collegamento elettrico [kollega**men**to ela**yt**treeko]
radio	radio [**rad**yo]
reduction	riduzione [reedoots**yo**nay]
repair	riparare [reepa**rar**ay]
rubbish	spazzatura [spatza**too**ra]
rubbish bin	secchio per la spazzatura [**sek**yo pair la spatza**too**ra]
safe	cassaforte [kassa**for**tay]
shower	doccia [**do**cha]
sink	lavandino [lavan**dee**no]
sleeping bag	sacco a pelo [**sak**ko a **pay**lo]
soap	sapone [sa**pon**ay]
sports ground	campo sportivo [**kam**po spor**tee**vo]
tea towel	straccio per i piatti [**stra**cho pair ee pee**at**tee]
television	televisore [telayvee**zor**ay]
telephone	telefono [te**lay**fono]
tent peg	picchetto [pee**ket**to]
toilet	gabinetto [gabee**net**to]
toilet paper	carta igienica [**kar**ta ee**jay**neeka]
towel	asciugamano [ashooga**ma**no]
wash	lavare [la**var**ay]
washing machine	lavatrice [lava**tree**chay]
water	acqua [**ak**wa]

There is nearly always somewhere nearby that sells ice-cream and a cool drink

Food and Drink

Is there ... around here?

a good restaurant
a reasonably cheap restaurant
a nice/a typical restaurant

with regional/
international cuisine?

C'é ... qui vicino
[chay ... kwee vee**chee**no]
un buon ristorante [oon b**won** reesto**ran**tay]
un ristorante economico
[oon reesto**ran**tay ekono**mee**ko]
un locale carino/tipico
[oon lo**ka**lay ka**ree**no/**tee**peeko]
con cucina nostrana/internazionale
[kon koo**chee**na nos**tra**na/eentairnatsyo**na**lay]

I'd like/We'd like

to have breakfast
to have lunch/dinner
a snack

just something to drink.

Io vorrei/Noi vorremmo
[**ee**-o vor**ray**ee/noy vor**ray**mo]
fare colazione [**far**ay kolats**yo**nay]
pranzare/cenare [pran**tzar**ay/che**nar**ay]
mangiare una piccolezza
[man**jar**ay **oo**na peeko**lay**tza]
solo bere qualcosa. [solo **bair**ray kwal**ko**za]

I'd like to reserve a table

for tonight/tomorrow night

at 7/8 o'clock

for 4/6.

The name is ...

Io vorrei ordinare un tavolo
[**ee**-o vor**ray**ee ordee**nar**ay oon **ta**volo]
per oggi/domani sera
[pair **oj**jee/do**ma**nee **sai**ra]
alle ore diciannove/venti
[**al**lay **o**ray deechan**no**vay/**ven**tee]
per quattro/sei persone
[payr **kwat**tro/**say**ee pair**so**nay]
a nome di ... [a **no**may dee]

I've reserved a table. The name is ...

Io ho ordinato un tavolo a nome di ...
[**ee**-o o ordee**na**to oon **ta**volo a **no**may dee]

40

A table for 2/4, please!	Un tavolo per due/quattro persone prego! [oon **ta**volo pair **doo**ay/**kwat**tro pair**so**nay **pray**go]
Is this table/seat taken?	Questo tavolo/posto è libero? [**kwes**to **ta**volo/**pos**to ay **lee**bairo]
Do you have high chairs?	Avete sedie per bambini? [a**vay**tay **say**deeay pair bam**bee**nee]
Excuse me, where's the toilet?	Dove sono i gabinetti per favore? [**do**vay **so**no ee gabee**net**tee pair fa**vo**ray]

How to Order

Excuse me, please! Could I have the menu/menu of the day/list of drinks/wine list/ice-cream menu, please!	Cameriere, prego! [kamair**yair**ay **pray**go] Il menù/menù del giorno/menù delle bevande/menù del vino/menù dei gelati prego! [eel me**noo**/me**noo** del **jor**no/me**noo** **del**lay be**van**day/me**noo** del **vee**no/me**noo** **day**ee je**la**tee **pray**go]
What can you recommend?	Che cosa mi consiglia? [kay **ko**za mee kon**seel**ya]
I'll have	**Io vorrei/Io prendo** [**ee**-o vor**ray**ee/**ee**-o **pren**do]

soup
  the dish of the day
  menu number 1/2
	una zuppa [**oo**na **tsoo**ppa]
	  il menù del giorno [eel me**noo** del **jor**no]
	  il menù numero uno/due
	  [eel me**noo** **noo**mairo **oo**no/**doo**ay]

this
    as a starter/as the main course/for dessert.
	questo qui [**kwes**to kwee]
	    come antipasto/piatto principale/dessert.
	    [**ko**may antee**pas**to/**pyat**to preenchee**pa**lay/des**sair**]

Do you have any regional specialities?	Quali sono i piatti tipici della regione? [**kwa**lee **so**no ee **pyat**tee **tee**peechee **del**la re**jo**nay]
Could I have pasta/rice instead of chips, please?	Io vorrei pasta/riso invece delle patatine fritte. [**ee**-o vor**ray**ee **pas**ta/**ree**zo een**vay**chay **del**lay pata**tee**nay **freet**tay]

Breakfast Italian-style

The notion of a family breakfast is alien to most Italian households. Before the children go to school, they are given a glass of warm milk and a few biscuits, but the menfolk will have a drink and a bite to eat on their way to work in one of the many bars which exist through-out Italy, north and south. The order is nearly always a coffee in the form of an *espresso* or *cappuccino*, accompanied by a *cornetto* (croissant).

In Italy, the bar is a meeting place, where people go to exchange news and gossip, pick up their cigarettes or make a phone call. Most Italians have their own favourite bar, where they pop in regularly for breakfast, a quick bite at lunchtime – maybe a slice of pizza or a *panino* (sandwich) – or to watch the football on TV in the evening.

As Italy is not generally well-supplied with public toilets, many people come in off the street to make use of the bar toilets. It is the done thing, however, to order a drink or buy at least something before using the WC.

FOOD AND DRINK

Coffee the Italian way

An Italian *caffè* is usually served strong, without milk and taken with lots of sugar. If you want something even stronger, then order a *ristretto*, which is a strong *espresso*. A *cappuccino* is a normal *caffè* or *espresso* with a topping of foamy milk and a sprinkling of cocoa. If you want coffee with milk then order a *caffè latte*. It is usually served in a glass or a cup without a handle. An *espresso corretto* has an added shot of brandy.

For the child/children
Per il bambino/i bambini
[pair eel bambeeno/ee bambeenee]

a small portion
una porzione piccola [oona portsyonay peekola]

a children's portion
un piatto per bambini
[oon peeatto pair bambeenee]

an extra plate
un piatto extra [oon peeatto extra]

extra cutlery, please.
posate extra [pozatay extra]

Do you have a vegetarian dish?
C'è una pietanza vegetale?
[chay oona peeaytantza vejetalay]

Is this dish (very) hot/sweet/rich?
Questa pietanza è (molto) piccante/dolce/grassa? [kwesta peeaytantza ay (molto) peekantay/dolchay/grassa]

To drink, I'd like/we'd like
Prego, vorrei/vorremmo
[praygo vorray/vorraymo]

a glass
un bicchiere [oon beekyairay]

a bottle
una bottiglia [oona botteelya]

a quarter of a litre
un quarto [oon kwarto]

half a litre/one litre of red/white wine, please.
mezzo litro/un litro di vino rosso/bianco.
[metzo leetro/oon leetro di veeno rosso/byanko]

Do you serve wine in carafes?
Avete anche vini aperti?
[avaytay ankay veenee apairtee]

Thank you, that's all.
Grazie, questo è tutto. [gratsyay kwesto ay tootto]

Could I have ..., please?
Posso avere ancora [posso avairay ankora]

some more bread
del pane [del panay]

another beer
una birra? [oona beerra]

Enjoy your meal!
Buon appetito! [bwon appayteeto]

Cheers!/Your health!
Salute!/Alla tua/Sua salute!
[salootay/alla tooa/sooa salootay]

Complaints

That's not what I ordered!
Questo non l'ho ordinato!
[kwesto non lo ordeenato]

I'm sorry but
Mi dispiace, ma [mee deespyachay ma]

the food is cold
il cibo è freddo [eel cheebo ay freddo]

the meat is tough/not cooked through.
la carne è dura/non è cotta bene.
[la karnay ay doora/non ay kotta baynay]

42

We still need ..., please?/ Could we have ..., please?	Manca ancora/Ci porti ancora [manka ankora/chee portee ankora]
some cutlery	posate [pozatay]
another knife/another fork	un coltello/una forchetta [oon koltello/oona forketta]
another tea spoon	un cucchiaino [oon kookyaeeno]
another plate	un piatto [oon pyatto]
another glass	un bicchiere [oon beekyairay]
oil and vinegar	aceto e olio [achayto ay olyo]
salt and pepper	sale e pepe [salay ay paypay]
an ashtray	un portacenere [oon portachaynairay]
napkins	tovaglioli [tovalyolee]
toothpicks	stuzzicadenti. [stootzeekadentee]
Have you forgotten my food/drink?	Ha dimenticato la mia pietanza/bevanda? [a deementeekato la mee-a peeatantsa/bevanda]
There seems to be a mistake in the bill	Io credo che il conto non sia preciso. [ee-o kraydo kay eel konto non seea precheezo]
What is this, please?	Cosa è questo? [koza ay kwesto]
I didn't have that!	Questo non l'ho avuto! [kwesto non lo avooto]

Paying the bill

Could I have the bill, please!	Il conto per favore! [eel konto pair favoray]
All together, please.	Pago tutto insieme. [pago tootto eensyaymay]
Separate bills, please.	Paghiamo separatamente. [pagyamo separatamentay]
Could I have a receipt, please?	Vorrei una ricevuta, prego. [vorrayee oona reechayvoota praygo]
Did you enjoy the meal?	È piaciuto? [ay peeachooto]
Was everything OK?	Sono soddisfatti? [sono soddeesfattee]
It was very good, thank you.	Grazie, è stato molto buono. [gratsyay ay stato molto bwono]
That's for you.	Questo è per Lei. [kwesto ay pair lay]
Keep the change!	Va bene così! [va baynay kozee]

Traditional Italian fare

If you want to sample authentic Italian food with the atmosphere to match, then go to one of the many *trattorie* or *osterie* where local families eat. These family-run restaurants usually serve regional dishes made with locally-produced ingredients, which are always seasonal. *Trattorie* and *osterie* don't always have signs outside, but wherever you see locals eating, you are more or less guaranteed that the food's going to be good.

If you just want something hot to keep you going, then go to a *rosticceria* or a *tavola calda* (a sort of snack bar). Here you will find the ubiquitous *pizza*, but also *calzone*, a parcel of pastry stuffed with cheese, tomatoes, mushrooms, artichokes or ham fillings and then fried in oil.

43

Food

Colazione	**Breakfast**
Burro [**boor**ro]	butter
Cacao [ka**ka**o]	cocoa
Caffè [ka**ffay**]	coffee
con dolcificante [kon dolcheefee**kan**tay]	with sweetener
con/senza latte [kon/**sen**dza **lat**tay]	with/without milk
con zucchero [kon **tsoo**kairo]	with sugar
senza caffeina [**sen**dza kaffay-**ee**na]	decaffeinated
Formaggio [for**maj**jo]	cheese
Jogurt [**yo**goort]	yogurt
Latte (caldo/freddo) [**lat**tay (**kal**do/**fred**do)]	(hot/cold) milk
Marmellata [marmel**la**ta]	jam
Miele [**myay**lay]	honey
Pane [**pa**nay]	bread
Pane integrale [**pa**nay eente**gra**lay]	wholemeal bread
Panini [pa**nee**nee]	bread roll
Tè [tay]	tea
alla menta [**al**la **men**ta]	peppermint tea
alle erbe [allay **air**bay]	herbal tea
con limone [kon lee**mo**nay]	with lemon
Toast [**tost**]	toast
Uovo [**wo**vo]	egg
Uovo à la coque [**wo**vo a la kok]	soft boiled egg
Merende	**Snacks**
Panino [pa**nee**no]	sandwich
Toast [**tost**]	toast
con formaggio [kon for**maj**jo]	with cheese
con prosciutto [kon pro**shoot**to]	with ham
con salame [kon sa**la**may]	with salami
Antipasti	**Starters**
Antipasto misto [antee**pas**to **mees**to]	mixed starters
Antipasto nostrano [antee**pas**to no**stra**no]	starters recommended by the chef
Caprese [ka**pray**zay]	tomatoes with mozzarella
Cocktail di gamberetti [**kok**ta-eel dee gambay**ret**tee]	prawn cocktail
Crostini di funghi [kros**tee**nee dee **foon**gee]	stuffed mushrooms on toasted bread
Giardiniera [jardeen**yai**ra]	mixed marinated vegetables
Insalata di frutti di mare [insa**la**ta dee **froot**tee dee **ma**ray]	seafood salad
Lumache [loo**ma**kay]	snails
Minestre	**Soups**
Brodo (con uovo) [**bro**do (kon oo-**o**vo)]	clear soup (with egg)
Minestrone [meenes**tro**nay]	vegetable soup
Pastina in brodo [pas**tee**na een **bro**do]	noodle soup
Stracciatella [stracha**tel**la]	clear soup with beaten egg

FOOD AND DRINK

Pasta e riso
Cannelloni ripieni [kannellonee reepyaynee]
Fettuccine ai quattro formaggi
[fettoocheenay a-ee kwattro formajjee]
Fettuccine alla Fiorentina
[fettoocheenay alla feeorenteena]
Maccheroni ai calamari
[makkaironee a-ee kalamaree]
Penne al pomodoro [pennay al pomodoro]
Ravioli [raveeolee]
Rigatoni alla Carrettiera
[reegatonee alla karrettyaira]
Rigatoni alla contadina
[reegatonee alla kontadeena]
Risi e bisi [reezee ay beezee]
Risotto alla milanese
[reezotto alla meelanayzay]
Spaghetti [spagettee]
  all'amatriciana [allamatreechana]

  alla bolognese [alla bolonyayzay]
  alla carbonara [alla karbonara]
  alla marinara [alla mareenara]

  alla palermitana [alla palairmeetana]
Tortellini alla panna [tortelleenee alla panna]

Pesci e frutti di mare
Calamari alla griglia [kalamaree alla greelya]
Calamari fritti [kalamaree freettee]
Calamari al ragù [kalamaree al ragoo]
Cozze al vino bianco
[kotzay al veeno byanko]
Grigliata mista di pesce
[greelyata meesta dee payshay]
Misto di frutti di mare
[meesto dee froottee dee maray]
Salmone alla pizzaiola
[salmonay alla peetzayola]
Scampi alla griglia [skampee alla greelya]
Sogliola alla griglia [solyola alla greelya]
Zuppa di pesce all'alloro
[tsooppa dee payshay allalloro]

Pizze
Calzone [kaltsonay]

Capricciosa [kapreechoza]
Margherita [margaireeta]
Marinara [mareenara]

Pasta and rice dishes
stuffed cannelloni
fettuccine with four different
types of cheese
fettuccine with spinach

macaroni with
squid sauce
penne with tomato sauce
ravioli
rigatoni with meat,
tuna and mushrooms
rigatoni with tomatoes,
olives and capers
rice with peas
regional rice dish with
saffron
spaghetti
  with tomato sauce
  and bacon
  with meat sauce
  with egg and bacon
  with fish and seafood in
  tomato sauce
  with aubergines
tortellini in cream sauce

Fish and seafood
grilled squid
deep fried squid
squid in tomato sauce
mussels in white wine

mixed grilled fish platter

mixed seafood

salmon in tomato sauce
with herbs
grilled king prawns
grilled sole
fish soup with bay leaf,
tomatoes and herbs

Pizzas
folded pizza, stuffed with
tomatoes, cheese, artichokes
and ham
with many different toppings
with tomato and mozzarella
with tomatoes, cheese
and seafood

Prosciutto [proshootto]	with tomatoes, cheese and cooked ham
Quattro stagioni [kwattro stajonee]	with tomatoes, cheese, sweet peppers, olives, ham and mushrooms
Romana [romana]	with anchovies
Salame [salamay]	with cheese and salami

Carni	**Meat**
Carne alla pizzaiola [karnay alla peetzayola]	beef in tomato sauce
Costata alla boscaiola [kostata alla boskayola]	loin with mushrooms in a cream sauce
Cotoletta alla bolognese [kotoletta alla bolonyayzay]	breaded escalope topped with cheese and ham
Cotoletta alla milanese [kotoletta alla meelanayzay]	escalope
Filetto alla griglia [feeletto alla greelya]	grilled fillet
Lombatina di maiale alla panna [lombateena dee mayalay alla panna]	pork loin in cream sauce
Ossobuco [ossobooko]	knuckle of veal
Rosbif [rosbeef]	beef stew
Saltimbocca alla Romana [salteembokka alla romana]	thinly cut loin with ham and sage in a wine sauce
Scaloppine al limone [skalopeenay al leemonay]	slices of veal in lemon sauce
Scaloppine al pepe [skalopeenay al paypay]	slices of veal in gorgonzola sauce with different types of pepper
Vitello trifolato [veetello treefolato]	finely chopped veal with mushrooms in a cream sauce

Selvaggina, pollame	**Game, poultry**
Anatra all'arancia [anatra allarancha]	duck with orange and ginger sauce
Cinghiale arrosto con carciofi e olive [cheengyalay arrosto kon karchofee ay oleevay]	wild boar with artichokes and olives
Fagiano arrosto con funghi misti [fajano arrosto kon foongee meestee]	roast pheasant with different types of mushrooms
Filetto di lepre in mantello di verza con funghi [feeletto dee lepray een mantello dee vairtsa kon foongee]	fillet of hare wrapped in savoy cabbage with mushrooms
Lombata di cervo con verdure primavera [lombata dee chairvo kon vairdooray preemavaira]	loin of venison served with a selection of vegetables
Pernice al vino bianco [pairneechay al veeno byanko]	partridge in white wine sauce
Pollo arrosto [pollo arrosto]	roast chicken
Quaglia alla cacciatora [kwalya alla kachatora]	quail served with tomato sauce, mushrooms and garlic

Contorni	**Side dishes**
Broccoli [**brok**koli]	broccoli
Fagiolini [fajo**lee**nee]	French beans
Finocchio [fee**nok**kyo]	fennel
Insalata di pomodori [insa**la**ta di pomo**do**ree]	tomato salad
Insalata mista [insa**la**ta **mis**ta]	mixed salad
Insalata verde [insa**la**ta **vair**day]	lettuce
Patatine fritte [pata**tee**nay **freet**tay]	chips

▶ **(Fruit and vegetables, see page 62)**

Formaggi	**Cheese**
Asiago [a**zy**ago]	hard cheese from the Asiago area
Caciocavallo [kachoka**val**lo]	ball-shaped cheese from southern Italy
Gorgonzola [gorgond**zo**la]	blue cheese
Mozzarella [motza**rel**la]	soft cheese made of buffalo or cow's milk
Parmigiano [parmee**ja**no]	hard cheese from the Parma area
Pecorino [peko**ree**no]	aromatic sheep cheese
Provola [**pro**vola]	smoked cheese
Ricotta [ree**kot**ta]	type of fromage frais

Dessert	**Desserts**
Bignè all'amaretto [been**yay** allama**ret**to]	Amaretto eclairs
Cannoli Siciliani [kan**no**lee seechee**lya**nee]	Sicilian rolls
Cassata [kas**sa**ta]	ice-cream with candied fruit
Coppa di melone [**kop**pa dee me**lo**nay]	melon salad
Favette [fa**vayt**tay]	deep fried pastry
Frutta di stagione [**froot**ta dee sta**jo**nay]	seasonal fruit
Gelato [je**la**to]	ice-cream
Macedonia [mache**don**ya]	fruit salad
Panna cotta [**pan**na **kot**ta]	cream dessert
Tortine alla frutta [tor**tee**nay alla **froot**ta]	fruit tartlets
Zabaione [tzaba**yo**nay]	marsala and egg cream

Gelati	**Ice-cream**
Gelato al cioccolato [je**la**to al choko**la**to]	chocolate ice-cream
Gelato al cocco [je**la**to al **kok**ko]	coconut ice-cream
Gelato al mandarino [je**la**to al manda**ree**no]	tangerine ice-cream
Gelato al pistacchio [je**la**to al pee**stak**yo]	pistachio ice-cream
Gelato alla banana [je**la**to **al**la ba**na**na]	banana ice-cream
Gelato alla vaniglia [je**la**to **al**la va**neel**ya]	vanilla ice-cream
Gelato alle castagne [je**la**to **al**lay ka**stan**yay]	chestnut ice-cream
Gelato alle mandorle [je**la**to **al**lay **man**dorlay]	almond ice-cream
Meringhe ripiene di gelato [me**reen**gay reep**yay**nay dee je**la**to]	meringue ice-cream

47

Sorbetti alla frutta [sorbettee alla frootta]	fruit sorbet
Sorbetto di albicocche [sorbetto dee albeekokay]	abricot sorbet
Sorbetto di ananas [sorbaytto dee ananas]	pineapple sorbet
Sorbetto di anguria [sorbetto dee angoorya]	melon sorbet
Sorbetto di fragole [sorbetto dee fragolay]	strawberry sorbet
Sorbetto di limoni [sorbetto dee leemonee]	lemon sorbet
Tartufo [tartoofo]	truffle ice-cream

Drinks

Bevande alcooliche	**Alcoholic drinks**
Acquavite [akwaveetay]	aquavite
Aperitivo [apaireeteevo]	apéritif
Cognac [konyak]	brandy
Birra [beerra]	beer
alla spina [alla speena]	draught
chiara/scura [kyara/skoora]	lager/brown ale
senza alcool [sendza alkool]	alcohol-free
Gin [jeen]	gin
Liquore [leekworay]	liqueur
Pònce [ponch]	punch
Rum [room]	rum
Sherri [shairree]	sherry
Spumante [spoomantay]	sparkling wine
Vermut [vairmoot]	vermouth
Vino [veeno]	wine
amabile/dolce [amabeelay/dolchay]	very sweet/sweet
bianco/rosso/rosato [byanko/rosso/rosato]	white/red/rosé
secco/mezzo secco [saykko/maytzo saykko]	dry/medium dry
Vino porto [veeno porto]	port
Whisky [veeskee]	whisky
con ghiaccio [kon gyacho]	on the rocks
soda [soda]	soda
Bevande rinfrescanti	**Soft drinks**
Acqua [akwa]	water
Acqua minerale [akwa meenairalay]	mineral water
gasata [gazata]	sparkling
naturale [natooralay]	still
Aranciata [aranchata]	orangeade
Frappé [frappay]	milk shake
Latte [lattay]	milk
Limonata [leemonata]	lemonade
Succo di arancia [sookko dee arancha]	orange juice
spremuta fresca [spremoota frayska]	freshly squeezed
Succo di frutta [sookko dee frootta]	fruit juice

▶ (Warm drinks, see breakfast, page 44)

Il Duomo, Milan's cathedral, towers over the city like a white marble mountain

Sightseeing

Tourist information

Is there/Are there	**C'è** [chay]
a tourist office	un ufficio di informazioni turistiche [oon ooffeecho dee eenformatsyonay tooreesteekay]
an information office	un ufficio informazioni [oon ooffeecho eenformatsyonay]
guided tours	una guida organizzata [oona gweeda organeetzata]
sightseeing tours of the city?	un giro della città? [oon jeero della cheetta]
Do you have	**Ha** [a]
a street map	una carta topografica della città [oona karta topografeeka della cheetta]
a map of the city centre/ the area	una carta del centro/dei dintorni [oona karta del chentro/dayee deentornee]
a map of the underground	un piano orario della metropolitana [oon peeyano orareeo della metropoleetana]
brochures	prospetti [prospettee]
a list of hotels/ a list of restaurants	un elenco degli hotel/dei ristoranti [oon elenko daylyee otel/dayee reestorantee]
a programme of events	un programma delle manifestazioni [oon programma dellay maneefestatsyonay]
for this week/for the festival?	per questa settimana/ per le settimane festive? [pair kwesta setteemana/ pair lay setteemanay festeevay]
Could you book a room for me?	Può riservarmi una camera? [pwo reesairvarmee oona kamaira]

49

Sightseeing

abbey	badia [ba**dee**a]
alley	vicolo [**vee**kolo]
altar	altare [al**tar**ay]
ancient	antico [an**tee**ko]
architecture	architettura [arkeetet**too**ra]
arena	arena [a**rayn**a]
art	arte [**art**ay]
artist	artista [ar**tees**ta]
arts and crafts	artigianato [arteeja**nat**o]
Baroque	barocco [ba**rok**ko]
botanical gardens	giardino botanico [jar**dee**no bo**tan**eeko]
bridge	ponte [**pon**tay]
building	edificio [edee**feech**o]
castle	castello [kas**tell**o]
catacomb	catacombe [kata**kom**bay]
cave	caverna [ka**vair**na]
ceiling fresco	affresco su soffitto [a**ffres**co soo so**ffee**to]
cemetery	cimitero [cheemee**tair**o]
century	secolo [**say**kolo]
chapel	cappella [ka**pell**a]
Christian	cristiano [krees**tyan**o]
church service	messa [**mes**sa]
cloister	via crucis [**vee**a **kroo**chees]
cross	croce [**kroch**ay]
drawing	disegno [dee**sen**yo]
emperor	imperatore [eempaira**tor**ay]
empress	imperatrice [eempaira**treech**ay]
excavations	scavi [**skav**ee]
facade	facciata [fa**chat**a]
fortress	fortezza [for**tet**za]
gallery	(galleria di) quadri [(gallai**ree**a dee) **kwad**ree]
garden	giardino [jar**dee**no]
gate	portone [por**ton**ay]
glass	vetro [**vay**tro]
gorge	burrone [boo**rron**ay]
Gothic	gotico [**got**eeko]
grotto	grotta [**grot**ta]
guide	guida [**gwee**da]
history	storia [**stor**ya]
inscription	iscrizione [eeskreets**yon**ay]
island	isola [**eez**ola]
king	re [ray]
lake	lago [**lag**o]
landscape	paesaggio [pa–ay**sajj**o]

library	biblioteca [beeblyot**ay**ka]
market	mercato [mair**ka**to]
medieval	medioevale [medeeoe**va**lay]
memorial	luogo commemorativo [**lwo**go kommemora**tee**vo]
monastery	convento [kon**ven**to]
mosque	moschea [mos**ka**ya]
mountain	montagna [mon**tan**ya]
national park	parco nazionale [**par**ko natsyo**na**lay]
nature reserve	zona protetta [**dzo**na pro**tet**ta]
old town	centro storico [**chen**tro **sto**reeko]
organ	organo [**or**gano]
original	originale [oreejee**na**lay]
painting	pittura [peet**too**ra]
panorama	panorama [pano**ra**ma]
park	parco [**par**ko]
pedestrian precinct	zona pedonale [**dzo**na pedo**na**lay]
picture	quadro [**kwa**dro]
port	porto [**por**to]
prehistoric	preistorico [prayee**sto**reeko]
queen	regina [ray**jee**na]
relief	rilievo [reel**yay**vo]
religion	religione [relee**jo**nay]
renaissance	rinascimento [reenashee**men**to]
restore	restaurare [rest-ow**ra**ray]
Romanesque	romanico [ro**ma**neeko]
roof	tetto [**tet**to]
ruin	rovina [ro**vee**na]
sculpture	scultura [skool**too**ra]
square	piazza [**pya**tza]
statue	statua [**sta**tooa]
temple	tempio [**tem**pyo]
theatre	teatro [tay**a**tro]
tomb	tomba [**tom**ba]
tower	torre [**tor**ray]
town hall	municipio [moonee**chee**pyo]
town wall	mura della città [**moo**ra **del**la **chee**tta]
traditions	usanze [oo**zan**tsay]
valley	valle [**val**lay]
view	vista [**vees**ta]
vineyard	vigneto [veen**yay**to]
waterfall	cascata [kas**ka**ta]
wine tasting	assaggio di vino [as**saj**jo dee **vee**no]
wood	bosco [**bos**ko]
zoo	zoo [tzo]

What are the places of interest around here? | Cosa c'é di interessante da queste parti? [**ko**za chay dee interes**san**tay da **kwes**tay **par**tee]

Visiting the sights

I'd like/We'd like to visit | **Io vorrei/Noi vorremmo vedere** [ee-o vor**ray**ee/noy vor**raym**mo ve**dair**ay]

the cathedral/the church the palace/the castle | la cattedrale/la chiesa [la katay**dra**lay/la **kyay**za] il palazzo/il castello. [eel pa**lat**zo/eel kas**tel**lo]

What are the opening hours of the exhibition/museum? | Quando è aperta la mostra/il museo? [**kwan**do ay a**pair**ta la **mos**tra/eel moo**zay**o]

Is there a guided tour in English? | C'è una guida (inglese)? [chay **oo**na **gwee**da (eeng**lay**zay)]

When does it start?/How much is it? | Quando comincia?/Quanto costa? [**kwan**do ko**meen**cha/**kwan**to **kos**ta]

How long does it take? | Quanto dura? [**kwan**to **doo**ra]

1/2 ticket(s) for adults/children, please. | Un biglietto/Due biglietti, per adulti/bambini. [oon beel**yet**to/**doo**ay beel**yet**tee pair a**dool**tee/bam**bee**nee]

Are there special rates for children/students/senior citizens? | C'è uno sconto per bambini/studenti/anziani? [chay **oo**no **skon**to pair bam**bee**nee/stoo**dayn**tee/ ants**ya**nee]

* Chiuso per rinnovo. [**kyoo**zo pair reen**no**vo] | Closed for renovation.

No cameras allowed! | Vietato fotografare! [vyay**ta**to fotogra**fa**ray]

Do you have a guide in English? | Avete una guida in lingua inglese? [a**vay**tay **oo**na **gwee**da een **leen**gwa eeng**lay**zay]

Excursions

How much is the excursion to … ? | Quanto costa il viaggio per …? [**kwan**to **kos**ta eel **vyaj**jo pair]

Do we have to pay extra for the meal/for admission charges? | Il vitto/I biglietti di entrata sono da pagare extra? [eel **veet**to/ee beel**yet**tee **so**no da pa**ga**ray **ay**xtra]

Two tickets for today's excursion/tomorrow's excursion/for the excursion at 10 o'clock to …, please. | Prego due posti per la gita a …, oggi/domani/ alle ore dieci. [**pray**go **doo**ay **pos**tee pair la **jee**ta a …, **oj**jee/do**ma**nee/**al**lay **or**ay **dyay**chee]

When/Where do we meet? | Quando/Dov'è il posto di incontro? [**kwan**do/**do**vay eel **pos**to dee een**kon**tro]

When do we get back? | Quando ritorniamo? [**kwan**do reetorn**ya**mo]

Do we have | **Abbiamo** [abb**ya**mo]

time to go shopping? time to ourselves? | tempo per le spese [**tem**po pair lay **spay**zay] tempo libero a disposizione? [**tem**po **lee**bairo a deesposeets**yo**nay]

Do we also visit …? | Visitiamo anche …? [veezeet**ya**mo **an**kay]

Taking it easy on one of Italy's many fine beaches

Active Pursuits

At the beach and at the swimming pool

s there ... around here?	**C'è ... qui vicino?** [chay kwee vee**chee**no]
an open air/indoor swimming pool	una piscina libera/coperta [**oo**na pee**shee**na **lee**baira/ko**pair**ta]
a place to hire boats?	un'affittabarche [oonaffeetta**bar**kay]
s there a strong current?	La corrente è pericolosa? [la kor**ren**tay ay paireeko**lo**za]
Are there jellyfish/sea urchins n the water?	Ci sono meduse/ricci in acqua? [chee **so**no me**doo**zay/**ree**chee een **ak**wa]
'd like/We'd like to hire	**Io vorrei/Noi vorremmo affittare** [**ee**-o vor**ray**ee/noy vor**ray**mo affeet**tar**ay]
a (pedal/motor/ rowing/sailing) boat	una barca (a pedale/motore/remi/vela) [**oo**na **bar**ka (a pe**da**lay/mo**tor**ay/**ray**mee/**vay**la)]
a deckchair	una sedia a sdraio [**oo**na **sayd**ya a **zdra**yo]
a surfboard	una tavola da surf [**oo**na **ta**vola da surf]
a pair of water skis.	sci da acqua. [shee da **ak**wa]
How much is it	**Quanto costa** [**kwan**to **kos**ta]
per half hour	per mezzora [pair met**zor**a]
per day	al giorno [al **jor**no]
per week?	per una settimana? [pair **oo**na settee**ma**na]
Are there ... around here?	**Ci sono** [chee **so**no]
sailing courses/schools	corsi/scuole per vela [**kor**see/**skwo**lay pair **vay**la]
surfing courses/schools	corsi/scuole per surf? [**kor**see/**skwo**lay pair surf]
'm a beginner/ 'm experienced.	Io sono principiante/pratico. [**ee**-o **so**no preencheep**yan**tay/**pra**teeko]

Danger signs

Avviso di tempesta	Storm warning!
Pericoloso	Danger
Solo per nuotatori	Swimmers only!
Vietato fare il bagno	No swimming!
Vietato tuffarsi	No jumping!

Sports

Is there ... around here?
  a place to hire bikes

  a (crazy) golf course

  a tennis court

C'è/Ci sono [chay/chee sono]
  biciclette da affittare
  [beecheeklettay da affeettaray]
  un campo per (mini)golf
  [oon kampo pair (mini)golf]
  un campo da tennis? [oon kampo da tennis]

Where can I

  go bowling/
  go horse riding
  play squash/table
  tennis/tennis?

Dov'è possibile
[dovay posseebeelay]
  giocare a birilli/cavalcare
  [jokaray a beereellee/kavalkaray]
  giocare a squash/ping-pong/tennis? [jokaray a
  squash/pingpong/tennis]

Is fishing/swimming allowed
here?

Si può pescare/fare il bagno qui?
[see pwo peskaray/faray eel banyo kwee]

I'd like/We'd like to hire

  cross-country skis/downhill
  skis
  ice skating boots
  a tennis racket.

Io vorrei/Noi vorremmo affittare
[ee-o vorrayee/noy vorraymo affeettaray]
  sci da fondo/sci da discesa
  [shee da fondo/shee da deeshayza]
  pattini [patteenee]
  una racchetta da tennis.
  [oona raketta da tennis]

Do you play chess?
Do you mind if I join in?

Giochi/Gioca a scacchi? [jokkee/jokka a skakkee]
Posso giocare anche io?
[posso jokkaray ankay ee-o]

Nature, environment, adventure

We'd like
  to go on a bicycle tour

  to go hiking

  to go trekking
    in the nature reserve

    in the national park.

Noi vorremo [noy vorraymo]
  fare un'escursione con la bicicletta
  [faray ooneskoorsyonay kon la beecheekletta]
  fare un giro in montagna
  [faray oon jeero een montanya]
  fare un'escursione [faray ooneskoorsyonay]
    attraverso il territorio protetto
    [attravairso eel tairreetoryo protetto]
    attraverso il parco nazionale.
    [attravairso eel parko natsyonalay]

Do you have
a hiking map?

Ha [a]
una mappa per escursioni?
[**oo**na **ma**ppa pair eskoorsy**o**nee]

Is the route
easy/difficult
well marked
suitable for children?

La gita è [la **jee**ta ay]
semplice/difficile [**sem**pleechay/dee**ffee**cheelay]
ben segnata [ben sen**ya**ta]
adatta per bambini? [a**dat**ta pair bam**bee**nee]

How long will it take?

Quanto dura la gita?
[**kwan**to **doo**ra la **jee**ta]

Is this the right way
to ...?

È questa la strada giusta per ...?
[ay **kwes**ta la **stra**da **joos**ta pair]

Active pursuits

aerobics	aerobica [a-airo**bee**ka]
arm bands	braccioli [bra**cho**lee]
badminton	volano [**vo**lano]
ball	palla [**pal**la]
basketball	palla da basket [**pal**la da **bas**ket]
bay	baia [**ba**ya]
billiards	bigliardo [beel**yar**do]
changing rooms	cabina [ka**bee**na]
danger of avalanches	pericolo di valanghe [pai**ree**kolo dee va**lan**gay]
diving equipment	attrezzatura da sommozzatore [attretza**too**ra da sommotza**to**ray]
flippers	pinne [**peen**nay]
gymnastics	ginnastica [jeen**nas**teeka]
health club	centro sportivo [**chen**tro spor**tee**vo]
horse	cavallo [ka**val**lo]
jogging	jogging [**jog**ging]
net	pallacanestro [pallaka**nes**tro]
playground	campo da gioco [**kam**po da **jok**ko]
pony	pony [**po**nee]
ride	passeggiata a cavallo [passay**ja**ta a ka**val**lo]
rubber dinghy	gommone [gom**mo**nay]
sauna	sauna [**sa**oona]
shade	ombra [**om**bra]
shells	conchiglie [kon**keel**yay]
shower	doccia [**do**cha]
skating	pattinare sul ghiaccio [pattee**na**ray sool **gya**cho]
sled	slitta [**zleet**ta]
snorkelling	immergersi con il respiratore [ee**mair**jairsee kon eel respeera**to**ray]
snow	neve [**nay**vay]
stadium	stadio [**stad**yo]
storm	tempesta [tem**pes**ta]
suntan lotion	crema da sole [**kray**ma da **so**lay]
volleyball	palla a volo [**pal**la a **vo**lo]
wave	onda [**on**da]

ACTIVE PURSUITS

How far is it to ...? Quanto è ancora lontano fino a ...?
[kwanto ay ankora lontano feeno a]

Courses

I'd like to attend **Io vorrei iscrivermi a**
[ee-o vorrayee eeskreevairmee a]

a language course un corso di lingua [oon korso dee leengwa]
a cookery/painting course un corso di cucina/di pittura
[oon korso dee koocheena/dee peettoora]

a dance workshop. un corso di ballo. [oon korso dee ballo]

Are there still places Ci sono ancora posti liberi?
available? [chee sono ankora postee leebairee]
Where does the course/ Dove si fa il corso/il seminario?
the seminar take place? [dovay see fa eel korso/eel semeenaryo]
How many people are taking Quanti partecipanti ha il corso?
part in the course? [kwantee partecheepantee a eel korso]
When does it start?/How Quando comincia/Quanto costa il corso?
much is the course? [kwando komeencha/kwanto kosta eel korso]
Do you have somebody to C'è un'assistenza per bambini?
look after the children? [chay oonasseestentsa pair bambeenee]
I have (good) previous Io ho (buone) conoscenze di base.
knowledge [ee-o o (bwonay) konoshenzay dee bazay]
I don't have any previous Io non ho conoscenze di base.
knowledge [ee-o non o konoshenzay dee bazay]

The oldest sports newspaper in the world

In Italy sport is not just another topic of conversation. For many Italians it is the only thing that matters. This obsession is exemplified by the oldest newspaper in the world to deal exclusively in sport, *La Gazzetta dello Sport*. On 3 April 1996 the pink sporting gazette celebrated its 100th birthday. It is a national institution which sells about 350,000 copies a day and yet still looks young and fresh. The editor-in-chief, Candido Cannovò, believes he runs more than just a newspaper. He says it actually provides an emotional focus for an entire nation. On a Monday morning after a weekend of sporting events, the *Gazzetta dello Sport* is the most-read and most-discussed daily newspaper in the country. Football fans wanting to read about the burning issues in Italy's footballing world may need to know the relevant terminology:

defeat sconfitta [skonfeetta]
defender difensore [deefensoray]
draw pareggio [paraydjo]
first/second half primo/secondo tempo [preemo/sekondo tempo]
football fan tifoso [teefozo]
forward attaccante [attakantay]
foul fallo [fallo]
goal goal [gol]
goalkeeper portiere [portyairay]
off fuori [fworee]
off-side fuori di campo [fworee dee kampo]
penalty calcio di rigore [kalcho dee reegoray]
player giocatore [jokkatoray]
referee arbitro [arbeetro]
result risultato [reezooltato]
team squadra [skwadra]
top goalscorer capocannoniere [kapokannonyairay]
victory vittoria [veettoreea]

Entertainment

Cinema, theatre, opera and concerts

Whats on at the cinema today/tomorrow?
Quali film danno oggi/domani al cinema?
[**kwa**lee film **danno** ojjee/doma**nee** al **chee**nayma]

s the film
Il film è [eel film ay]

  dubbed
  sincronizzato
  [seenkronee**tza**to]

  shown in the original version with subtitles?
  in versione originale con sottotitoli?
  [een vairsyonay oreejeena**lay** kon sotto**teet**olee]

When does ... start?
Quando comincia
[**kwan**do komeencha]

  the show
  la presentazione
  [la presentats**yo**nay]

  the film
  il film principale
  [eel film preencheepa**lay**]

  the concert
  il concerto [eel kon**chair**to]

  the matinée
  la matinée [la matte**enay**]

  the ballet performance
  la rappresentazione del balletto
  [la rappresentats**yo**nay del bal**let**to]

  the cabaret
  il cabaret [eel kaba**ret**]

  the opera
  l'opera [**lo**paira]

  the operetta
  l'operetta [lopai**ret**ta]

  the musical
  il musical [eel **moo**zeekal]

  the play
  la rappresentazione
  [la raprezentats**yo**nay]

  the ticket sale
  la vendita anticipata dei biglietti
  [la **ven**deeta anteechee**pa**ta **day**ee beely**et**tee]

    for the festival ?
    per il festival? [pair eel **fes**teeval]

At the theatre

Centro centre	**Loggia** box
Destra/Sinistra right/left	**Platea** stalls
Fila row	**Posto** seat
Gabinetti toilets	**Prima/Seconda categoria**
Galleria gallery	dress/upper circle
Lato aisle	**Uscita di emergenza** emergency exit

What's on

tonight/tomorrow night
this weekend

at the theatre/at the opera

Is there a concert on (this evening)?

Where do I get/How much are tickets?

Are there still tickets at the box office?

Are there special rates?

* Tutto venduto.
[**too**tto ven**doo**to]

Two tickets/seats ..., please.

for the show

for the concert
tonight/tomorrow night
at 8 o'clock

How long does the show last?

I would like a programme, please.

Che cosa si dà
[kay **ko**za see da]
oggi/domani sera [**oj**jee/do**ma**nee **sai**ra]
questo fine settimana
[**kwes**to **fee**nay sette**ma**na]
a teatro/all'opera [a ta**ya**tro/allo**pai**ra]

C'è un concerto stasera [chay oon con**chair**to
(sta**sai**ra)?]

Dove si ricevono/Quanto costano i biglietti?
[**do**vay see ree**chay**vono/**kwan**to **kos**tano ee
beel**yet**tee]

Ci sono ancora biglietti alla cassa?
[chee **so**no an**ko**ra beel**yet**tee **al**la **kas**sa]

Ci sono biglietti ridotti?
[chee **so**no beel**yet**tee ree**dot**tee]

Sold out.

Prego due biglietti/posti
[**pray**go **doo**ay beel**yet**tee/**pos**tee]
per la rappresentazione
[pair la rappresentats**yo**nay]
per il concerto [pair eel kon**chair**to]
oggi/domani sera [**oj**jee/do**ma**nee **sai**ra]
alle ore venti. [**al**lay **o**ray **ven**tee]

Quanto dura la rappresentazione?
[**kwan**to **doo**ra la rappresentats**yo**nay]

Io vorrei un programma.
[**ee**-o vor**ray**ee oon pro**gram**ma]

Nightlife

Is there ... around here?
a discotheque
a (nice) pub
a bar
a casino
with live music?

C'è ... da queste parti [chay da **kwes**tay **par**tee]
una discoteca [**oo**na deesko**tay**ka]
una cantina (carina) [**oo**na kan**tee**na (ka**ree**na)]
un bar [oon bar]
un casinò [oon kaze**e**no]
con musica (live)? [kon **moo**zeeka (live)]

s this seat taken? | È ancora libero qui? [ay an**ko**ra **lee**bairo kwee]

Could I see the wine list, please. | La carta delle bevande, prego. [la **ka**rta **del**lay be**van**day **pray**go]

Shall we | **Vorrebbe** [vor**reb**bay]
dance | ballare [bal**la**ray]
have a drink | bere qualcosa [**bair**ay kwal**ko**za]
get a bit of fresh air? | prendere aria fresca? [**pren**dairay **ar**ya **fres**ka]

This one's on me. | Io la invito. [**ee**-o la een**vee**to]

Entertainment

actor	attore [at**to**ray]
actress	attrice [at**tree**chay]
band	banda [**ban**da]
bar	bar [bar]
bouncer	usciere [oosh**yai**ray]
box office	cassa [**kas**sa]
cabaret	cabaret [kaba**ret**]
chamber music	musica da camera [**moo**zeeka da **ka**maira]
choir	coro [**ko**ro]
circus	circo [**cheer**ko]
comedy	commedia [kom**med**eea]
concert	concerto [kon**chair**to]
conductor	direttore [deeret**to**ray]
dance hall	locale da ballo [**lo**kalay da **bal**lo]
dancer	ballerino/ballerina [ballai**ree**no/ballai**ree**na]
director	regista [ray**jees**ta]
folk concert	serata folcloristica [**sai**rata folkloree**stee**ka]
go out	uscire [oo**shee**ray]
interval	pausa [**pow**za]
jazz concert	concerto jazz [kon**chair**to jazz]
open-air theatre	teatro all'aperto [tay**a**tro alla**pair**to]
opera glasses	binocolo [bee**nok**kolo]
orchestra	orchestra [or**kes**tra]
play (vb)	suonare [swon**a**ray]
play (noun)	rappresentazione [rapprezentats**yo**nay]
pop music	musica pop [**moo**zeeka pop]
première	prima [**pree**ma]
presentation	rappresentazione [rapresentats**yo**nay]
singer	cantante [kan**tan**tay]
stage	palcoscenico [palko**shen**eeko]
stage set	scenario [shen**ar**yo]
ticket	biglietto di entrata [beel**yet**to dee en**tra**ta]

ENTERTAINMENT

Can I	Posso accompagnarti/accompagnarla
	[**posso** akompan**yar**ti/akompan**yar**la]
walk a bit with you	un pezzo [oon **pet**zo]
walk you home	a casa [a **ka**za]
walk you to the hotel?	in albergo/hotel?
	[een al**bair**go/o**tel**]

Would you like to come to my place?	Vorresti/Vorrebbe venire ancora da me?
	[vor**res**tee/vor**reb**bay ven**eer**ay an**ko**ra da may]

Thank you very much for the nice evening.	Grazie per questa bella serata.
	[**grats**yay pair **kwes**ta **bel**la sai**ra**ta]

Good-bye./ See you tomorrow!	Arrivederci./A domani.
	[arreevay**dair**chee/a do**ma**nee]

Festivals and events

When does ... start?	Quando comincia
	[**kwan**do ko**meen**cha]
the festival	la festa (popolare)
	[la **fes**ta (popo**la**ray)]
the festival programme	il programma festivo
	[eel pro**gram**ma fes**tee**vo]
the (trade) fair	la fiera [la fee**ai**ra]
the matinée	la matinée [la matee**nay**]
the parade/procession	il corteo/la processione
	[eel kor**tay**o/la prochess**yo**nay]
the show/performance	lo show/la rappresentazione
	[lo show/la raprezentats**yo**nay]
the circus?	la presentazione del circo?
	[la presentats**yo**nay del **cheer**ko]

Where does the show take place?	Dove si dà la manifestazione?
	[**do**vay see da la maneefestayts**yo**nay]

How long will it last?	Quanto durerà?
	[**kwan**to doo**rai**ra]

Do you have to pay to get in?	Si deve pagare l'entrata?
	[see **day**vay pa**ga**ray len**tra**ta]

Where do I get/ How much are the tickets?	Dove ricevo/Quanto costano i biglietti?
	[**do**vay ree**chay**vo/**kwan**to **kos**tano ee beel**yet**tee]

La Passeggiata

During the warm summer evenings and Sunday afternoons, Italians love to take a stroll. After 4pm, when the shops re-open, people pour on to the shopping streets, squares and into the bars. After work friends and families gather for their *cena fuori*, a meal in a restaurant. The early evening stroll, known as *la passeggiata*, is the opportunity to meet, chat and to see and be seen. The piazza and side streets become a parade ground for young men and women to show off their new clothes and flirt. Despite the distractions of television, *la passeggiata* is for many people still an essential everyday ritual.

The markets are still the main shopping centres for both locals and tourists alike

Shopping

General

Where can I get	**Dove ci sono/Dove posso trovare** [**do**vay chee **so**no/**do**vay **pos**so trovaray]
films	pellicole [pelleekolay]
papers?	giornali? [jornalee]
Is there ... around here?	**C'è ... qui vicino?** [chay kwee veecheeno]
a bakery	una panetteria [**oo**na panettaireea]
a food store	un negozio di generi alimentari [oon ne**got**syo dee **jay**nairee aleementaree]
a butcher's shop	una macelleria [**oo**na machellaireea]
a supermarket	un supermercato [oon soopairmair**ka**to]
* Cosa desidera? [**ko**sa desee**dai**ra]	What would you like?
* Posso aiutarla? [**pos**so ayoo**tar**la]	Can I help you?
I'm just looking, thanks.	Io vorrei solo dare un'occhiata. [ee-o vor**ray**ee **so**lo **dar**ay oonokyata]
I'd like ..., please.	**Per favore vorrei** [pair favoray vorrayee]
stamps	francobolli [franko**bol**lee]
suntan lotion	una crema da sole. [**oo**na **kray**ma da **so**lay]
How much is this?	Quanto costa? [**kwan**to **kos**ta]
That's (too) expensive.	È (troppo) caro. [ay (**trop**po) **ka**ro]
I (don't) like that.	Questo (non) mi piace. [**kwes**to (non) mee **pya**chay]
I'll take it.	Lo prendo. [lo **pren**do]

61

Groceries

baby food	alimenti per neonati [aleementee pair nayonatee]
biscuits	biscotti [beeskottee]
butter	burro [boorro]
cake	dolce [dolchay]
chocolate	cioccolata [chokkolata]
(without) colouring	(senza) coloranti [(sendza) kolorantee]
cream	panna [panna]
eggs	uova [wova]
fish	pesce [payshay]
flour	farina [fareena]
fruit	frutta [frootta]
juice	succo [sooko]
ketchup	ketchup [ketchup]
margarine	margarina [margareena]
mayonnaise	maionese [mayonayzay]
meat	carne [karnay]
(full-cream/semi-skimmed)	latte (intero/scremato)
milk	[lattay (eentairo/skremato)]
mortadella	mortadella [mortadella]
mustard	senape [saynapay]
nuts	noci [nochee]
oil	olio [olyo]
paprika	peperone [pepaironay]
pepper	pepe [paypay]
porridge oats	fiocchi di avena [fyokkee dee avayna]
(without) preservatives	(senza) conservanti [(sendza) konsairvantee]
rusk	fette biscottate [fettay beeskottatay]
salt	sale [salay]
spices	spezie [spetsyay]
sugar	zucchero [tsukkairo]
tinned foods	conserve [konsairvay]
toast	toast [tost]
vegetable	verdura [vairdoora]
vinegar	aceto [achayto]

▶ (See also food, page 44)

Fruit and vegetables

apple	mela [mayla]
apricot	albicocca [albeekokka]
artichoke	carciofo [karchofo]
aubergine	melanzana [melantsana]

62

avocado	avocado [avo**ka**do]
banana	banana [ba**na**na]
basil	basilico [ba**zee**leeko]
beans	fagioli [fa**jo**lee]
broccoli	broccoli [**brok**kolee]
cabbage	cavolo [**ka**volo]
carrots	carote [ka**rot**tay]
cherries	ciliegie [cheel**yay**jay]
chick peas	ceci [**chay**chee]
chicory	cicoria [chee**ko**rya]
chilli	peperoncini [pepairon**chee**nee]
courgettes	zucchini [tsoo**kee**nee]
cucumber	cetriolo [chet**ree**olo]
dates	datteri [**dat**tairee]
fennel	finocchio [fee**nok**kyo]
figs	fichi [**fee**kee]
garlic	aglio [**al**yo]
grapes (white/red)	uva (bianca/nera) [**oo**va (**byan**ka/**nai**ra)]
kiwi	kiwi [**kee**wee]
leeks	porro [**por**ro]
lemon	limone [lee**mo**nay]
mandarin orange	mandarino [manda**ree**no]
mango	mango [**man**go]
melon	melone [me**lo**nay]
nectarine	mandarino dolce [manda**ree**no **dol**chay]
olives	olive [o**lee**vay]
onion	cipolla [chee**pol**la]
orange	arancia [a**ran**cha]
parsley	prezzemolo [pret**zay**molo]
peanuts	arachidi [a**ra**keedee]
pear	pera [**pai**ra]
peas	piselli [pee**zel**lee]
pineapple	ananas [**a**nanas]
plum	prugna [**proon**ya]
potatoes	patate [pa**ta**tay]
raspberries	lamponi [lam**po**nee]
runner beans	fagiolini [fajo**lee**nee]
sweetcorn	granoturco [grano**toor**ko]
sweet pepper	peperone [pepai**ro**nay]
spinach	spinaci [spee**na**chee]
tomato	pomodoro [pomo**do**ro]
watermelon	anguria [an**goor**ya]

The market

The market (mercato) is still the place Italians prefer to get their shopping – much more so than the supermarket. Towns and villages have a market day at least once a week. Every market has its own special character and local specialities. As well as food, there are usually stalls selling clothes, household goods, farming and DIY tools, livestock and much more, depending on the size of the market.

The range of goods on offer is often wider and more varied than you'll find in a department store or a supermarket. It is not unusual to see customers haggling with traders over prices.

Do you have anything else cheaper/larger/smaller?

Ha qualcos'altro di più economico/più grande/più piccolo? [a kwalko**zal**tro dee pyoo eko**no**meeko/pyoo **gran**day/pyoo **peek**kolo]

Can I
pay by cheque/ traveller's cheque/credit card

exchange this?

Posso [**pos**so]
pagare con assegno/traveller's cheque/carta di credito [**pos**so pa**ga**ray kon as**sen**yo/travellers**sheks**/**kar**ta dee **kre**deeto]
cambiare questo? [kamb**ya**ray **kwes**to]

Where's the nearest cash dispenser/the nearest bank?

Dov'è il prossimo bancomat/la prossima banca? [do**vay** eel **pros**seemo **ban**komat/la **pros**seema **ban**ka]

* Ancora qualcosa? [an**ko**ra kwal**ko**za]

Anything else?

That's all, thanks.
Could you pack it for me, please?
Do you have a carrier bag?

Grazie è tutto. [**grats**yay ay **toot**to]
Mi può fare un pacchetto? [mee pwo **fa**ray oon pak**ket**to]
Posso avere una busta? [**pos**so a**vai**ray **oo**na **boos**ta]

Groceries

I'd like/Could I have ..., please?
a piece of ...
100 grams of...
half a kilo of ...
a kilo of ...
a litre of ...
a tin of ...
a bottle of ...

Vorrei/Mi dia per favore
[vor**ray**ee/mee **dee**a pair fa**vo**ray]
un pezzo di ... [oon **pet**zo dee]
cento grammi di ... [**chen**to **gram**mee dee]
mezzo chilo di ... [**met**zo **kee**lo dee]
un chilo di ... [oon **kee**lo dee]
un litro di ... [oon **lee**tro dee]
una lattina di ... [**oo**na lat**tee**na dee]
una bottiglia di ... [**oo**na bot**tee**lya dee]

Could I try some please?

Ne posso assaggiare? [nay **pos**so assa**ja**ray]

* Va bene un po' in più? [va **bay**nay oon po een pyoo]

It's a bit over. Is that all right?

A bit more/less, please.

Un po di più/di meno prego. [oon po dee pyoo/dee **may**no **pray**go]

It's all right!

Lasci così! [**la**shee ko**zee**]

64

Books, stationery and newspapers

Do you sell	**Ha [a]**
English papers/magazines	giornali/riviste in inglese [jornalee/reeveestay een eenglayzay]
postcards	cartoline illustrate [kartoleenay eelloostratay]
stamps	francobolli [frankobollee]
envelopes	buste per lettera [boostay pair lettaira]
pens/pencils	penne a biro/matite [pennay a beero/mateetay]
English books	libri in inglese [leebree een eenglayzay]
glue/adhesive tape?	colla/nastro adesivo? [kolla/nastro adayzeevo]

I'd like	**Io vorrei [ee-o vorrayee]**
a map of ...	una carta geografica di ... [oona karta jayografeeka dee]
a street map	una carta della città [oona karta della cheetta]
a travel guide	una guida turistica [oona gweeda tooreesteeka]
an Italian–English dictionary.	un dizionario italiano-inglese. [oon deetseeonareeo eetalyano-eenglayzay]

Clothes and shoes

I'm looking for	**Io cerco [eeo chairko]**
a blouse/a shirt	una camicetta/una camicia [oona kameechetta/oona kameecha]
a T-shirt	una maglietta [oona malyetta]
a pair of trousers/a skirt/ a dress	dei pantaloni/una gonna/un vestito [dayee pantalonee/oona gonna/oon vesteeto]
a sweater/a jacket	un maglione/una giacca [oon malyonay/oona jakka]
underwear/socks	biancheria intima/calzini [byankaireea eenteema/kaltseenee]
a raincoat	una giacca impermeabile [oona jakka eempairmayabeelay]
a pair of shoes.	scarpe. [skarpay]

I take size 40/I take size 39.	Io ho la taglia quaranta/il numero di scarpe trentanove. [**ee**-o la **tal**ya kwa**ran**ta/eel **noo**mairo dee **skar**pay trenta**no**vay]
Could I try this on?	Posso provare? [**pos**so pro**va**ray]
Do you have a mirror?	Dov'è uno specchio? [**do**vay **oo**no **spek**yo]
It fits/doesn't fit nicely.	Questo (non) mi sta bene. [**kwes**to (non) mee sta **bay**nay]
I like/I don't like it/this colour.	Questo/Questo colore (non) mi piace. [**kwes**to/**kwes**to ko**lo**ray (non) mee **pya**chay]
I'll take it.	Io lo prendo. [**ee**-o lo **pren**do]
Do you have other models/colours?	Ci sono ancora altri modelli/colori? [chee **so**no an**ko**ra **al**tree mo**del**lee/ko**lo**ree]

It is	È [ay]
too small/big	troppo piccolo/grande [**trop**po **pee**kolo/**gran**day]
too long/short	troppo lungo/corto [**trop**po **loon**go/**kor**to]

Is this	Questo/Questa è [**kwes**to/**kwes**ta ay]
real leather	vera pelle [**vai**ra **pel**lay]
cotton/wool/silk/linen?	cotone/lana/seta/lino? [ko**to**nay/**la**na/**say**ta/**lee**no]

Laundry and dry cleaning

I'd like to have these things cleaned/washed.	Io vorrei fare pulire/lavare questo. [**ee**-o vor**ray**ee **fa**ray poo**lee**ray/la**va**ray **kwes**to]
How much is it?	Quanto costa? [**kwan**to **kos**ta]
When can I pick it up?	Quando posso venire a prenderlo? [**kwan**do **pos**so ve**nee**ray a **pren**dairlo]

Jewellery and watches

My necklace/my alarm clock is broken.	La mia catenina/La mia sveglia è rotta. [la **mee**-a katay**nee**na/la **mee**-a **svel**ya ay **rot**ta]
My watch is broken.	Il mio orologio è rotto. [eel **mee**-o oro**lo**jo ay **rot**to]
Could you repair it?	Può riparare questo/-a? [pwo reepa**ra**ray **kwes**to/-a]

I'd like	Io avrei bisogno di [**ee**-o av**ray** beezon**yo** dee]
a new battery	una nuova batteria [**oo**na **nwo**va battai**ree**a]
a bracelet	un bracciale [oon bra**cha**lay]
a brooch	una spilla [**oo**na **speel**la]
a ring	un anello [oon a**nel**lo]
some earrings.	orecchini. [orek**kee**nee]

Buying clothes in Italy

When buying clothes and shoes in Italy, you'll find that the Italian sizing system is different to the British. With women's clothing, add 32 to your UK size, so a woman's 12, for example, becomes 44.

The difference in men's shirt sizes is 23, so a size 16 collar becomes a 39. With suits simply add 10 (UK40 is 50 in Italy). Shoe sizes are different too. Add 33 to your UK size (UK6 = 39).

Clothes and shoes

anorak	anorak [anorak]
belt	cintura [cheentoora]
bikini	bikini [beekeenee]
boots	stivali [steevalee]
bra	reggiseno [rejeesayno]
cap	berretto [bairretto]
gloves	guanti [gwantee]
hat	cappello [kappello]
panties	slip [zleep]
sandals	sandali [sandalee]
scarf	foulard [foolar]
sunhat	cappello da sole [kappello da solay]
swimming trunks	slip da bagno [zleep da banyo]
swimsuit	costume da bagno [kostoomay da banyo]
tie	cravatta [kravatta]
tights	collant [kollan]
tracksuit	tuta da ginnastica [toota da jeennasteeka]
waistcoat	gilet [jeelay]

Is this   È/Sono [ay/sono]
  genuine   vero/veri [vairo/vairee]
  silver/gold   d'argento/d'oro [darjento/doro]
  silver-plated/gold-plated?   argentato/dorato? [arjentato/dorato]

Electrical appliances and photography

I'm looking for/I need   Io cerco/Ho bisogno di
       [ee-o chairko/o beezonyo dee]
  an adapter   una spina di riduzione
       [oona speena dee reedootsyonay]
  a battery   una batteria [oona battaireea]
    for a torch   per torcia elettrica [pair torcha elettreeka]
    for a camera   per macchina fotografica
       [pair makkeena fotografeeka]
    for a video camera   per videocamera [pair veedeokamaira]
    for a radio.   per radio. [pair radyo]

I'd like   Io avrei bisogno di [ee-o avrayee beezonyo dee]
  a colour film/a black and   una pellicola a colori/bianco e nero
  white film   [oona pelleekola a koloree/byanko ay nairo]
  a slide film   una pellicola per diapositiva
       [oona pelleekola pair deeapozeeteeva]
    with 24/36 exposures   per ventiquattro/trentasei riprese
       [pair venteekwattro/trentasayee reeprayzay]
  a video casette (VHS)   una cassetta video (VHS)
       [oona kassetta veedeo (voo-akka essay)]
  a standard lens   un obiettivo standard [oon obyetteevo standard]
  a wide-angle/   un obiettivo grandangolare/tele/zoom.
  telephoto/zoom lens.   [oon obyetteevo grandangolaray/taylay/tzoom]

Could you . . ., please? Può/Potete [pwo/potaytay]
  put the film in the camera mettere la pellicola [**met**tairay la pel**lee**kola]
  develop this film for me sviluppare questa pellicola
    [sveeloo**pa**ray **kwes**ta pel**lee**kola]

  do prints sviluppare delle foto [sveeloo**pa**ray **del**lay **fo**to]
    9 by 13 in formato nove per tredici
    [een for**ma**to **no**vay pair **tray**deechee]

    gloss/matt lucido/opaco? [**loo**cheedo/o**pak**ko]

Do you do passport photos? Lei fa foto per tessera? [lay fa **fo**to pair **tes**saira]
When will the prints be Quando sono pronte le foto?
ready? [**kwan**do **so**no **pron**tay lay **fo**to]

. . . doesn't work. **. . . non funziona bene.** [non foont**syo**na **bay**nay]
  My camera La mia macchina fotografica
    [la **mee**-a **mak**keena fotogra**fee**ka]

  My flash Il mio flash [eel **mee**-o flash]

Could you have a look at Può controllarlo/-la/ripararlo/-la?
it?/Can you repair it? [pwo kontrol**lar**lo/la/reepa**rar**lo/la]

When can I pick it up? Quando posso venire a prenderlo/prenderli?
    [**kwan**do **pos**so venee**ray** a **pren**dairlo/**pren**dairlee]

Souvenirs and arts and crafts

I'm looking for **Io cerco** [ee-o **chair**ko]
  a souvenir un souvenir [oon soove**neer**]
  folk costumes vestiti folcloristici [ves**tee**tee folklo**rees**teechee]
  ceramics ceramica [chai**ra**meeka]
  art oggetti artistici [o**jet**tee ar**tees**steechee]
    modern/antique/folk moderni/antichi/popolari
      [mo**dair**nee/an**tee**kee/poppo**la**ree]

  leather goods oggetti in pelle [o**jet**tee een **pel**lay]
  jewellery. gioielli. [jo**yel**lee]

What's typical of **Cosa è tipico per** [**ko**za ay **tee**peeko pair]
  this town questa città [**kwes**ta chee**tta**]
  this area questa regione [**kwes**ta re**jo**nay]
  this country? questo paese? [**kwes**to pa-ay**zay**]

Is this **Questo è** [**kwes**to ay]
  handmade fatto a mano [**fat**to a **ma**no]
  genuine/antique vero/antico [**vai**ro/an**tee**ko]
  artisan work artigianato artistico [arteeja**na**to ar**tees**teeko]
  local? della regione? [**del**la re**jo**nay]

Optician

My glasses are broken. I miei occhiali sono rotti.
    [ee m**yay**ee ok**kya**lee **so**no **rot**tee]

Can you let me have a Può darmi degli occhiali di riserva?
substitute pair? [pw**o** **dar**mee **day**lyee ok**kya**lee dee ree**sair**va]

Chemist

baby powder	talco per bambini [**tal**ko pair bam**bee**nee]
baby's bottle	biberon [beebai**ron**]
body lotion	lozione per il corpo [lots**yo**nay pair eel **kor**po]
brush	spazzola [**spat**zola]
comb	pettine [**pet**teenay]
condom	profilattico [profee**lat**teeko]
cotton wool	ovatta [o**vat**ta]
deodorant	deodorante [dayodo**ran**tay]
detergent	detersivo [detair**see**vo]
dummy	succhietto [sook**yet**to]
elastic hairband	elastico per capelli [e**las**teeko pair ka**pel**lee]
hair gel	gel per capelli [jel pair ka**pel**lee]
hairspray	lacca per capelli [**lak**ka pair ka**pel**lee]
insect repellent	antizanzare [anteetsant**za**ray]
nail file	limetta per le unghie [lee**met**ta pair lay **oong**yay]
nail scissors	forbici per le unghie [**for**beechee pair lay **oong**yay]
nappies	pannolini [panno**lee**nee]
perfume	profumo [pro**foo**mo]
razor-blade	lamette da barba [la**met**tay da **bar**ba]
sanitary towels	pannolini (da donna) [panno**lee**nee (da **don**na)]
saftey pin	spilla di sicurezza [**speel**la dee seekoo**ret**za]
shaving foam	schiuma da barba [**skyoo**ma da **bar**ba]
shower gel	gel per doccia [jel pair **doch**ha]
soap	sapone [sa**po**nay]
tampons	tamponi [tam**po**nee]
toilet paper	carta igienica [**kar**ta eejye**nee**ka]
tweezers	pinzetta [peent**set**ta]
toothbrush	spazzolino da denti [spatzo**lee**no da **den**tee]
toothpaste	dentifricio [dentee**free**cho]
washing-up liquid	detersivo per i piatti [detair**see**vo pair ee p**yat**tee]

When can I pick up the glasses?	Quando posso venire a prendere gli occhiali? [**kwan**do **pos**so ve**nee**ray a **pren**dairay lyee ok**kya**lee]
I'm shortsighted/ longsighted.	Io sono miope/presbite. [ee-o **so**no **mee**opay/**prez**beetay]
I have	**Io ho** [ee-o o]
lost my glasses/contact lens	perso i miei occhiali/una lente a contatto [**pair**so ee **mya**yee ok**kya**lee/**oo**na **len**tay a kon**tat**to]
... dioptre in the right/left eye.	a destra/sinistra ... diottrie. [a **des**tra/seen**ees**tra ... dee**ot**treeay]

SHOPPING

I need
a pair of sunglasses
a spectacle case

a pair of binoculars
cleansing solution/rinsing
solution
  for hard/soft contact
  lenses.

Io ho bisogno di [ee-o o beezonyo dee]
occhiali da sole [okkyalee da solay]
un astuccio per occhiali
[oon astoocho pair okkyalee]
un binocolo [oon beenokolo]
una soluzione per pulire/conservare
[oona solootsyonay pair pooleeray/konsairvaray]
  per lenti a contatto dure/morbide.
  [pair lentee a kontatto dooray/morbeeday]

Chemist

I'd like
some plasters
some tissues
a hand/skin creme

a suntan lotion with
protection factor 6/12

an after sun lotion
a shampoo
  for normal hair

  for dry hair
  for greasy hair
  for dandruff.

Io vorrei [ee-o vorrayee]
cerotti [chairottee]
fazzoletti di carta [fatzolettee dee karta]
una crema per le mani/per la pelle
[oona krayma pair lay manee/pair la pellay]
una crema per il sole con fattore protettivo
sei/dodici
[oona krayma pair eel solay kon fattoray
protetteevo say/dodeechee]
un doposole [oon doposolay]
uno sciampo [oono shampo]
  per capelli normali
  [pair kapellee normalee]
  per capelli secchi [pair kapellee sekkee]
  per capelli grassi [pair kapellee grassee]
  contro la forfora. [kontro la forfora]

Tobacconist

. . . please.

A packet/carton of cigarettes

  with/without filters.

A packet of pipe tobacco

A box of matches
A lighter

. . ., prego [praygo]

Un pacchetto/Una stecca di sigarette
[oon pakketto/oona stekka dee seegarettay]
  con/senza filtro
  [kon/sendza feeltro]
Tabacco da pipa
[tabakko da peepa]
Fiammiferi [fyammeefairee]
Un accendino
[oon achendeeno]

Sale e Tabacchi

The words *Sale e Tabacchi* can still sometimes be read on old-fashioned signs above tobacconists' shops. In the old days, the sale of salt was controlled by the state. Only those shops, bars and restaurants displaying the sign *Sale e* *Tabacchi* were allowed to sell salt and tobacco, both of which were highly taxed. This restriction now only applies to tobacco and stamps. Look for the sign with the large, white T on a blue background.

Most public phone boxes now only accept phonecards

Practical Information

Medical assistance

At the doctor's surgery

I need a doctor (urgently).

Io ho bisogno (subito) di un medico.
[**ee**-o o bee**zon**yo (**soo**beeto) dee oon **may**deeko]

Please call a doctor/an ambulance.

Prego telefoni al medico di emergenza/ad una autoambulanza. [**pray**go te**lay**fonee al **may**deeko dee emair**jen**tsa/ad **oo**na owtoamboo**lant**sa]

Is there a ... around here?
gynaecologist
paediatrician
dentist
English-speaking

Dove trovo [**do**vay **tro**vo]
un ginecologo [oon jeenay**ko**logo]
un pediatra [oon pedy**a**tra]
un dentista [oon den**tee**sta]
che parla inglese?
[kay **par**la een**glay**zay]

Can the doctor come here?

Può venire qui il medico?
[pwo ve**neer**ay kwee eel **may**deeko]

When are his surgery hours?

Quando è aperto l'ambulatorio?
[**kwan**do ay a**pair**to lamboola**tor**eeo]

Can I have an appointment immediately?
When can I come?

Posso venire subito nell'ambulatorio?
[**pos**so ve**neer**ay **soo**beeto nellamboola**tor**eeo]
Quando posso venire? [**kwan**do **pos**so ve**neer**ay]

* Che cosa posso fare per Lei?
[kay **ko**za posso **far**ay pair lay]

What can I do for you?

I feel sick (all the time).

Mi sento (continuamente) male.
[mee **sen**to (konteenooa**men**tay) **ma**lay]

I had a fall.

Sono caduto. [**so**no ka**doo**to]

72

've got	**Io ho** [ee-o o]
a cold	il raffreddore [eel raffred**dor**ay]
an allergy	un'allergia [oonallair**jee**a]
diarrhoea	la diarrea [la deear**ray**a]
the flu	l'influenza [leenfloo**ent**sa]
a cough	la tosse [la **tos**say]
a headache	mal di testa [mal dee **tes**ta]
stomach-ache	mal di pancia [mal dee **pan**cha]
earache	mal di orecchi [mal dee o**rek**kee]
a sore throat	mal di gola [mal dee **go**la]
cystitis	un'infezione alla vescica [ooneenfetsy**on**ay **al**la ve**shee**ka]
shooting pains in the heart	fitte al cuore [**feet**tay al **kwor**ay]
a (high) temperature.	la febbre (alta). [la **feb**bray (**al**ta)]

I have vomited. — Io ho vomitato [ee-o o vomee**ta**to]

* Quanto è alta la febbre? [**kwan**to ay **al**ta la **feb**bray] — How high is the temperature?

* Da quando ha la febbre? [da **kwan**do a la **feb**bray] — When did the fever start?

Two days ago. — Da due giorni. [da **doo**ay **jor**nee]

* Dove fa male? [**do**vay fa **ma**lay] — Where does it hurt?

* Non è niente di grave. [non ay **nyen**tay dee **gra**vay] — It's nothing serious.

Is the leg broken?	È fratturata la gamba? [ay frattoo**ra**ta la **gam**ba]
Is the arm/ the finger broken?	È fratturato il braccio/il dito? [ay frattoo**ra**to eel **bra**cho/eel **dee**to]

I've got digestion problems. — Io non digerisco il mangiare [ee-o non deejai**rees**ko eel man**ja**ray]

I am allergic to penicillin. — Io non sopporto la penicillina. [ee-o non sop**por**to la peneechee**lleen**a]

I'm	**Io sono** [eeo **so**no]
pregnant/4 months pregnant	incinta/nel quarto mese di gravidanza [in**cheen**ta/nel **kwar**to **may**zay dee gravee**dant**za]
a diabetic	malato di diabete [ma**la**to dee deea**bay**tay]
chronically ill.	malato cronico *(m)*/malata cronica *(f)*. [ma**la**to **kron**eeko/ma**la**ta **kron**eeka]

Directions for use of medicine

digiuno	on an empty stomach
due/tre volte al giorno	twice/three times a day
esterno/interno	external/internal
prima/dopo i pasti	before/after food
sciogliere in acqua	dissolve in water
sciogliere in bocca	dissolve on the tongue
senza masticare	swallow whole

Could you
prescribe this for me
prescribe something for ...,
please?

Mi può [mee pwo]
prescrivere questo [pre**scree**vairai **kwes**to]
prescrivere qualcosa contro ...?
[pre**scree**vairay kwal**ko**za **kon**tro]

At the dentist

I've got (terrible) toothache.

Io ho (un forte) mal di denti.
[**ee**-o o (oon **for**tay) mal dee **den**tee]

I've lost a filling.

Io ho perso una piombatura.
[**ee**-o o **pair**so **oo**na pyomba**too**ra]

Could you
see me immediately
give me something for the
pain, please?

Può [pwo]
visitarmi subito [veezee**tar**mee **soo**beeto]
darmi un antidolorifero?
[**dar**mee oon anteedolo**ree**fairo]

Medical assistance

aids	aids [**aeeds**]
allergy	allergia [aller**jee**a]
antibiotic	antibiotico [anteeb**yo**teeko]
appendicitis	appendicite [appendee**chee**tay]
aspirin	aspirina [aspee**ree**na]
(strong) bleeding	emorragia (forte) [emmora**jee**a (**for**tay)]
blood test	controllo del sangue
	[kon**trol**lo del **san**gway]
burn	bruciatura [broocha**too**ra]
certificate	certificato medico [chairteefee**ka**to **may**deeko]
circulatory problems	disturbo di circolazione
	[dees**toor**bo dee cheerkolat**syo**nay]
cold	raffreddore [raffred**do**ray]
condom	profilattico [profee**lat**teeko]
concussion	commozione cerebrale
	[kommot**syo**nay chairay**bra**lay]
constipation	stitichezza [steetee**kay**tza]
cough mixture	sciroppo per la tosse [shee**rop**po pair la **tos**say]
cramp	crampo [**kram**po]
eardrops	gocce per le orecchie [**go**chay pair lay orek**yay**]
eyedrops	collirio [kol**lee**reeo]
flu	influenza [eenfloo**en**tsa]
fracture	ernia [**air**neea]
fungus (infection)	(infezione da) fungo [(eenfet**syo**nay da) **foon**go]
gastroenteritis	malattie dell'apparato digerente
	[malat**tee**ay delappa**ra**to deejai**ren**tay]
HIV-positive	sieropositivo [syairopozee**tee**vo]
infection	infezione [infet**syo**nay]
infectious	contagioso/-a [konta**jo**zo/-a]

Could you do a temporary repair on the tooth/the bridge/the crown.

Per favore ripari solo provvisoriamente il dente/il ponte/la corona.
[pair favoray reeparee solo proveezoreeamentay eel dentay/eel pontay/la korona]

Could you give me an/no injection, please.

Io (non) vorrei una iniezione.
[ee-o (non) vorrayee oona eenyetsyonay]

At the hospital

Where is
the nearest hospital
accident and emergency?

Dov'è [dovay]
l'ospedale più vicino [l'ospedalay pyoo veecheeno]
l'ambulanza? [lamboolantsa]

Please call
Mr/Mrs ...
at the ... Hotel!

Prego informi [praygo eenformee]
il signor/la signora ... [eel seenyor/la seenyora]
all'hotel ...! [al-otel]

inflammation	infiammazione [eenfyammatsyonay]
migraine	emicrania [emmeekranya]
ointment	unguento [oongwento]
operation	operazione [opairatsyonay]
painkiller	pillole contro il dolore [peellolay kontro eel doloray]
plaster	cerotto [chairotto]
poisoning	avvelenamento [avelaynamento]
pulled muscle	strappo muscolare [strappo mooskolaray]
pulled tendon	stiramento del tendine [steeramento del tendeenay]
pus	pus [poos]
rash	sfogo [sfogo]
seasickness	mal di mare [mal dee maray]
sleeping pills	pillole contro l'insonnia [peellolay kontro leensonya]
snakebite	morso da serpente [morso da sairpentay]
sprained	slogato/-a [slogato/-a]
sunstroke	colpo di sole [kolpo dee solay]
temperature	febbre [febbray]
tranquilizer	calmante [kalmantay]
travel sickness	malattia da viaggio [malateea da vyajjo]
vomiting	vomito [vomeeto]
vaccinate	vaccinare [vacheenaray]
vaccination	vaccinazione [vacheenatsyonay]
virus	virus [veeroos]
wound	ferita [faireeta]
x-ray	radiografia [radeeografeea]

Do you have private/two-bed rooms?

Avete camere private/camere a due letti? [avaytay kamairay preevatay/kamairay a dooay lettee]

What's the diagnosis?
Which treatment/therapy do you propose?
How long will I have to stay?

Qual'è la diagnosi? [kwalay la deeanyozee]
Quale terapia è necessaria? [kwalay tairapeea ay nechessareea]
Quanto devo rimanere? [kwanto dayvo reemanairay]

When can I get up?

(Quando) Posso alzarmi? [(kwando) posso altsarmee]

I feel (don't feel any) better.

(Non) Sto meglio. [(non) sto maylyo]

I need
    a painkiller
    sleeping pills.

Ho bisogno di [o beezonyo dee]
    un antidolorifero [oon anteedoloreefairo]
    pillole per l'insonnia. [peellolay pair leensonya]

Am I well enough to travel?

Posso viaggiare? [posso vyajjaray]

I'd like ...
    to see the doctor
    to be discharged
    a medical report

    a certificate
        for my medical insurance

        for my doctor.

Io vorrei [ee-o vorrayee]
    parlare con il medico [parlaray kon eel maydeeko]
    essere rilasciato [essairay reelashato]
    un rapporto di malattia
    [oon rapporto dee malatteea]
    un certificato [oon chairteefeekato]
        per la mia cassa malattia
        [pair la mee-a kassa malatteea]
        per il mio medico di fiducia.
        [pair eel mee-o maydeeko dee feedoocha]

At the pharmacy

I'm looking for a pharmacy.

Io cerco una farmacia
[ee-o chairko oona farmacheea]

I have (I don't have) a prescription.

Io (non) ho una ricetta.
[ee-o (non) o oona reechetta]

I need
    some plasters
    an insect repellent

    something for a cough/
    for a (head) ache
        for me
        for adults/for children.

Io ho bisogno di [ee-o o beezonyo dee]
    cerotti [chairottee]
    qualcosa contro le zanzare
    [kwalkoza kontro lay tzantzaray]
    qualcosa contro la tosse/il dolore (di testa)
    [kwalkoza kontro la tossay/eel doloray (dee testa)]
        per me [pair may]
        per adulti/bambini. [pair adooltee/bambeenee]

Is the medicine strong/weak?

Questa medicina è forte/leggero?
[kwesto medeecheena ay fortay/lejairo]

How many tablets/drops do I have to take?

Quante pastiglie/gocce devo prendere?
[kwantay pasteelyay/gochay dayvo prendairay]

Could you give me
a receipt/a copy of the prescription, please!

Prego mi dia una ricevuta/una copia
della ricetta.
[praygo mee deea oona reechayvoota/oona kopya della reechetta]

Holidays and festivals

Is there a (national) holiday today?	Oggi è festa (nazionale)? [**oj**jee ay **fes**ta (natsyo**na**lay)]
What's being celebrated today?	Quale festa si festeggia oggi? [**kwa**lay **fes**ta see fes**tej**ja **oj**jee]
When does the festival start?	Quando comincia il programma festivo? [**kwan**do ko**meen**cha eel pro**gram**ma fes**tee**vo]
How long does it last?	Quanto dura? [**kwan**to **doo**ra]
Where does the festival take place?	Dove si fa la manifestazione? [**do**vay see fa la maneefestats**yo**nay]

Money matters

Can I pay with ... here?	**Posso pagare con** [**pos**so pa**ga**ray kon]
cheques	assegno [as**sen**yo]
traveller's cheques	traveller's cheques [travellers sheks]
my cheque card	carta assegni [**kar**ta as**sen**yee]
credit card	carta di credito? [**kar**ta dee **kray**deeto]
Where's the nearest	**Dov'è/C'è** [do**vay**/chay]
bank	una banca [**oo**na **ban**ka]
bureau de change	un ufficio di cambio [oon oo**fee**cho dee **kam**byo]
cash dispenser?	un bancomat? [oon **ban**komat]
What time does the bank close?	Quando/Fino a quando è aperta la banca? [**kwan**do/**fee**no a **kwan**do ay a**pair**ta la **ban**ka]
* Quanto desidera? [**kwan**to de**see**daira]	How much do you want?
300 000 lire.	Trecentomila lire. [traychento**mee**la **lee**ray]
What's the current exchange rate?	Quanto è il cambio attuale? [**kwan**to ay eel **kam**byo at**twa**lay]
What's the maximum amount per cheque?	Quanto è la somma massima per assegno? [**kwan**to ay la **som**ma **mas**seema pair as**sen**yo]
I'd like to change 100 pounds sterling/dollars into lire, please.	Io vorrei cambiare cento sterline/dollari in Lire. [**ee**-o vor**ray**ee kamb**ya**ray **chen**to stair**lee**nay/**dol**laree een **lee**ray]
Please give me small notes/some coins as well!	Mi dia per favore biglietti di piccolo taglio/anche moneta! [mee **dee**a pair fa**vo**ray beel**yet**tee dee **pee**kolo **tal**yo/**an**kay mo**nay**ta]
Can I use my credit card to get cash?	Posso avere soldi con la mia carta di credito? [**pos**so a**vai**ray **sol**dee kon la **mee**-a **kar**ta dee **kray**deeto]
* Il Suo assegno prego. [eel **soo**-o as**sen**yo **pray**go]	Can I see your cheque card, please?
* Prego firmi qui [**pray**go **feer**mee kwee]	Sign here, please.

78

* Prego dia il Suo numero
di codice! [**pray**go **dee**a eel
soo-o **noo**mairo dee **ko**deechay]

Enter your pin number, please!

Has my bank transfer/money
order arrived yet?

È arrivato il vaglia bancario dalla mia banca/
il vaglia postale dal mio ufficio postale?
[ay arree**va**to eel **val**ya ban**kar**yo **dal**la **mee**-a **ban**ka/
eel **val**ya pos**ta**lay dal **mee**-o oo**fee**cho pos**ta**lay]

Crime and police

Where's the nearest police
station?

Dov'è la prossima stazione di polizia?
[**do**vay la **pros**seema stats**yo**ne dee pollet**see**a]

Please call the police!

Prego telefoni alla polizia!
[**pray**go te**lay**fonee **al**la pollet**see**a]

I've been
  robbed
  mugged on the road/
  at the beach.

Sono stato/stata [**so**no **sta**to/**sta**ta]
  derubato/derubata [dairoo**ba**to/dairoo**ba**ta]
  aggredito/aggredita sulla strada/
  sulla spiaggia. [agray**dee**to/agray**dee**ta **sool**la
  strada/**sool**la **spyaj**ja]

This man is
bothering/following me.

Questo uomo mi dà fastidio/mi segue.
[**kwes**to **wo**mo mee da fas**teed**yo/mee **sayg**way]

My car has been broken into.

La mia macchina è stata scassinata.
[la **mee**-a **mak**keena ay **sta**ta skassee**na**ta]

... has been stolen!

È stato rubato/stata rubata
[ay **sta**to roo**ba**to/**sta**ta roo**ba**ta]

  My passport

  la mia carta di identità
  [la **mee**-a **kar**ta dee eeden**tee**ta]

  My car/bicycle

  la mia macchina/bicicletta
  [la **mee**-a **mak**keena/beechee**klet**ta]

  My wallet

  il mio portafoglio [eel **mee**-o porta**fol**yo]

  My camera

  la mia macchina fotografica
  [la **mee**-a **mak**keena foto**gra**feeka]

  My handbag

  la mia borsa [la **mee**-a **bor**sa]

  My cheques/
  My cheque card

  i miei assegni/la mia carta assegni
  [ee **myay**ee as**sen**yee/la **mee**-a **kar**ta as**sen**yee]

  My watch

  il mio orologio. [eel **mee**-o oro**lo**jo]

I'd like to report
  a theft
  a fraud
  a robbery
  a rape

Io vorrei denunciare [**ee**o vor**ray**ee denoon**char**ay]
  un furto [oon **foor**to]
  un imbroglio [oon eem**brol**yo]
  un'aggressione [oonagress**yo**nay]
  uno stupro [**oo**no **stoo**pro]

I'd like to
  report an accident

  speak to a lawyer/
  call my embassy

Io vorrei [**ee**-o vor**ray**ee]
  riferire un incidente
  [reefair**eer**ay dee oon eenchee**den**tay]
  parlare con un avvocato/con la mia
  ambasciata [par**lar**ay kon oon avvo**ka**to/
  kon la **mee**-a amba**sha**ta]

79

Opening times

Shops are open Monday to Saturday from 9am to 1pm and from 4pm to 7pm. Many boutiques close on Monday morning. Banks open Monday to Friday from 8.30am to 1pm and again from 2.45pm to 3.45pm.

The *siesta* break from 1pm to 4pm is a long-established nationwide tradition.

During these hours, most things come to a standstill (except for in the big towns and cities where the siesta is slowly becoming a thing of the past).

When planning your trip to Italy, it's worth remembering that the whole country takes its summer holiday in August and many public services close.

Does anyone here speak English?	C'è qualcuno che parla inglese? [chay kwal**koo**no kay **par**la een**glay**zay]
I need	**Io ho bisogno di** [ee-o o bee**zon**yo dee]
an interpreter	un interprete [oon een**tair**pretay]
a written document for insurance purposes.	un certificato per la mia assicurazione. [oon chairteefee**ka**to pair la **mee**-a asseekoorats**yo**nay]
It wasn't my fault	Io non ho colpa. [ee-o non o **kol**pa]
I've got nothing to do with it	Io non ho niente a che vedere. [ee-o non o **nyen**tay a kay ve**dair**ay]
* Quando/Dove è successo? [**kwan**do/**do**vay ay soo**ches**so]	When/Where did it happen?

Emergencies

▶ **(See also breakdown, accident, page 25, and at the hospital, page 75)**

* Attenzione! [attents**yo**nay]	Caution!
* Pericolo (di morte)! [pai**ree**kolo dee (**mor**tay)]	Danger (of death)!
* Uscita di emergenza [u**shee**ta dee emair**jayn**tsa]	Emergency exit
Help!	Aiuto! [a**yoo**to]/Soccorso! [sok**kor**so]

Opening times

When does ... open/close?	Quando apre/chiude [**kwan**do apray/**kyoo**day]
the supermarket	il supermercato [eel soopairmair**ka**to]
the shop	il negozio [eel ne**gots**yo]
the bank	la banca [la **ban**ka]
the post office	l'ufficio postale [loo**fee**cho post**a**lay]
the museum?	il museo? [eel moo**za**yo]
Are you closed at lunch time?	Ha aperto a mezzogiorno? [a a**pair**to a metzo**jor**no]
Is there a day you are closed?	Ha un giorno di riposo? [a oon **jor**no dee ree**po**zo]

Post office

Where can I find	**Per favore dov'è** [pair favoray dovay]
a post office	l'ufficio postale [loofeecho postalay]
a post-box?	una cassetta postale? [oona kassetta postalay]

I'd like	**Io vorrei** [ee-o vorrayee]
some/10 stamps/	di francobolli/una serie speciale
special issue stamps	[dee frankobollee/oona sairyay spechalay]
for postcards/letters	per cartoline/lettere [pair kartoleenay/lettairay]
to England/the United	per l'Inghilterra/per gli Stati Uniti [pair
States	leengeeltairra/pair lyee statee ooneetee)]
a phonecard.	una carta telefonica. [oona karta telayfoneeka]

By airmail.	Per via aerea, prego. [pair veea a-airea praygo]
Express, please.	Per espresso, prego. [pair espresso praygo]

* Fermo posta. [**fair**mo **pos**ta]	Poste restante.

Do you have any mail for me?	C'è posta per me? [chay posta pair may]
My name is ...	Il mio nome è ... [eel mee-o nomay ay]

I would like to send a packet/	Io vorrei mandare un pacchetto/un telegramma.
a telegram.	[ee-o vorrayee mandaray oon paketto/oon telegramma]

How much do you charge for	Quanto costano dieci parole?
ten words?	[kwanto kostano dyaychee parolay]

I'd like to make a phone call	Vorrei telefonare in Inghilterra/negli Stati Uniti.
to England.	[vorrayee telefonaray een eengeeltairra]
Can I call direct?	Posso telefonare direttamente?
	[posso telefonaray deerettamentay]

▶ **(See also telecommunications, page 82)**

Can I send a fax to ... from	Si può mandare da qui un telefax a ...?
here?	[see pwo mandaray da kwee oon telefax a]
How much is it?	Quanto costa? [kwanto kosta]

Vatican City postboxes are blue instead of the usual red seen in the rest of Italy

Radio and television

On which wavelength can I pick up
  the traffic report

  English radio programmes?

What time is the news?

Do you have a TV guide?

What channels do you get?

Da quale frequenza si può ricevere
[da **kwa**lay frek**wen**tsa see pwo ree**chay**vairay]
  il programma sul traffico
  [eel pro**gram**ma sool **traf**feeko]
  i programmi in inglese?
  [ee pro**gram**mee een een**glay**zay]

A che ora ci sono le notizie?
[a kay **o**ra chee **so**no lay no**teet**syay]

Ha un giornale con i programmi televisivi?
[a oon jor**na**lay kon ee pro**gram**mee telay**vee**zeevee]

Quali canali ricevono?
[**kwa**lee ka**na**lee see ree**chay**vono]

Telecommunications

(Where) can I
  make a phone call
  buy a phonecard?

Can I send an e-mail (from here)?

Is there ... near here?
  a phone box
  a public phone
  a payphone/cardphone

  a cyber café

Can you change this?

I need coins for the telephone.

Do you have a phonebook for ...?
Can I dial direct to ...?

A long-distance call to ..., please!
How long do I have to wait?
What's the charge per minute to ...?
Is there a cheap rate at night time?
I'd like to make a reversed charge call.

(Dove) Posso [(**do**vay) **pos**so]
  telefonare [telay**fo**naray]
  comprare una carta telefonica?
  [kom**pra**ray **oo**na **kar**ta telay**fo**neeka]
Posso mandare un e-mail da qui? [**pos**so man**da**ray oon e-mail (da kwee)]

C'è ... da queste parti [chay da **kwes**tay **par**tee]
  una cabina telefonica [**oo**na ka**bee**na telay**fo**neeka]
  un telefono pubblico [oon te**lay**fono **poo**bleeko]
  un telefono a gettoni/con tessera
  [oon te**lay**fono a jet**to**nee/kon **tes**saira]
  un cyber café [oon **sy**ber kaf**fay**]

Per favore può cambiare?
[pair fa**vo**ray pwo kamb**ya**ray]

Ho bisogno di moneta per telefonare.
[o bee**zon**yo dee mo**nay**ta pair telefo**na**ray]

Posso avere un elenco telefonico di ... ?
[**pos**so a**vai**ray oon e**len**ko telay**fo**neeko dee]
Posso telefonare direttamente a ...?
[**pos**so telay**fo**naray deeretta**men**tay a]

Prego una telefonata interurbana a ...!
[**pray**go **oo**na telay**fo**na**ta** eentairoor**ba**na a]
Quanto devo aspettare? [**kwan**to **day**vo aspet**ta**ray]
Quanto costa un minuto per ...?
[**kwan**to **kos**ta oon mee**noo**to pair]
C'è una tariffa economica notturna?
[chay **oo**na ta**reef**fa ekono**mee**ka not**toor**na]
Io vorrei annunciare una telefonata a carico del ricevente [**ee**-o vor**ray**ee anoon**cha**ray **oo**na telefo**na**ta a **ka**reeko del reeche**ven**tay]

* Occupato. [okko**opa**to]
* Non risponde nessuno.
[non ree**spon**day nes**soo**no]

Engaged.
There's no reply.

Making phone calls

In addition to the telephone offices run by the national telephone company, Telecom, there are phone boxes everywhere. Most of these now only accept phonecards *(scheda/carta telefonica),* but some still take *gettoni* (tokens) and coins (100, 200 or 500 lira).

Phonecards to the value of 5,000 or 10,000 lira and *gettoni* (200 lira) can be bought from tobacconists and Telecom offices.

The international dialling code for the United Kingdom is 00 44, the Republic of Ireland 00 353 and the United States 00 1.

The following numbers are free of charge: police: 113; fire brigade: 112; information: 110.

Hello!	Pronto! [**pron**to]
Who's calling?	Chi parla? [kee **par**la]
This is ...	Qui parla ... [kwee **par**la]
Can I speak to Mr/Mrs ... ?	Posso parlare con il signor/la signora ...? [**pos**so par**la**ray kon eel seen**yor**/la seen**yora**]
* Sono io. [**so**no **ee**-o]	Speaking.
* Lui/Lei purtroppo non è qui. [**loo**-ee/lay poor**trop**po non ay kwee]	Sorry, he/she is not here at the moment.
Do you speak English?	Lei parla inglese? [lay **par**la een**glay**zay]
When can I speak to him/her?	Quando si può parlare con lui/lei? [**kwan**do see pwo par**la**ray kon **loo**-ee/lay]
Please tell him/her that I called.	Gli/le Dica per favore che io ho telefonato. [lyee/lay **dee**ka pair fa**vo**ray kay **ee**-o o telefo**na**to]
My number is ...	Il mio numero è ... [eel **mee**-o **noo**mairo ay]
Thanks, good-bye.	Grazie, a risentirci! [**grats**yay a reesen**teer**chee]

Toilets

Where are the toilets please?	Dove sono i gabinetti per favore? [**do**vay **so**no ee gabee**net**tee pair fa**vo**ray]
Is there a public toilet around here?	Ci sono gabinetti pubblici qui vicino? [chee **so**no gabee**net**tee **poo**bleechee kwee vee**chee**no]
* Donne/Uomini [**don**nay/**wom**meenee]	Ladies/Gentlemen

Tipping

Is service included?	Il servizio è compreso nel prezzo? [eel sair**veets**yo ay kom**pray**zo nel **pret**zo]
How much does one tip?	Quant'è la mancia di solito? [kwan**tay** la **man**cha dee **so**leeto]
That's for you!	Questo è per Lei! [**kwes**to ay pair lay]
Keep the change!	Tenga pure il resto! [**ten**ga **poo**ray eel **res**to]
That's fine!	Va bene così! [va **bay**nay ko**zee**]

English–Italian A–Z

A

accident incidente [eencheedentay] 25, 79, 80

accommodation alloggio [allojo] 32

address indirizzo [eendeereetzo] 15, 27

admission ticket biglietto di entrata [beelyetto dee entrata] 49, 57

adult adulto [adoolto] 29, 77

age età [eta] 14

agreed d'accordo [dakkordo]

air conditioning aria condizionata [aarya kondeetsyonata] 26, 38

air mattress materasso pneumatico [matairasso pnayoomateeko] 53

air aria [aarya]

aircraft aereo [a-airayo] 30

airport aeroporto [a-airoporto] 30

alarm clock sveglia [svelya] 66

alcohol level (parts per thousand) quantità pair mille [kwanteeta pair meellay]

all tutti [toottee]

alone solo/-a [solo/-a]

ambulance ambulanza [amboolantsa] 25, 75, 80

America l'America [amaireeka] 13

American americano [amereekano] 13

angry furioso/-a [fooreeozo/-a]

animal animale [aneemalay] 35

anorak anorak [anorak] 67

answering machine segreteria telefonica [segretairee-a telayfoneeka] 82

antiques antichità [anteekeeta] 69

apology scusa [skooza] 13

appointment appuntamento [appoontamento] 14

arena arena [arayna] 50

arm braccio [bracho] 73

art gallery galleria d'arte [gallaireea dartay] 50

aunt zia [tseea] 13

Australia l'Australia [owstralya] 13

Australian australiano [owstralyano] 13

autumn autunno [owtoonno] 17

avenue viale [vee-alay]

B

baby food alimenti per neonati [aleementee pair nayonatee] 62

baby neonato [nayonato]

baby's bottle biberon [beebairon] 71

bachelor scapolo [skappolo] 14, 15

back indietro [eendyaytro]

bad cattivo/-a [katteevo/-a]

bakery panetteria [panettaireea] 61

ball palla [palla] 55

bank holiday giorno di festa [jorno dee festa] 78

bank banca [banka] 78

bar cantina [kanteena] 58

bath bagno [banyo] 33, 53

battery batteria [battaireea] 26, 66, 67

bay baia [baya] 53

beach spiaggia [spyajja] 33, 53

beautiful bello/-a [bello/-a]

beauty (salon) (salone di) cosmetica [(salonay dee) kozmeteeka] 71

bed letto [letto] 32, 38

bedcover coperta [kopairta] 38

beer birra [beerra] 48

beginning inizio [eeneetsyo]

behind indietro [eendyaytro]

belt cintura [cheentoora] 67

bicycle bicicletta [beecheekletta] 22

bikini bikini [beekeenee] 67

bill conto [konto]

birthday compleanno [komplayanno] 14

black nero/-a [nairo/-a] 20

blame colpa [kolpa]

blood sangue [sangway] 72

blouse camicetta [kameechetta] 65

boat barca [barka] 53, nave [navay] 31

body (lotion) (lozione per il) corpo [(lotsyonay pair eel) korpo] 71

book libro [leebro] 65

bookshop libreria [leebraireea] 65

boots stivali [steevalee] 67

border confini [konfeenee] 21

boring noioso [noyozo]

born nato/-a [nato/-a]

bottle opener apribottiglia [apreebotteelya] 61

bottle bottiglia [bot**tee**lya] 43, 64
bowl terrina [tair**ree**na]
boy ragazzo [ra**gat**zo]
boy-friend amico [a**mee**ko] 13, 14
bra reggiseno [rejee**say**no] 67
breakdown panne [**pan**nay] 25, 79, 80
breakfast colazione [kolats**yo**nay] 33,
   41, 44
bridge ponte [**pon**tay] 50, 75
briefcase portafoglio [porta**fol**yo] 79
broken rotto/-a [**rot**to/-a]
brooch spilla [**speel**la] 66
brother fratello [fra**tel**lo] 13
brother-in-law cognato [kon**ya**to] 13
bureau de change cambio
   [**kam**byo] 78
bus autobus [**ow**toboos] 28, 29
bus station stazione dei pullman
   [stats**yo**nay **day**ee **pool**man] 28, 29
bus-stop fermata [fair**ma**ta] 28, 29
butcher macelleria [machel**lai**reea] 61
button bottone [bot**to**nay]
buy [vb] comprare [kom**pra**ray] 61

C

cabin (boat) cabina [ka**bee**na] 31
cabin (on a camp-site) capanna
   [ka**pan**na] 37
café caffè [kaf**fay**] 40
cake-shop pasticceria
   [pasteech**ai**reea] 61
camera macchina fotografica
   [**mak**keena fotogra**fee**ka] 67, 69
camper van camper [**kam**pair] 22, 37
camp-site campeggio [kam**pay**jo] 37
cap berretto [bai**ret**to] 67
car auto [**ow**to]; macchina
   [**mak**keena] 22, 24
caravan roulotte [roo**lott**] 37
car-park parcheggio [par**kay**jo] 23, 33
cash contanti [kon**tan**tee] 78
cash-desk cassa [**kas**sa] 57, 61
castle castello [kas**tel**lo] 50,51
cat gatto [**gat**to] 35
cathedral cattedrale [kattay**dra**lay] 50
cause causa [**kau**sa]; motivo [mo**tee**vo]
centimetre centimetro
   [chen**tee**metro] 19
centre centro [**chen**tro] 22
certificate certificato
   [chairteefee**ka**to] 77, 79
chain catena [ka**tay**na] 26
chair sedia [**say**dya]

charges spese [**spay**zay]
charter flight volo charter
   [**vo**lo **char**ter] 30
cheap economico [eko**no**meeko]
cheeky impertinente
   [eempairtee**nayn**tay]
chemist farmacia [farma**chee**a] 77
cheque assegno [as**sen**yo] 33, 78
child bambino [bam**bee**no] 29, 42, 77
church chiesa [**kyay**za] 50
cigarette sigarette [seega**ret**tay] 71
cinema cinema [**chee**nayma] 57
circular tour giro turistico
   [**jee**ro too**ree**steeko] 49, 52
city centre centro [**chen**tro] 22
clean pulito/-a [poo**lee**to/-a]
cleaning pulizia [poo**leet**seea] 66
clear chiaro/-a [**kya**ro/-a]
clock orologio [oro**lo**jo] 66, 79
closed chiuso/-a [**kyoo**zo/-a] 80
clothing abbigliamento
   [abbeelya**men**to] 65
coast costa [**kos**ta] 53
coat cappotto [kap**pot**to] 67
coins monete [mo**nay**tay] 39, 78, 82
cold freddo/-a [**fred**do/-a]
collar colletto [kol**let**to] 65
colour colore [ko**lo**ray] 20
comb pettine [**pet**teenay] 71
compartment scompartimento
   [skompartee**men**to] 29
compensation risarcimento danni
   [reesarchee**men**to **dan**nee]
complaint lagnanza [lan**yant**sa] 34, 42
concert concerto [kon**chair**to] 57
condom profilattico [profee**lat**teeko] 71
connecting (flight/train) coincidenza
   (per l'aereo/treno) [koeenchee**den**tsa
   (pair la-**ay**rayo/**tray**no)] 29, 30
connection collegamento
   [kollega**men**to] 28, 30
consulate consolato [konso**la**to] 79
contraceptive anticoncezionali
   [anteekonchetsyo**na**lee] 72, 77
contract contratto [kon**trat**to]
cook [f] cuoca [**kwok**ka] 40
cook [m] cuoco [**kwok**ko] 40
cooked cucinato/-a [koochee**na**to/-a]
corkscrew cavatappi [kava**tap**pee] 61
corner angolo [**an**golo]
cost [vb] assaggiare [assa**ja**ray]
cotton buds bastoncini di ovatta
   [baston**chee**nee dee o**vat**ta] 71

cotton wool ovatta [ovatta] 71
cotton cotone [kotonay] 66
counter sportello [sportello] 29, 57
country house tenuta [tenoota];
    possedimento rurale
    [possedeemento ruralay] 32
country road strada provinciale
    [strada proveenchalay] 22
country paese [pa-ayzay]
court tribunale [treeboonalay]
cousin [f] cugina [koojeena] 13
cousin [m] cugino [koojeeno] 13
credit card carta di credito
    [karta dee kraydeeto] 33, 78
cruise crociera [krochaira] 31
culture cultura [kooltoora] 57
cup tazza [tatza] 43
currency valuta [valoota] 78
customs dogana [dogana] 21
cutlery posate [pozatay] 38, 43

D
dance [vb] ballare [ballaray] 59
dangerous pericolo
    [paireekolo] 23, 54, 80
dark scuro/-a [skooro/-a] 20
date data [data] 17
daughter figlia [feelya] 13
day giorno [jorno] 12, 15, 19
day-ticket carta del giorno
    [karta del jorno] 28
dear caro/-a [karo/-a]
debt debito [daybeeto]
deep profondo/-a [profondo/-a]
degree grado [grado] 20, 73
delicatessen delicatezza
    [deleekatetza] 40
dentist dentista [denteesta] 72, 74
deodorant deodorante
    [dayodorantay] 71
departure partenza [partentsa] 28, 31
deposit cauzione [kowtsyonay] 23
dessert dessert [dessair] 47
destination meta [mayta] 54
dialling code prefisso [prefeesso] 82
die morire [moreeray]
diesel diesel [deezel] 24
difference differenza [deeffairentsa]
different diverso/-a [deevairso/-a]
difficult difficile [deeffeecheelay]
direct flight volo diretto
    [volo deeretto] 30
direction direzione [deeretsyonay] 22

directly diretto [deeretto]
director direttore [deerettoray] 32, 57
dirty sporco/-a [sporko/-a]
discotheque discoteca [deeskotayka] 58
discount sconto [skonto] 61
dismissal congedo [konjaydo] 12
display window vetrina
    [vetreena] 61
diversion deviazione
    [deveeatsyonay] 23
dizzy (to feel) avere le vertigini
    [avairay lay vairteejeenee] 72
doctor medico [maydeeko] 72
dog cane [kanay] 35
donkey asino [azeeno]
door porta [porta]
double doppio [doppyo]
doubt dubbio [doobbyo]
drink (noun) bevanda [bevanda] 48
drinking water acqua potabile
    [akwa potabeelay] 29, 39, 48
driver autista [owteesta]; conducente
    [kondoochentay] 28, 29
driving licence patente di guida
    [patentay dee gweeda] 21, 79
drunk ubriaco/-a [oobreeako/-a]
dummy succhiotto [sookkyotto] 71

E
earrings orecchini [orekkeenee] 66
earth terra [tairra]
east est [est]; oriente [oreeayntay] 22
easy leggero/-a [lejairo/-a]
eat mangiare [manjaray] 40, 43
edible mangiabile [manjabeelay]
education educazione [edookatsyonay]
electrical store negozio di
    elettrodomestici [negotsyo dee
    elettrodomaysteechee] 67
embassy ambasciata [ambashata] 79
emergency brake freno di emergenza
    [frayno dee emairjayntsa] 29
emergency exit uscita di emergenza
    [usheeta dee emairjayntsa] 58
emergency phone colonna per
    chiamata di soccorso [kolonna pair
    kyamata di sokkorso]
empty vuoto/-a [vwoto/-a]
engaged occupato/-a [okkoopato/-a]
engine motore [motoray] 26, 27
England Inghilterra [eengeeltairra] 13
English inglese [eenglayzay] 13
enter avanti [avantee]

entertainment trattenimento
[trattenee**men**to] 57

entrance entrata [en**tra**ta] 49, 57

environment ambiente [amby**en**tay] 54

environmental protection protezione
ecologica [protetsy**o**nay ekolo**jee**ka] 54

estate agent (mediatore di) immobili
[(medy**a**toray dee) eem**mo**beelee]

evening sera [**sai**ra] 12, 19

events (calender of) (calen**da**rio delle)
manifestazioni [(kalen**da**ree-o del**la**y)
maneefestatsy**o**nee] 49

everything tutto [**too**tto]

excursion escursione [eskoorsy**o**nay] 52

exhausted esaurito/-a [esow**ree**to/-a]

exit uscita [u**shee**ta] 23, 29

expensive caro/-a [**ka**ro/-a]

F

factory fabbrica [**fa**bbreeka]

faithful fedele [fe**da**ylay]

family famiglia [fa**mee**lya] 13

fan belt cinghia [**cheen**gya] 26, 67

far lontano/-a [lon**ta**no/-a]

fashion moda [**mo**da] 65

fast veloce [velo**cha**y]

father padre [**pa**dray] 13

faulty difetto/-a [dee**fet**to/-a]

fax telefax [**te**layfax] 35, 82

fear paura [**pow**ra] 72, 79

fee tariffa [ta**ree**ffa] 78

ferry traghetto [tra**get**to] 31

festival festa [**fays**ta] 78

few poco [**po**ko]

field campo [**kam**po] 54

finger dito [**dee**to] 73

fire brigade pompiere [pomp**yai**ray] 80

fire extinguisher estintore
[esteen**to**ray] 80

fire fuoco [**fwo**kko]; incendio
[een**chen**dyo] 80

firm fermo/-a [**fair**mo/-a]

firm (company) ditta [**dee**tta]

fishmonger pescheria [peska**ire**ea] 64

flat appartamento [apparta**men**to] 35

flea market mercatino delle pulci
[mairka**tee**no del**la**y **pool**chee] 61

flight volo [**vo**lo] 30

flirt [vb] flirtare [fleer**ta**ray)]

floor pavimento [pavee**men**to]

flower fiore [**fyo**ray] 61

fly mosche [**mo**skay]

food viveri [**vee**vairee] 62, 64

foot piede [**pyay**day] 73

football calcio [**kal**cho] 54, 56

foreigner straniero [stran**yai**ro] 14, 21

forest foresta [for**res**ta] 54

fork forchetta [for**ket**ta] 43

form modulo [**mo**doolo] 21, 79

fragile fragile [**fra**jeelay]

free of charge gratuitamente
[gratooeeta**men**tay]

free libero/-a [**lee**bairo/-a]

French francese [fran**chay**zay] 13

fresh fresco/-a [**fres**ko/-a]

Friday venerdì [venair**dee**] 17

fruit frutta [**froo**tta] 62

full board pensione completa
[pensy**o**nay kom**plet**ta] 33

full up sazio/-a [**sat**syo/-a]

full pieno/-a [**pyay**no/-a]

fun divertimento [deevairtee**men**to] 57

furniture shop mobilificio
[mobeelee**fee**cho] 61

furniture mobili [**mo**beelee] 61

fuse valvola di sicurezza
[**val**vola dee seekoo**ret**za] 26

G

garage garage [ga**ra**jay] 23, 33, 38

garden giardino [jar**dee**no] 50

garment vestito [ves**tee**to] 65

gentlemen signori [seeny**o**ree]

gents' toilet uomini [**wo**meenee] 83

genuine vero [**vai**ro];
genuino [jenoo**ee**no]

girl ragazza [ra**gat**za]

girl-friend amica [a**mee**ka] 13, 14

gladly volentieri [volent**yai**ree]

glass vetro [**ve**tro]; (tumbler) bicchiere
[beek**kyai**ray] 43, 50

glasses occhiali [ok**kya**lee] 69

glove guanti [**gwan**tee] 67

good bene [**bay**nay]

government governo [go**vair**no]

gram grammo [**gram**mo] 19, 64

grandchild nipote [nee**po**tay] 13

grandfather nonno [**non**no] 13

grandmother nonna [**non**na] 13

grass erba [**air**ba]

greengrocer's fruttivendolo
[frootteeven**do**lo] 61

grocer's drogheria
[droga**ire**ea] 70

ground-floor piano terra
[pyano **tair**ra] 32

group gruppo [**groopo**]
guarantee garanzia [garan**see**a] 22, 61
guard controllore
  [kontrol**loray**] 28, 29
guesthouse pensione
  [pen**syo**nay] 32, 39
guide guida [**gwee**da] 49, 52

H
hair capelli [ka**pellee**]
hair-brush spazzola per capelli
  [spat**zo**la pair ka**pellee**] 71
hairdresser parrucchiere
  [parrookk**yairay**]
hairspray lacca per capelli
  [**lak**ka pair ka**pellee**] 71
half mezzo [**metzo**]
hand-bag borsetta [bor**setta**] 69, 79
handicrafts artigianato artistico
  [arteeja**na**to ar**teesteeko**] 69
hand-luggage bagaglio a mano
  [ba**gal**yo a **ma**no] 30
hand-towel fazzoletto
  [fatzo**letto**] 38
happy felice [fe**leechay**]
hard duro/-a [**dooro**/-a]
hat cappello [ka**pello**] 67
head testa [**testa**] 73
healthy sano/-a [**sano**/-a]
heating riscaldamento
  [reeskalda**mento**] 38
heavy pesante [pe**zan**tay]
Help! Soccorso! [sok**korso**] 25, 80
Help! Aiuto! [a**yooto**] 79, 80
high alto/-a [**alto**/-a]
hobby hobby [**obbee**]
holiday villa casa per le vacanze
  [**ka**za pair lay va**kan**tsay] 35
holiday vacanze [va**kan**tsay]
home domicilio [domee**chee**lyo] 13
homeland patria [**patreea**] 13
home-made fatto in casa
  [**fat**to een **ka**za]
hope [*vb*] sperare [spai**raray**]
hospital ospedale [ospe**dalay**] 74
hot caldo/-a [**kaldo**/-a]
hotel room camera [**ka**maira] 32
hotel hotel [o**tel**] 32
hour ora [**ora**] 19
house casa [**ka**za] 35
household goods articoli da casa
  [ar**teekolee** da **ka**za] 61
hovercraft hovercraft [hover**craft**] 31

humid umido/-a [**oo**meedo/-a]
hunger fame [**famay**] 40
husband marito [ma**reeto**] 13
hydrofoil aliscafo [alees**kafo**] 31

I
identity card carta d'identità
  [**karta** deeden**teeta**] 21, 79
ill malato/-a [ma**lato**/-a]
important importante [impor**tan**tay]
impossible impossibile
  [imposse**beelay**]
inclusive incluso [een**kloozo**]
information informazione
  [eenformat**syo**nay] 29, 49
inhabitant abitante [abee**tan**tay]
injured ferito/-a [fai**reeto**/-a] 25, 72
innocent innocente [eenno**chen**tay]
insurance assicurazione
  [asseekoorat**syo**nay] 22
intelligent intelligente [eentelleejentay]
interesting interessante
  [eentairess**an**tay] 52
invalid non valido/-a
  [non va**leedo**/-a]
investigation esame [e**zamay**] 72, 79
invoice conto [**konto**] 39, 43
Ireland l'Irlanda [eer**landa**]
Irish irlandese [eerlan**day**zay]
island isola [**eezola**] 50

J
jacket giacca [**jak**ka] 65, 67
jellyfish medusa [me**dooza**] 53, 72
jeweller gioielliere [joyell**yairay**] 66
jewellery gioielli [joy**ellee**] 66, 69
job professione [professyonay] 14
journey viaggio [**vyaj**jo]
jumper pullover [**pool**lover] 65
junk shop rigattiere
  [reegatt**yairay**] 61, 69
justice giudizio [joo**deet**syo]

K
key chiave [**kya**vay] 39
kilo chilo [**keel**o] 19, 64
kilometre chilometro
  [**keelo**metro] 19, 23
kiosk chiosco [**kyosko**] 61
kiss bacio [**bacho**]
knife coltello [kol**tello**] 43
knitwear maglieria
  [malyai**reea**] 67

L

ladies' toilet donne [donnay] 71, 83
lady signora [seenyora]
landing sbarco [sbarko]; atterraggio
[attairrajjo] 30
landlord oste [ostay] 40
landscape panorama [panorama] 51
language lingua [leengwa] 13
large grande [granday]
laundry lavanderia [lavandaireea] 66
lazy pigro/-a [peegro/-a]
leather goods articoli di pelle
[arteekolee dee pellay] 69
leather pelle [pellay] 66
left luggage office deposito bagagli
[depozeeto bagalyee]
left sinistra [seeneestra]
leg gamba [gamba] 73
length lunghezza [loongetza] 19
letter lettera [lettaira] 65, 81
letter-box cassetta per lettera
[kassetta pair lettaira] 81
lifebelt salvagente
[salvajentay] 31, 53
lifeboat battello di salvataggio
[battello dee salvatajjo] 31, 53
life-jacket giubbotto di salvataggio
[joobbotto dee salvatajjo] 31, 55
lift ascensore [ashensoray] 38
light luce [loochay] 34, 39
lightning fulmine [foolmeenay] 20, 69
linen lino [leeno] 66
lip-stick rossetto [rossetto] 71
litre litro [leetro] 19, 64
little (a) (un) poco [(oon) poko]
live [vb] vivere [veevairay]
locker cassetta di sicurezza
[kassetta dee seekooretza] 29
long lungo [loongo]
lorry camion [kamyon] 23
lost property office ufficio degli
oggetti smarriti [ooffeecho delyee
ojettee zmarreetee] 79
lounger sedia a sdraio
[sedya a zdrayo] 53
love [vb] amare [amaray]
low basso/-a [basso/-a]
luggage bagaglio [bagalyo] 29, 32, 38
lunch pranzo [prandzo] 34, 40

M

magazine rivista [reeveesta] 65
make-up trucco [trooko] 71

man uomo [womo] 13
many molto [molto]
map carta geografica
[karta jeografeeka] 49
market hall mercato coperto
[mairkato kopairto] 61
market mercato [mairkato] 51, 61, 64
marriage matrimonio [matreemonyo]
married couple coppia sposata
[koppya spozata] 13
married sposato/-a [spozato/-a] 14, 15
mass (church) messa [messa]
matches fiammiferi [fyammeefairee] 71
material stoffa [stoffa] 66
meal pasto [pasto] 40
medication medicina
[medeecheena] 73
memory ricordo [reekordo]
menu menù [menoo] 44
metre metro [metro] 19
midday mezzogiorno
[metzojorno] 17, 19
minute minuto [meenooto] 19
misfortune disgrazia
[deesgratsya] 25, 80
miss signorina [seenyoreena] 12
mistake (by) per sbaglio [pair zbalyo]
mistake errore [airroray] 25, 79
misunderstanding equivoco
[ekweevoko]
modern moderno/-a [modairno/-a]
moment momento [momento] 14
monastery convento [konvento] 51
Monday lunedì [loonaydee] 17
money soldi [soldee] 78
month mese [mayzay] 17
morning (in the) il mattino
[eel matteeno] 12, 15
morning mattina [matteena] 19
mosquito net mo rete per le mosche
[rettay pair lay moskay]
mosquito repellent rimedio
antizanzare [reemedyo
anteetzantzaray] 71, 77
mosquito zanzara [tzantzara]
mother madre [madray] 13
motor-cycle moto [moto] 22
mountain montagna
[montanya] 50
Mr signore [seenyoray] 12
much molto [molto]
museum museo [moozayo] 51
music musica [moozeeka] 57, 58

N

nail clippers forbici per unghie [**for**beechee pair lay **oon**gyay] 71

nail file limetta per le unghie [lee**met**ta pair lay **oon**gyay] 71

nail polish smalto per unghie [**zma**lto pair lay **oon**gyay] 71

nail polish remover acetone per smalto delle unghie [ache**to**nay pair **zma**lto **del**lay **oon**gyay] 71

nail-brush spazzola per le unghie [**spat**zola pair lay **oon**gyay] 71

naked nudo/-a [**noo**do/-a]

name nome [**no**may] 12, 40

nappies pannolini [panno**lee**nee] 71

nation stato [**sta**to]

nationality nazionalità [natsyona**lee**ta] 13

natural fibre fibra naturale [**fee**bra natoo**ra**lay] 66

nature natura [na**too**ra] 54

nausea nausea [**now**zay-a] 72

near vicino/-a [vee**chee**no/-a]

nearest prossimo/prossima [**pros**seemo/**pros**seema]

necessary necessario [neches**sa**reeo]

neckerchief fazzoletto da collo [fatzo**let**to da **kol**lo] 67

neighbour vicino [vee**chee**no] 13

nephew nipote [nee**po**tay] 13

never mai [**ma**ee]

New Zealand la Nuova Zelanda [**nwo**va tzay**lan**da]

New Zealander neozelandese [nayotzelan**day**zay]

new nuovo/-a [**nwo**vo/-a]

news notizie [no**teet**syay] 82

newspaper giornale [jor**na**lay] 65

next prossimo/prossima [**pros**seemo/**pros**seema]

nice gentile [jen**tee**lay]

niece nipote [nee**po**tay] 13

night notte [**not**tay] 12, 19

nightshirt camicia da notte [ka**mee**cha da **not**tay] 67

no no [no]

nobody nessuno [nes**soo**no]

noise rumore [roo**mo**ray]

noisy rumoroso [roomo**ro**zo]

non-smoker non fumatore [non fooma**to**ray] 30, 31

normal normale [nor**ma**lay]

north nord [nord] 22

not non [non]

notary notaio [no**ta**yo] 79

nothing niente [**nyen**tay]

nowhere da nessuna parte [da nes**soo**na **par**tay]

number numero [**noo**mairo] 22, 82

O

obvious chiaro/-a [**kya**ro/-a]

office ufficio [oo**ffee**cho] 49, 81

often spesso [**spes**so]

old vecchio [**vek**kyo]

once una volta [**oo**na **vol**ta]

only solo [**so**lo]

open aperto/-a [a**pair**to/-a] 80

opening times orari di apertura [o**ra**ree dee apair**too**ra] 49, 80

optician ottico [**ot**teeko] 69

other altro/altra [**al**tro/**al**tra]

otherwise diversamente [deevairsa**men**tay]

owner proprietario [propree-e**ta**ryo]

P

pain scherzo [**skair**tso]

pains dolori [do**lo**ree] 72

pair coppia [**kop**pya] 20

palace palazzo [pa**lat**zo] 51

papers documenti [doko**men**tee] 21, 79

parasol ombrellone [ombrel**lo**nay] 53, 61

parcel pacchetto [pak**ket**to] 81

parents genitori [jenee**to**ree] 13

park parco [**par**ko] 51

part parte [**par**tay]

passage passaggio [pas**saj**jo] 23

passenger passeggiero [passe**jai**ro] 30, 31

passport passaporto [passa**por**to] 21, 79

past passato [pas**sa**to]

pedestrian pedone [pe**do**nay] 49, 52

people popolo [**po**polo]

percentage percento [pair**chen**to]

performance presentazione [presentatsyo**na**y] 12, 57

perfume profumo [pro**foo**mo] 71

petrol benzina [bend**zee**na] 24

petrol station distributore [deestreeboo**to**ray] 24

photography shop negozio fotografico [ne**got**syo fota**gra**feeko] 67

picture quadro [**kwa**dro] 50, 69
piece pezzo [**pettzo**] 20
pillow cuscino [koo**shee**no] 38
pity (it's a) peccato [pek**ka**to]
place posto [**po**sto]; luogo [**lwo**go] 22
plain pianura [pya**noo**ra] 54
plant pianta [**pyan**ta] 54, 61
plate piatto [**pyat**to] 43
platform binario [bee**nar**yo] 29
please prego [**pray**go]
poisonous velenoso/-a [vele**no**zo/-a]
police officer poliziotto
  [poleets**yot**to] 79
police polizia [poleet**see**a] 79
politics politica [po**lee**teeka]
poor povero [**po**vero]
port porto [**por**to] 31, 50
porter portiere [port**yai**ray] 32
possible possibile [pos**see**beelay]
postcard cartolina postale
  [karto**lee**na po**sta**lay] 81
postcode codice di avviamento postale
  [**ko**deechay dee avvee**a**mento
  po**sta**lay] 81
post-office ufficio postale [oo**ffee**cho
  po**sta**lay] 81
pottery ceramica [chai**ra**meeka] 69
powder talco [**tal**ko] 71
prefix prefisso [pre**fees**so] 82
pregnant incinta [een**cheen**ta] 73
present regalo [re**ga**lo] 69
pretty carino/-a [ka**ree**no/-a]
price prezzo [**pret**zo] 61
priest prete [**pret**tay]
programme programma
  [pro**gram**ma] 82
pub cantina [kan**tee**na] 40
public pubblico [**poob**bleeko]
pullover pullover [**pool**lover] 65
punctual puntuale [poont**wa**lay]
punishment multa [**mool**ta] 79
purse portamonete
  [portamo**nay**tay] 79
pyjamas pigiama [pee**ja**ma]

Q

quality qualità [kwalee**ta**] 40, 61
quarter quartiere
  [kwart**yai**ray] 22, 51
question domanda [do**man**da] 16
quiet tranquillo/-a [trank**weel**lo/-a]
quiet(ly) a bassa voce
  [a **bas**sa **voch**ay]

R

radio radio [**rad**yo] 39, 82
rain pioggia [**pyoj**ja] 20
raincoat impermeabile
  eempairmay**abee**lay] 65
rape stupro [**stoo**pro] 79
rare raro/-a [**ra**ro/-a]
razor blade lamette da barba
  [la**met**tay da **bar**ba] 71
ready pronto/-a [**pron**to/-a]; finito/-a
  [fee**nee**to/-a]
receipt ricevuta [reeche**voo**ta] 43, 77
reception ricezione [reechets**yo**nay] 32
records dischi [**dees**kee] 61
relative parente [pa**ren**tay] 13
responsible responsabile
  [responsa**bee**lay]
rest riposo [ree**po**zo]; tranquillità
  [trankweel**lee**ta]
restaurant ristorante [reesto**ran**tay] 40
result risultato [reezool**ta**to] 54
rich ricco/-a [**reek**ko/-a]
right (correct) giusto/-a [**joo**sto/-a]
right destra [**de**stra]
risk rischio [**rees**kyo] 23, 54, 80
river fiume [**fyoo**may] 50, 54
riverbank riva [**ree**va] 53
road strada [**stra**da] 22
roadside restaurant posto di ristoro
  [**po**sto dee ree**sto**ro] 32
room sala [**sa**la] 51; spazio [**spat**syo] 51
round rotondo/-a [ro**ton**do/-a]
rubbish spazzatura [spatza**too**ra] 39
rucksack zaino [tza-**ee**no] 54

S

sad triste [**tree**stay]
safe sicuro/-a [see**koo**ro/-a]
safety belt cintura di sicurezza
  [cheen**too**ra dee seekoo**ret**za] 26
sale saldi [**sal**dee] 61
sandals sandali [**san**dalee] 67
sanitary towel pannolino
  [panno**lee**no] 71
satisfied soddisfatto/-a [soddees**fat**to/-a]
Saturday sabato [**sa**bato] 17
saucepan pentola [**pen**tola] 39
scheduled flight volo di linea
  [volo dee **lee**nay-a] 30
scissors forbici [**for**beechee] 71
Scotland la Scozia [**skot**sya]
Scottish scozzese [skot**say**zay]
sea mare [**ma**ray] 53

seafood frutti di mare
[**froot**tee dee ma**ray**] 45
seasickness mal di mare
[mal dee ma**ray**] 31, 72
season stagione [sta**jo**nay] 17;
(high/low) season (alta/fuori)
stagione [(**alta/fwor**ee) sta**jo**nay] 17
seat posto a sedere
[**po**sto a se**dair**ay] 28, 40
sea-urchin riccio di mare
[**ree**cho dee ma**ray**] 53, 72
second secondo [se**kon**do] 19
self-service autoservizio
[owtosair**veet**syo] 40, 61
separate diviso/-a [dee**vee**zo/-a]
series fila [**fee**la]
serious serio/-a [**sair**eeo/-a]
service personale di servizio
[pairso**na**lay dee sair**veet**syo] 41, 61
sex sesso [**ses**so]
shaver rasoio elettrico
[ra**zo**yo e**let**treeko] 67, 71
shawl scialle [**shal**lay] 67
shirt camicia [ka**mee**cha] 65
shoe cream crema per scarpe
[**kray**ma pair **skar**pay] 65
shoe shop calzoleria [kaltsolai**ree**a] 65
shoelaces legaccioli [lega**chol**ee] 65
shoes scarpe [**skar**pay] 65
shop negozio [ne**got**syo] 61
shore riva [**reev**a] 53
short corto [**kor**to]
shorts pantaloncini *(m/Pl)*
[pantalon**cheen**ee] 67
shower doccia [**do**cha] 33, 38, 55
shy timido/-a [**tee**meedo/-a]
sick malato/-a [ma**la**to/-a]
side lato [**la**to]
sign insegna [een**sen**ya] 23, 29, 54
signature firma [**feer**ma] 21, 78
signpost indicatore stradale
[eendeeka**tor**ay stra**da**lay] 22
silk seta [**say**ta] 66
single celibe *(m)* [**chel**eebay]/nubile *(f)*
[**noo**beelay] 14
sister sorella [so**rel**la] 13
sister-in-law cognata [kon**ya**ta] 13
situation situazione [seetooats**yon**ay]
skirt gonna [**gon**na] 65
sleeper car carrozza a cuccette
[kar**rot**za a koo**chet**tay] 29
sleeve manica [**man**eeka] 65
slim snello/-a [**znel**lo/-a]

slowly lentamente [lenta**men**tay]
small piccolo/-a [**peek**kolo/-a]
smell odore [o**dor**ay] 40
smoke *[vb]* fumare [foo**mar**ay] 71
snack spuntino [spoon**teen**o] 40
soap sapone [sa**pon**ay] 39
socks calzini [kalt**seen**ee] 65
soft morbido/-a [**mor**beedo/-a]
solicitor avvocato [avvo**ka**to] 79;
notaio [no**ta**yo] 79
some alcuni [al**koon**ee]
something qualcosa [kwal**ko**za]
son figlio [**feel**yo] 13
sorry! scusi tanto! [**skoo**zee **tan**to] 13
south sud [sood]; meridione
[mairee**dyon**ay] 22
souvenirs ricordini [reekor**deen**ee] 69
special offer offerta speciale
[of**fair**ta spe**chal**ay] 61
special rate tariffa speciale
[ta**reef**fa spe**chal**ay] 30
speciality specialità [spechalee**ta**] 40
speed velocità [veloche**ta**] 19
spoon cucchiaio [kook**kya**yo] 43
sport sport [sport] 54, 56
sports articles articoli sportivi
[ar**tee**kolee spor**tee**vee] 61
sportsground campo sportivo
[**kam**po spor**tee**vo] 54
spring primavera [preema**vair**a] 17
spring sorgente [sor**jen**tay] 51, 54
square piazza [**pyat**za] 22, 30, 41, 51
staircase scala [**ska**la] 38
stamp francobollo [franko**bol**lo] 81
starter antipasto [antee**pas**to] 44
station stazione [stats**yon**ay] 29
stationery cartoleria [kartolai**ree**a] 65
stay soggiorno [so**jor**no] 15
steward cameriere di bordo
[kamir**yair**ay dee **bor**do] 30, 31
stewardess hostess [**ost**ess] 30, 31
stockings calze [**kalt**say] 67
stone pietra [**pyay**tra]
stopover scalo [**ska**lo] 30
storey piano [**pya**no] 32
storm tempesta [tem**pes**ta] 20, 55;
temporale [tempo**ral**ay] 20
story racconto [rak**kon**to]
straight on dritto [**dreet**to]
street strada [**stra**da] 22
stupid stupido/-a [**stoo**peedo/-a]
subway sottopassaggio
[sottopas**saj**jo] 23

suede camoscio [ka**mosho**] 65, 69
suit (for men) vestito da uomo
[ve**steeto** da **wo**mo] 67
suit (for women) costume
[kos**toomay**]
suitcase valigia [va**lee**ja] 29, 32, 79
summer estate [es**ta**tay] 17
sun sole [**so**lay] 20
sunburn scottatura da sole
[skotta**toora** da **so**lay] 72, 77
suncream latte solare
[**lat**tay so**la**ray] 71
Sunday domenica [dome**nee**ka] 17
sunglasses occhiali da sole
[ok**kya**lee da **so**lay] 70
suntan lotion crema solare
[**kray**ma so**la**ray] 71
supermarket supermercato
[soopairmair**ka**to] 61
supper cena [**chay**na] 34, 40
supplement (for train ticket)
supplemento [soo**play**mento] 29
surprise sorpresa [sor**pray**za]
sweets dolciumi [dol**choo**mee]
swimming costume costume da bagno
per donna
[kos**toomay** da **ban**yo pair **don**na] 67
swimming pool piscina
[pee**shee**na] 33, 53
swimming trunks costume da bagno
per uomo
[kos**toomay** da **ban**yo pair **wo**mo] 67
synthetic material sintetico
[seen**tet**eeko] 66

T

table tavolo [**ta**volo] 40
tablets pastiglie [pas**teel**yay] 73, 77
take-off decollo [de**kol**lo] 30; partenza
[par**tent**sa] 54
tampons tamponi [tam**po**nee] 71
taste gusto [**goo**sto] 40
telegram telegramma [tele**gram**ma] 81
telephone telefono [te**lay**fono] 82
telephone conversation chiamata
interurbana
[kya**ma**ta eentairoor**ban**a] 82
telephone directory elenco telefonico
[e**len**ko tele**fo**neeko] 82
temperature temperatura
[tempair**a**toora] 20, 73
terminus l'ultima stazione
[**lool**teema stats**yo**nay] 28, 29

terrible spaventoso/-a [spaven**tozo**/-a]
thank you grazie [**grats**yay] 13
theatre teatro [tay**a**tro] 57
theft furto [**foor**to] 79
thick grosso/-a [**gros**so/-a]
thin sottile [sot**tee**lay]
thing cosa [**ko**sa]; oggetto [o**jet**to]
thirst sete [**say**tay] 48
through-carriage vagone diretto
[va**go**nay dee**ret**to] 29
Thursday giovedì [jovay**dee**] 17
ticket biglietto [beel**yet**to] 28, 29, 57
tide mareggiata [maray**ja**ta] 31
tie cravatta [kra**vat**ta] 67
tights calzamaglia [kaltsa**mal**ya] 67
timber legno [**lay**nyo] 37
time tempo [**tempo**] 17, 19
timetable orario di viaggio
[o**rar**yo dee **vyaj**jo] 28, 29
tip mancia [**man**cha] 43, 83
tired stanco/-a [**stan**ko/-a]
tiring faticoso/-a [fatee**kozo**/-a]
tobacco tabacco [ta**bak**ko] 71
tobacconist's tabaccheria
[tabak**kai**ree-a] 71
together insieme [een**syay**may]
toilet paper carta igienica
[**kar**ta ee**jen**eeka] 39, 71
toilet gabinetto [gabee**net**to] 39
tomorrow domani [do**ma**nee] 17
too much troppo [**trop**po]
toothbrush spazzolino [spatzo**lee**no] 71
toothpaste dentifricio
[dentee**free**cho] 71
total somma [**som**ma] 43
tourist turista [too**ree**sta] 21, 49
tourist guide guida turistica [**gwee**da
too**ree**steeka] 49, 65
tourist office ufficio di informazioni
turistiche [oo**fee**cho dee
eenformats**yo**nee too**ree**steekay] 49
tourist sight monumento
[monoo**men**to] 52
towel tovagliolo [toval**yo**lo] 43
tower torre [**tor**ray] 51
town città [**chee**tta] 22, 51
town hall municipio
[moonee**chee**pyo] 51
town map carta della città
[**kar**ta **del**la **chee**tta] 49, 65
toy giocattolo [jo**kat**tolo] 61
toyshop negozio di giocattoli
[ne**got**syo dee jo**kat**tolee] 61

traffic lights semaforo [se**ma**foro] 22
traffic traffico [**traff**eeko] 23
train treno [**tray**no] 29
trainers scarpe da ginnastica
   [**skar**pay da jeen**na**steeka] 67
tram tram [tram] 28
translator interprete
   [eentair**pre**tay] 80
travel agent agenzia di viaggi
   [ajent**see**a dee **vyaj**jee] 49, 52
traveller's check assegno turistico
   [as**sen**yo too**ree**steeko] 33, 78
tree albero [**al**bairo] 54
trip into the country gita campestre
   [**jee**ta kam**pay**stray] 31
trousers pantaloni *(m/Pl)*
   [panta**lo**nee] 65
truck camion [**kam**eeon] 23
true vero/-a [**vai**ro/-a]
T-shirt T-Shirt [T-shirt] 65
Tuesday martedì [marta**ydee**] 17
tunnel tunnel [**toon**nayl] 23
tweezers pinzetta [peent**sett**a] 71
tyre pneumatico [pnayoo**ma**teeko] 26

U

ugly brutto/-a [**broot**to/-a]
umbrella ombrello [om**bre**llo] 61
uncle zio [**tsee**o] 13
underground metropolitana
   [metropol**ee**tana] 28
underpants mutande [moo**tan**day] 67
understand capire [ka**pee**ray]
underwear biancheria intima
   [byankai**ree**a een**tee**ma] 65
unhappy infelice [eenfe**lee**chay]
urgent urgente [oor**jen**tay]

V

valid valido/-a [**va**leedo/-a]
value valore [va**lo**ray]
vegetables verdura [vair**doo**ra] 62
very molto [**mol**to]
vest maglia [**mal**ya] 67
video (cassette) (cassette) video
   [(kas**set**tay) video] 67
view vista [**vee**sta]50
viewpoint punto di vista
   [**poon**to dee **vee**sta] 50
village paese [pa–**ay**zay] 22, 50
visa visto [**vee**sto] 21
visible visibile [vee**zee**beelay]
visit visita [**vee**zeeta] 49, 52

W

waistcoat gilè [jeelay] 67
waiter cameriere [kamair**yai**ray] 41
waiting room sala di attesa
   [sala dee at**tay**za] 72
waitress cameriera [kamair**yai**ra] 41
Wales il Galles [**gall**es]
walk passeggiata [passay**ja**ta] 49, 54
warm caldo/-a [**kal**do/-a]
warning attenzione [attents**yo**nay] 23
washing powder detergente
   [detair**jen**tay] 71
washing-up liquid detersivo per i
   piatti [detair**see**vo pair ee **pyatt**ee]
watchmaker orologiaio [orolo**ja**yo] 66
water acqua [**ak**wa] 37, 39, 48
wave onda [**on**da] 55
weather forecast previsioni del tempo
   [preveez**yo**nee del **taym**po] 20, 82
weather tempo [**tem**po] 20
Wednesday mercoledì [mairkolay**dee**] 17
week settimana [sette**ema**na] 17, 19
weight peso [**pay**zo] 19, 61
welcome benvenuto [benve**noo**to]
wellington boots stivale di gomma
   [**stee**valay dee **gom**ma] 65
Welsh gallese [gal**lay**zay]
west ovest [**ovest**] 21
wet bagnato/-a [ban**ya**to/-a]
wide largo/-a [**lar**go/-a]
wife moglie [**mol**yay] 13
wind vento [**ven**to] 20
winter inverno [een**vair**no] 17
witness testimone [testee**mo**nay] 25, 79
woman signora [seen**yo**ra] 12, 13
wood bosco [**bos**ko] 51, 54
wool lana [**la**na] 66
word parola [pa**ro**la]
work lavoro [la**vo**ro] 14
workshop officina [offee**chee**na] 25, 27
world mondo [**mon**do]
written scritto/-a [**skreet**to/-a]
wrong falso/-a [**fal**so/-a]

Y

year anno [**an**no] 17, 20
yes sì [see]
young giovane [**jo**vanay]
youth hostel ostello [os**tel**lo] 38

Z

zip chiusura lampo
   [kyoo**zoo**ra lampo] 61

Italian–English A–Z

A

acqua (non) potabile (not) drinking water
aeroporto airport
albergo hotel
ambulanza ambulance
annuncio display
arrivo arrival
attenzione caution
autogrill motorway services
autostrada motorway

B

banca bank
barbiere gent's hairdresser
benvenuti welcome
benzina petrol
biblioteca library
biglietteria ticket office
binario platform

C

cabina cabin
cabina telefonica telephone box
calzolaio shoemaker
cambio bureau de change
camping camp-site
casello autostradale toll-booth
cassa cash desk
centro centre
chiuso closed
cimitero cemetery
cinema cinema
coda traffic jam
cognome surname
cuccetta sleeper carriage

D

deviazione diversion
distributore petrol station
divieto di sorpasso no overtaking
divieto di transito no through road
donne ladies' toilet

E

edicola kiosk
entrata libera admission free

F

fabbrica factory
famiglia family
fare la fila to queue
farmacia chemist
fatto a mano hand-made
fermata bus-stop
fermo posta poste restante
festivo holiday
freno di emergenza emergency brake
frontiera border
frutta e verdura fruit and vegetables
fumatori smokers

G

gas gas
giornali newspapers
giorni feriali weekdays
girare to turn off

I

importante important
imposta di valore aggiunto (IVA) value added tax
informazioni information

L

lago lake
lettera letter
libero free
libreria bookshop
listino prezzi price list

M

macelleria butcher's
meccanico mechanic
metropolitana underground
mostra exhibition

N

nave boat
nome name
non fumatori non-smokers

O

offerta speciale special offer
ospedale hospital
ottico optician

P
pacco package
panetteria bakery
parcheggio car-park
parrucchiere hairdresser
partenza departure
pedaggio motorway toll
pericolo di morte danger of death
pericoloso danger
pittura fresca wet paint
polizia police
porto port
premere to press
prenotazione reservation
prevendita advance ticket sales
programma programme

R
ricevuta fiscale invoice, bill
riduzione reduction
rifiuti rubbish
ritardo delay

S
sala d'attesa waiting room
salumeria cooked meat shop
scontrino receipt
senso unico one-way street

senza piombo lead-free
signori gentlemen
società society; company
spettacolo presentation
sposato/-a married
spremuta fruit juice
supermercato supermarket

T
tabacchi tobacco goods
teatro theatre
teatro comunale municipal theatre
tirare to pull
trattoria restaurant
tutto compreso everything included

U
ufficio office
ufficio postale post office
urgente urgent
uscita exit, way out

V
via road
vietato fumare no smoking

Photo Credits

All pictures Veit Haak except APA Publications/Frances Gransden: 81; Rainer Hackenberg: 17, 25 (right), 40; Herbert Hartmann: 37; Gerold Jung: 32, 53, 65 (right); Markus Kirchgeßner: 61, 72; Daniele Messina: 77; The Stock Market: cover.